THE
Great Religions

ABOVE Achaemenid cylinder seal from Iran, 6th to 4th centuries BC.
At the top is the winged symbol of Ahura Mazda, the supreme
God of Zoroastrianism. The figure has the wings and tail of a bird
and the right hand is raised in blessing.

ENDPAPERS Muslims praying in a mosque in Nairobi.

OVERLEAF St Mark writing his gospel, from an 11th-century
Byzantine gospel lectionary. Almost all that is known about the life
of Jesus comes from the four gospels. Mark, the shortest of them,
is now generally believed to be the oldest. It may date from soon
after AD 70, about forty years after the death of Jesus.

OVERLEAF RIGHT Stone carving expressing reverence for the
Bodhi-Tree. It was after many days and nights of meditation
beneath this tree, according to tradition, that the Buddha attained
enlightenment.

ἘΚ ΚΑ ΜΑΡ.

τῶν ἀπορίμων ✝
Καὶ ἤρξατο ποίει
θιται ἀυτοῦ ὁδὸν
ποιεῖν τίλλον
τὸ τοὺς στάχυας ✝

τοῦ καιρῶ ἐκ ἀμοῦ
ἐπορεύετο τοῖς
τοῖς σάμμασι διὰ

THE
Great Religions

RICHARD CAVENDISH

ARCO PUBLISHING, INC.
New York

Published by Arco Publishing, Inc.
219 Park Avenue South, New York, N.Y.
10003

Printed in Italy
Library of Congress Cataloging in
Publication Data

Cavendish, Richard.
  The great religions.

  1. Religions.   I. Title.
BL80.2.C38   1980   291   79–28659
ISBN 0–668–04929–4

Contents

17th-century figure of Krishna playing the flute, with an appreciative audience of animals. Krishna is the most popular and most widely worshipped of all the gods of India.

1. Religion

Religion is one of the things which distinguishes man from the other animals. Apes and dolphins, as far as we know, have no religions, but no group of human beings has ever been discovered which did not have religious beliefs. Religion is so old that its origins are shrouded in the darkness of prehistoric times, when our early ancestors trod the earth, and it has exerted so immense an influence on human behaviour ever since that there is no hope of understanding history and human nature without taking religion into account. Religions have taught men and women how to lead their lives on the earth and have given them hope for a happier life after death. They have supported human beings in times of danger, pain, bewilderment and despair. They have inspired nobility, self-sacrifice, courage and endurance, and they have also inspired wars, persecutions and abominable cruelty. They have created compelling and magnificent rituals and a massive wealth of literature, architecture, art, music and philosophy. Great civilizations have grown up round them and even in the modern world, when the religious impulse is supposed to be dying, it is in fact vigorously expressing itself in new forms and disguises.

The principal living religions of the world originated in three geographical areas: in India, Hinduism, Buddhism, Jainism and Sikhism; in China and Japan, Confucianism, Taoism and Shinto; in the Middle East, Judaism, Zoroastrianism, Christianity and Islam. Five of these — Christianity, Islam, Hinduism, Buddhism and Judaism — are generally classified as the major religions of the world as they have exercised the greatest influence on the largest numbers of people. The membership figures given later should be taken with large lumps of salt. They are extremely rough estimates and they exaggerate the extent of genuine religious commitment. For what they are worth, however, the latest figures indicate that rather more than half the people in the world (about fifty-seven per cent) belong to one or other of the five major religions. Of every 1000 people alive today, 239 are Christians, 140 are Muslims, 126 are Hindus, 63 are Buddhists and 4 are Jews.

The nature of prehistoric religion can only be guessed at, because our early ancestors left no written records. This limestone figure from Austria, the Venus of Willendorf, is not much more than four inches high. The swollen belly and emphasized sexual features, together with the blank face, suggest that it represents woman, in general, in her role as mother, and possibly a great goddess believed to be the source of all life.

7

What is Religion?

It is quite widely believed today that all religions are fundamentally the same, that behind their surface differences, adapted to the circumstances of different peoples and historical periods, they all bring essentially the same message. This must be more of a pious hope than anything else, for although similar teachings do occur in more than one religion, fundamental differences of belief, attitude and behaviour are so marked that it is extremely hard to pin down exactly what religion is.

For example, the attitudes of the major religions to salvation and the purpose of life are quite different. In Judaism, Christianity and Islam salvation means the survival of the individual personality in a happy existence in heaven after death. In Hinduism and Buddhism, on the other hand, salvation may mean the opposite, not the survival but the obliteration of the individual personality. Christianity believes in a divine Saviour, who came into the world to rescue man, but Judaism and Islam strongly disapprove of this belief as a gross breach of monotheism, the belief in a single god. Christianity, Judaism and Islam all agree, however, that human beings live only once on the earth and so have only one chance to make sure of a happy afterlife. Life on earth is therefore a profoundly serious affair and it is essential to get it right. But in Hinduism and Buddhism human beings live over and over again on the earth, born and reborn again indefinitely, and there is literally all the time in the world to get things right. It is hardly surprising, consequently, that Hinduism and Buddhism are far more tolerant than Judaism, Christianity and Islam.

Fundamental differences occur not only between one religion and another, but within each religion itself. All religions contain internal contradictions and inconsistencies. All contain sects and groups and schools of thought which reflect varying psychological attitudes on the part of believers. The American philosopher William James drew a distinction between what he called the 'healthy-minded' and the 'morbid-minded' religious temperaments. The first enjoys life, sees it as something to be grateful for and produces a religion of cheerful thanksgiving and praise. The second is deeply conscious of the evils of life and the viciousness of human nature, and produces a religion of guilty repentance and dread. Both attitudes coexist inside every religion, and so do other psychological categories: tough-minded and tender-minded, for instance, or emotional and unemotional, or individualist and collectivist.

Cutting across psychological differences of this kind is another contrast. Each religion has what might be called a high register and a low register. The high register is the level of intellectual, educated and sophisticated belief, high-minded, philosophical and concerned with correct doctrine and the spiritual life. The low register is the level of widespread popular belief, which is far more down to earth and concerned with practical matters. The main purpose of religion at this level is to obtain the good things of life, ward off life's evils – suffering, poverty, disease, deprivation, bad luck – and secure a more enjoyable physical life after death or next time round. Trouble is therefore taken to conciliate and win the favour of the supernatural powers which have the good things of life in their gift.

ABOVE The religious significance of Stonehenge is uncertain, but it was aligned with risings and settings of the sun and moon, and is now widely believed to have been used as an astronomical observatory, and perhaps as an astronomical computer. Prehistoric men were evidently better equipped intellectually and better able to cope with their environment than was formerly recognized, and the origin of religion is unlikely to lie in simple fear of the unknown.

LEFT Canaanite stele from Hazor in Palestine, dated to the 14th century BC and thought to be connected with the worship of a prehistoric moon deity. The symbol of the moon is at the top of the stele and the two raised hands might stand for veneration and thanksgiving.

Popular religion tends to be polytheistic, a belief in many gods, and this is why the worship of many divine powers occurs within a monotheistic system, as in Christianity or Islam, or in an atheistic system, a disbelief in any gods, as in Buddhism. Accounts of religions vary considerably according to which of the two registers is stressed, but all religions contain both.

Religion is difficult to define, not only because different religions are different, and give house-room to widely varying beliefs, but because they are part of the entire life of a community, part of its ethics, its art, its politics, its whole organization and outlook. Religions explain why the world and the human condition are as they are, and justify society's institutions and values. They tell people what to do or not to do, and this can extend far beyond telling you that you must not murder or steal to deciding what you may eat, who you may eat with, whom you may marry, how you are or are not allowed to enjoy yourself.

What is it that separates religion from other areas of activity? The obvious answer is belief in gods or a God, but unfortunately this answer raises problems. One is that early Buddhism did not require any belief in gods or a God, and yet it is difficult not to regard the Buddha as a religious teacher. Another is that the objects of reverence in the various religions, or at different levels of the same religion, vary enormously. They may be animals or trees, or forces sensed in the wind and the rain or in the growth of crops in the spring; or dead or living human beings, like the god-men of India or the Christian and Muslim saints; or supernatural powers conceived of as larger-than-life human beings, like the gods of ancient Egypt, Greece or Rome; or an eternal Father or Mother, powerful and loving; or a vast impersonal It, with no human characteristics whatever.

There is no simple satisfactory definition of religion, but what seems to lie at the heart of it is a sense of the sacred, a feeling that there is another dimension to life besides the material and temporal one of ordinary, everyday experience. Behind and beyond the visible and palpable objects and creatures and phenomena of the world, there is sensed a reality which is more important, more lasting, more real, and which arouses emotions of awe and reverence. This ultimate reality may be a being or beings, a force, a principle, or something indefinable, but whatever it is, it gives a meaning and purpose to life, which without it would be a tale told by an idiot, signifying nothing.

The German writer Rudolf Otto pointed out that it is only in the sphere of religion that the terms 'holy' and 'sacred' are used. He traced the idea of the sacred to what he called the 'numinous', objects or places or experiences which inspire a sense of being in the presence of something, outside oneself, which is overwhelmingly mysterious, uncanny or sublime. An example is a bolt of lightning, striking suddenly, violently and destructively from a threatening sky, and lightning, or the power in the lightning, has been deified all over the world. The numinous provokes sensations ranging from stark terror to awe to fascination and a need to draw closer to the sacred and commune with it. Some people see the origin of all religion in experiences of the numinous, but it is doubtful whether this allows sufficiently for another facet of religious experience, the ability of human beings to think rationally about their situation in the world.

The reactions aroused by the sacred are naturally expressed in behaviour: in rituals, prayers, sacrifices, offerings, processions, pilgrimages; in the telling of myths, the writing of scriptures, the construction of systems of doctrine, or correct belief; in art and symbolism; in institutions, priesthoods, temples, churches, monasteries; in codes of morals and rules of conduct. One of the most important functions of religion is to encourage people to lead good moral lives. Morality varies from one society to another, but murder, treachery, greed, stealing, lying and unkindness are almost everywhere condemned as wrong. It is almost universally believed that the good ought to be rewarded and the wicked punished, but it is a matter of common observation that in reality the good frequently suffer while the wicked flourish. The unfairness of life raises an awkward problem for religion, because it suggests that the divine powers which rule the world are cruel and unjust. The solution, in all the major religions, is a system of justice which extends beyond this life. The good are rewarded and the wicked punished in the life after death or in the next life on earth.

The Origin of Religion

How religion first began is again extremely difficult to pin down, and again there may be no simple answer. Because religion is so old and so widespread, it is sometimes suggested that a religious impulse is embedded in human nature, that human beings are naturally religious. The trouble with this theory is that, if you look around you, a good many people plainly have no such impulse and are temperamentally irreligious. A different approach finds the source of religion not in man but in God, who has revealed himself to man, but this usually applies to the true religion (one's own religion), not to religion in general.

An explanation which many people nowadays accept traces religion to fear of the unknown, but this is an oversimplification which exaggerates the helplessness of early man. Prehistoric men very likely had a strong sense of the numinous and no doubt did fear the unknown, but the picture of them starting with terror at every shadow is overdrawn. In fact they coped successfully with their environment. They buried their dead and put food and useful equipment in the graves, which suggests belief in a life after death of some kind, and possibly a cult of each group's ancestors, but also shows that early man could abstract himself from the business of living, consider the meaning of death and think beyond the obvious conclusion. Like other animals, man has a powerful urge to survive. Unlike them, he knows he will die. The way out of this dilemma is another life after death.

Because prehistoric men left no written records behind them, we can only speculate about what they believed. They survived by hunting, fishing and gathering wild fruits, and crucial factors in their survival were outside their control. They needed a continuing supply of game and fruit every year, which depended on the annual cycle of nature, the birth of young animals and fresh vegetation in the spring. The continuance of each human group similarly required the birth of children to replace the adults who

One of the prehistoric cave paintings from Lascaux in France which indicate prehistoric man's concern with the animals he hunted for food. The bull on the left is apparently pierced with an arrow, perhaps as a magical aid to successful hunting.

The figure known as 'the dancing sorcerer', from deep in the cave of the Trois Frères in France. A man disguised as an animal, with an owlish mask and the antlers of a stag; he may represent a god who was lord of beasts, or possibly a priest-magician believed to have power over animals.

died. Early man may have sensed a pattern, an order in nature, not attributable to men or animals, and so attributed to unseen powers, superhuman and superanimal. The prehistoric 'Venus' figures of obese pregnant women, with the faces left blank, may represent 'woman', a goddess, as the source of all life. In the cave paintings, which seem to have been magical aids to hunting, there are figures of dancers disguised as animals in skins and masks. They may portray a god who was lord of animals, or a priest representing the god.

The beliefs which so-called 'primitive' peoples have broadly in common also throw some light on the wellsprings of religion. A particularly important point is the widespread disinclination to believe in chance and accident. When things happen, they are believed to happen by design, which implies a strong demand for order in nature. All events whose causes are not obvious are put down to supernatural agencies, not so much out of fear as to make sense of life. Linked with this, and with the knowledge that life is subject to factors beyond human control, are a deep respect for the numinous and a belief in many gods, spirits and unseen forces, on which human beings are dependent. Among them are the ancestors. People whose control over their environment is limited naturally try to establish good relations with their ancestors, from whom they inherit such techniques as they possess. It is widely believed that physical death is not the end of life and that the ancestors are still present and take an interest in their descendants, from whom they require loving and respectful offerings.

Communication with the ancestors and the world of spirits is achieved through shamans. A shaman, who often undergoes a long training, has the capacity to put himself into trance, in which he is believed to visit the spirit-world. In trance he may assume a different and eerily impressive personality, in which he speaks as the mouthpiece of a god or spirit. He has strange powers, and there is evidence now that some of them can be genuine. He may be able to read people's minds, to know what is happening far away, to catch glimpses of the future, and because he is confidently believed in he can frequently cure the sick. Shamanism has convinced people all over the world that an apparently supernatural dimension exists, in addition to that of ordinary, everyday life.

The shaman is the spiritual ancestor of the prophet and the mystic, and trance-experience, visions and ecstatic states have played an important role in the history of religions. Many of the founders and major inspiring figures of religions – including, for example, the Buddha, Moses, Muhammad, St Paul and Zoroaster – discovered the truth they subsequently proclaimed in experiences of this kind. It does not follow that all religion can be written off as absurd, for it is exceedingly unlikely that truth is limited to what reason will certify. It looks, indeed, as if the factors that are close to the roots of religion include a recognition of order in the world and a need to make sense of life, experiences of the numinous, the uncanny and impressive powers of peculiarly gifted individuals, the urge to survive and the consequent need for a life after death, the realization that man depends for survival on forces greater than himself, and the human capacity to think.

2. Hinduism

There are estimated to be about 520 million Hindus in the world today, which means that one of every eight people alive is a Hindu. All religions shelter a variety of beliefs and practices under one umbrella, but Hinduism accommodates so many that it is doubtful whether there is any religious belief or activity known to man which has not occurred somewhere in its history. There are many paths to truth in the Hindu view of things, and human beings are like rivers winding their different courses to the same sea. Hinduism consists of an enormous number of groups, sects and schools of thought, some with many followers, some with few, some dating from time immemorial, some founded by sages and holy men during the last thousand years, and some founded in the last hundred years. There is no Hindu creed or statement of faith, no Hindu Church with a hierarchy of priests, nothing which a Hindu is required by religion to think.

Some Hindus believe in many deities, some in none. Some believe in a single deity, but not all of them in the same one. Most often it will be Vishnu or Siva, but belief in a single deity does not imply rejection of the others. For those who worship Vishnu as the one God, Siva is not a false god but a secondary manifestation of Vishnu, and for the worshippers of Siva the converse is true. Besides the major deities, known all over India, there are the cults of numerous local gods and goddesses. The majority of Hindus live in villages which have their own deities, ancestor spirits, sacred trees, deified animals, forest and mountain godlings.

Hinduism is the oldest religious tradition of India. The word Hindu comes from the name of a river, the Indus, and essentially means Indian. Hinduism is almost entirely an Indian phenomenon, though Hindus who have settled in Africa, South-East Asia, the West Indies and Europe have naturally taken their religious traditions with them. Hindus have shown far less appetite for missionary work and the making of converts than Buddhists, Christians and Muslims. The conventional Hindu attitude is that it is each man's business to look after his own spiritual welfare and leave other people to look after theirs.

What holds Hinduism together, in all its astonishing and engaging variety, is first its Indian-ness and second its rites and ceremonies. There is nothing a Hindu must think but, traditionally at least, there are many things which he must do. The religion permeates a whole way of life and following this way of life, rather than any particular doctrine, constitutes orthodox, old-fashioned Hinduism.

Most of the rites take place at home, because every action of daily life, from getting up to going to bed, is part of the religion. Actions which in the West are mere matters of habit and social convention are religious actions for the orthodox Hindu. Washing first thing in the morning, for instance, is a religious duty and part of a complex of morning rites which includes repeating the name of one's god on getting out of bed, and saying prayers. Later in the day, liquid butter is poured on to the domestic fire, which is sacred, or pieces of wood are put on it, not merely to keep it burning but as offerings to it. Prayers are said before the image or symbol of the family deity, who lives in the house as an honoured guest and to whom simple offerings of food and flowers are made. The sacred dimension pervades everyday living in a way which is uncommon in the West. Having a bath, for example, the devout Hindu may think of the bath-water as the sacred water of the Ganges and pray to the Ganges to keep him safe from harm.

Purification rites bulk large, because of the emphasis which Hinduism places on spiritual and physical purity. Cleanliness is not merely next to godliness, it almost is godliness. Many actions are traditionally regarded as contaminating, including eating and drinking, urination and defecation, sexual intercourse, menstruation and pregnancy, and attending a funeral. The pollution must be removed by the correct ritual. After eating, for instance, the mouth should be rinsed out twelve times, with prayer to a god and taking care to spit the water out to the left, not to the right.

There are also ceremonies at home for each stage of a person's life, from those which protect an unborn baby in its mother's womb to those performed at the child's birth, when he is named, when he first sees the sun and when he first eats solid food. Later there are ceremonies for the main events of life through marriage to death. Worship in temples is less important. Some Hindus go to a temple every day, some go now and again, some never go at all.

Rebirth and Karma

Hinduism is famous in the West for its lofty philosophy, its mysticism, its ferocious asceticism and its eroticism, but the great majority of Hindus are not and never have been philosophers, mystics, ascetics or voluptuaries. As long ago as the eleventh century a Muslim named Alberuni wrote a book about India in which he commented on the gulf between the high register of Hindu religion and the religion at its popular level. The one philosophical idea which has thoroughly permeated popular Hinduism is the belief in rebirth.

In Christianity, Judaism and Islam each soul has a single life on earth, which comes to an end with the death of the body. In Hinduism – and in

Hundreds of religious festivals are celebrated every year in Hindu India, so many that it is said that if a Hindu observed them all he would have no time to do anything else. At this village festival the images of the local gods have been garlanded with flowers, and clay figures of horses watch the proceedings.

Pool in a temple of Vishnu at
Kanchipuram in the south,
the only Indian city sacred to
both Vishnu and Siva.
Hinduism places a strong
emphasis on spiritual and
physical cleanliness. Frequent
washing is an important ritual
requirement and at most
temples there is a 'tank', in
which worshippers wash
themselves and their clothes,
and which is regarded as a
place where heaven and earth
meet.

Buddhism, which is descended from it – the souls of human beings and all living things live and die and are reborn again and again in a succession of bodies, bound to 'the wheel of existence' which turns for ever. Linked with this is the law of *karma*. The behaviour of each soul in each life determines the type of body it will have and the type of experience it will undergo in its next life. Those who do good are reborn in a higher condition of life. Those who do not are reborn as human beings of lower status: or even, in theory, as animals, insects or plants, though in practice Hindus do not take this notion very seriously. The system was set up long ago by the gods. It works automatically and the effect is that people are not rewarded or punished for their actions so much as by them. Those who do good become good and those who do evil become evil.

Only the most spiritual of human beings can escape from the wheel of existence, and in Hindu philosophy and mysticism the true goal of life is to achieve the escape. At popular levels, however, the attitude tends to be very different and life is widely regarded as something so potentially excellent that the powers that be have beneficently arranged for it never to end. The emphasis on salvation, on liberation from life in the body, which is so dominant in the theology, is far less evident in the popular religion. The ordinary believer is not expected to be a spiritual athlete. Tradition lays down three aims for him: acquiring wealth; enjoying life; and accumulating religious merit, primarily through the correct observance of rituals. Only in later life is he supposed to withdraw somewhat from the world and meditate upon his salvation. In practice, the main purpose of religion for most Hindus is to achieve material prosperity and the good things of life. These are granted or withheld by the gods, who can abate or even override the effects of karma.

After death, according to the prevailing belief, the souls of those who have accumulated good karma go for a time to lead a happy life in one of the heavens, where they receive part of their reward, before being reborn on earth in a better condition than before. Those who have piled up bad karma pay part of it off in one of the hells, where they are punished before being reborn on a lower rung of the ladder than before. Cutting across this belief, however, is the belief that through loving faith in a particular god the worshipper can be saved from death and rebirth, and live for ever in happiness in the god's heaven.

The Aryans and Vedism

Hinduism has no founder and its early history is obscure because it extends so far back into the past and is clouded by extreme uncertainty about dates. The earliest discernible influences which seem to have helped to create Hinduism come from the civilization flourishing in the Indus valley from about 2500 BC. No temples or buildings which can be identified as religious have been discovered, but numerous female figurines suggest the worship of a fertility goddess. A seal has been found which seems to represent a horned god squatting in a yoga position and surrounded by animals, perhaps a prototype of the god Siva. There is also evidence of veneration of

Seal from the Indus valley civilization, which was overwhelmed by the Aryan invasions. It may depict a prototype of Siva in his character as Pasupati, the beneficent lord of animals, but the extent to which pre-Aryan beliefs influenced Hinduism is disputed.

the phallus and of ritual bathing, both of which occur in medieval and modern Hinduism.

From about 1500 BC waves of tribes speaking Sanskrit and equipped with horses and chariots invaded India from the north-west and overwhelmed the Indus valley civilization. From the Punjab they moved slowly eastwards to conquer the northern plains. Over many hundreds of years the culture they established in the north, with its heartland in the central Ganges area, spread southwards through the Indian peninsula to Sri Lanka and eastwards to Bengal and Assam. The invaders called themselves Aryans and came originally from somewhere in the steppe country of southern Russia and Central Asia. They were a branch of the Indo-European peoples, having much in common with the Persians, Greeks, Romans, Celts, Slavs, Germans and Scandinavians. They were fair-skinned and tall, in contrast to the dark-skinned, flat-nosed aboriginal inhabitants of India, whom they regarded with contempt and described as noseless dwarfs and monkeys.

The invaders believed in Aryan racial supremacy long before Hitler. To be Aryan was to be 'noble'. To be non-Aryan was to be ignoble, uncouth and savage. This distinction has affected Indian attitudes ever since and the approved, traditional Hindu way of life is still called 'the Aryan way'. The early development of Hinduism is regarded by most western historians as an interaction between Aryan and aboriginal, non-Aryan ideas, but this is foreign to the traditional Hindu view, in which Hinduism is of exclusively Aryan descent.

The Aryans were led by rajas, or tribal chieftains, and later by kings. The aristocracy reckoned their wealth principally in cattle and, unlike most later Hindus, were great eaters of beef. They enjoyed fighting, hunting, feasting, gambling and all the physical pleasures of life. Their priest-magicians and learned men, the Brahmins, were a separate class of specialists in the sacred.

There seem to have been no temples or images of the Aryan gods. Animals were sacrificed to them in the open air, burned on fires. An intoxicating drink called *soma*, personified as a god and possibly derived from the mushroom, fly agaric, was drunk by the worshippers and poured out to the gods. These were cheerful occasions at which the gods and their human worshippers feasted together and in return for their offerings the worshippers hoped to obtain the favour of the gods, strong sons, increase of cattle and crops, good fortune in life and an entry into heaven at death. They were perhaps a magical imitation and foretaste of heaven on earth and the hallucinogenic effects of drinking soma would create an ecstatic sense of rising above the human condition and being at one with the gods.

Some of the rituals were extremely elaborate. An example is the *asvamedha*, or horse sacrifice, performed only for kings and then only rarely because it was difficult and expensive. A young stallion, preferably white, was ritually consecrated and allowed to wander about the country for a year, followed by an escort of warriors. Any ruler into whose territory the horse strayed was required either to fight or to submit. The horse was finally adorned with pearls, anointed with oil and killed, after which the king's chief wife went through a mimic copulation with it. Its flesh was then cooked and part of it was eaten and the rest burned. The rite was presumably intended to promote the fertility and power of both the royal family and the land. The last asvamedha on record was celebrated for the ruler of Jaipur in the eighteenth century.

Human victims were offered to the gods on occasion. In one ritual, resembling the horse sacrifice, the chosen victim lived royally for a year, except that he had to remain chaste. He was then stabbed or strangled and, again, the queen pretended to copulate with the corpse. Human sacrifices continued in India into the nineteenth century. A human victim was offered every week to the goddess Kali in the temple at Tanjore, and the custom of sacrificing children on an island south of Calcutta continued until 1803.

The religion of the Aryans is known as Brahmanism or Vedism. Its principal scriptures, the four Vedas (Veda means knowledge), are the oldest sacred books of any living religion in the world. They are collections of hymns to the gods, prayers and spells, handed on by word of mouth for centuries before being written down. The most important of them, the *Rig Veda* (Royal Veda), contains more than a thousand hymns. The Vedas are profoundly revered as the foundation of Hinduism, and sacrifices are offered to them. They are not regarded as the compositions of priests and poets put together gradually over many generations, but as divinely inspired, 'not of human origin', revealed complete as they stand to certain great sages.

The Aryans worshipped the powers of nature, personified as larger-than-life human beings. They were a warlike, patriarchal people and, though they recognized goddesses, their principal deities were male. The Vedic deities, the Devas or 'shining ones', were mainly connected with the sky and the weather. Their leader, Indra, was lord of storm, thunder, rain and war. Pictured in the image of the ideal Aryan war-chief, he was an invincible fighter, aggressive, boisterous, boastful and jovial, bull-like in his virility, given to gigantic eating and magnificent drunkenness, and he welcomed warriors to feast with him in his heaven after death. It was Indra who led the Aryans to victory and conquest, but all the Vedic gods battled against the powers of darkness and evil, the Asuras, who on one level represented cosmic forces of drought, death and chaos, and on another represented the human enemies of the Aryans.

Agni, the personification of fire, was another important god. He was the lightning which flashed from the sky down to the earth, and conversely the fire which carried the burned offerings of sacrifice from the earth up to the gods in the sky. He was the fire on the domestic hearth, the god who lived among human beings as the warm centre of home and family. Reverence for fire and light has remained a characteristic of Hinduism ever since. There is a beautiful hymn in the *Rig Veda* to Ushas, goddess of the dawn, the brilliant brightness, who personifies the coming of light to a world shrouded in darkness.

The *Rig Veda* already shows signs of the trend towards monotheism and the bent for philosophical speculation which come to the fore in the later Sanskrit scriptures. One text says that the supreme reality is One, though called by many names, and there is a hymn to 'the unknown god' who is

18th-century figure of the old Vedic god of fire, Agni, from southern India. He rides the ram, his 'vehicle', and stylized flames issue from his two heads, which symbolize the fire of sacrifice and the fire on the hearth at home.

lord of all that exists. Another text speaks of a great primeval sacrifice when the gods dismembered the cosmic man, Purusha. From the parts of his body everything in the universe was made. In this myth the sacrifice is the foundation of the order of the universe, and the practical effect of the myth was to emphasize the importance of sacrificial rituals, which were believed to repeat the primeval sacrifice and so magically to recreate and perpetuate the world-order. The effect was also to give the Brahmins, who alone knew how to perform the elaborate rituals correctly, a position of supreme dominance. The gods, who are part of the world-order, are themselves dependent on the rituals and become the subordinates of the priests who celebrate them. The Brahmins claimed to be gods themselves, and throughout the subsequent history of Hinduism priests have enjoyed high prestige and influence, and ritual has been the centre of the religion.

The Upanishads

Over the centuries the Vedic religion slowly altered, partly it seems through the absorption of non-Aryan ideas from the conquered peoples. The doctrines of rebirth and karma are stated clearly for the first time in the *Upanishads* (Sittings with a Teacher), which are believed to have been delivered to selected pupils by certain notable *gurus*, or spiritual instructors. The *Brihadaranyaka Upanishad*, for instance, is attributed to Yajnavalkya, a famous semi-legendary hermit, said to have demonstrated his mastery as a theologian at a gathering of sages from all over India, where he trounced his own teacher so thoroughly in debate that the latter's head fell off.

According to the *Upanishads*, all things die and are reborn in an endless cycle, to which even the gods are subject. Behind this, however, is something which is not born and does not die, which remains timeless and unchanging at the heart of time and change, a supreme reality or Absolute, not a being but a principle, not He but It. It is called Brahman, a word used earlier to mean 'sacred'. The true goal of existence is to escape from the wheel of successive lives and merge with the Absolute. This is possible because Brahman exists within each human being as the innermost self, called Atman. The self and the Absolute, Atman and Brahman, are identical, a doctrine summed up in the phrase, 'Thou art That'. Brahman, which is the whole universe and pervades the whole universe, is also the self within the heart, smaller than a grain of rice yet greater than the earth and sky (*Chandogya Upanishad*). The realization of this truth is the key to achieving liberation from life in the world, and in some of the *Upanishads* the realization by itself brings liberation.

This enormously powerful and inspiring idea became the central theme of Hindu philosophy, and has been examined and re-examined by thinkers and mystics for more than 2000 years. The main thrust of the Hindu religion in its high register became the search for liberation from life. The two systems of Hindu spirituality best known in the West, Vedanta and Yoga, are both founded on the *Upanishads*.

The ideas expressed in the *Upanishads* spread rapidly among the higher social classes. Their inevitable effect was to devalue the Vedic gods. If the only permanent reality is an impersonal Absolute, then any personal deity is at best second-rate. A new god, Brahma, now appeared as the personal manifestation of Brahman, but whether he attracted much enthusiasm outside the ranks of priests is uncertain. The old Vedic deities had already been undermined by the Brahmins' claim to control them. Gods who are subservient to men, even to god-men, have lost the power which made them worth worshipping in the first place. Though the process took many centuries, the Vedic gods faded slowly away until most of them were forgotten.

Heaven was also devalued, because it was no longer an eternal state of happiness after death, but a kind of temporary rest-camp or amusement park between one life on earth and the next. The sacrifices were devalued as well, because all they were now seen to do was to perpetuate the world-order from which the new impulse was to escape.

The *Upanishads* were intended for, and helped to create, a spiritual elite. The longed-for liberation is not achieved by the ordinary person, who goes on leading his succession of lives indefinitely. It is achieved by the mystic, the ascetic, the athlete of the spirit. The *Upanishads* gave a powerful impetus to asceticism. If the goal of the religious life is to gain liberation from existence in the world in a physical body, then an apparent way of escape is to slight the body and withdraw from the world. One form of this is renunciation, giving up possessions and refusing to own things, abstaining from sex and physical pleasures, remaining silent, abstracting oneself from the bustle and scurry of everyday living. The more active form is positive mortification of the flesh, which the Vedas had already taught as a way of obtaining superhuman powers. Hence the long tradition of Hindu asceticism, in which the body is subjected to pain and stress. The awesome austerities of the Hindu *sadhu*, or holy ascetic, have always fascinated people in the West. Some sadhus mutilate or lacerate themselves, some lie on beds of nails, some remain standing or sitting motionless for years, some keep their hands clenched until their nails grow into their palms.

In the wake of the *Upanishads* came the principle of *ahimsa*, of doing no harm to living things, because all life was believed to share in the sacredness of Brahman. In practice it chiefly meant vegetarianism and the offering of vegetable substances instead of animals in sacrifice, both of which became characteristic of Hinduism, though not adopted by all Hindus. The principle has been much admired in the West, but in real life cruelty to human beings and animals has been no rarer in India than in the western world. In the eastern religions ahimsa is classified as a type of renunciation, and from this negative point of view it has frequently meant that refraining from actively causing harm is all that is required, while positive efforts to alleviate suffering are left to other people, chance or death. The law of karma, after all, makes sure that people and animals get only what they deserve.

By the sixth century BC the Vedic religion was under serious attack. The new emphasis on the individual and his need to find the path to salvation had little use for priests and complicated rituals standing between the worshipper and the divine. The authority of the Vedas and the Brahmins

10th-century figure of the god Brahma, from the Khmer kingdom of South-East Asia. He personified Brahman, the Absolute or supreme reality. He was depicted with four heads, to indicate his control of the four quarters of the world, but he was never popular and was seldom worshipped. The devotees of Vishnu and Siva subordinated him to their own gods.

was challenged by ascetics and reformers, including Gautama and Mahavira, the founders of Buddhism and Jainism. They gained support among aristocrats and merchant families and among young intellectuals.

Vishnu, Siva and the Goddess

The first definite date in Indian history is 327 BC, when Alexander the Great invaded from the north-west. He was soon forced to withdraw when his Greek troops, who had conquered half the known world and wanted to go home, refused to follow him any further to the east. Soon afterwards, Chandragupta I Maurya, who had met the great Macedonian and admired him, seized the throne of Magadha, a kingdom in the north-east. He extended his sway to all northern India from Afghanistan to Bengal and founded the first Indian empire. His grandson, Asoka, ruled all India except the far south from his capital at Pataliputra (modern Patna) on the Ganges. Asoka became a Buddhist and in his time Buddhism was the most dynamic religious force in India.

After Asoka's death his empire began to break up, and the late centuries before the Christian era saw a reaction against both Upanishadic philosophy and Buddhism. An impersonal Absolute is hard to love and losing one's cherished identity by merging with it is not everyone's ideal. A new religious trend appeared in groups who turned to *bhakti*, love of a deity who is the Absolute but who is also a tender and merciful person. According to one tradition, the new movement came from the south, from peninsular, tropical India.

Bhakti means both man's love for God and God's love for man. In the *Bhagavad Gita* (Song of the Lord), the most admired of the Hindu classics, the Supreme Being is the god Vishnu, appearing on earth in his human form as Krishna, and the way to salvation is to do one's duty in one's station in life, to fear God and to love God. God is the whole universe and the innermost self of each human being is a tiny particle of God, but the ultimate absorption of the self in God no longer means the loss of personal identity. 'Who sees Me everywhere, who sees the All in me, for him I am not lost, nor is he lost to me.'

The bhakti movement valued emotion above cerebration. It rejected thinking about God is favour of heartfelt and concentrated adoration of God and submission to his will. It preferred simple devotions, such as chanting God's name and singing his praises, to elaborate rituals, and though at first the Brahmins were consequently antagonistic, in time they came to terms with it. Some bhakti teachers regarded good moral behaviour as less important than, and even possibly a hindrance to, fervent devotion to the divine. A cautionary story was told about the legendary King Bharata, who saved a fawn from drowning and became so fond of it that his loving concentration on God was impaired. He was punished by being reborn as a doe, and in this form he repaired his mistake.

To what extent, if at all, this idea of a loving God appearing on earth in human form was influenced by Christianity is a disputed question, bedevilled by uncertainty about dates. No one knows when the bhakti

movement first grew up, or when Christianity first reached India. Usually, however, Christian influence is denied and the *Bhagavad Gita* is generally dated well before the time of Christ.

Bhakti was a far more popular movement than the religion of the *Upanishads*. It is closely linked with the worship of Vishnu and Siva, who became the two great gods of medieval and modern Hinduism. Vishnu, who had been a minor deity in the Vedas, became for his worshippers the one true God, the creator and preserver of the universe and the saviour of mankind. The belief grew up that he had manifested himself on earth in a number of animal and human forms, his avatars or 'descents', each time to save the world and man from destruction by evil forces. The Hindu

Vishnu reclining on the coils of Ananta, the serpent of infinite time, who rests on the waters of the primeval ocean. The god, the serpent and the water are all manifestations of the divine energy which underlies life. At the god's feet is his consort, the beautiful goddess Lakshmi. A lotus springs from the god's navel and in it Brahma is born. Painted clay, 19th century.

reaction against Buddhism is clear from the doctrine that Vishnu came to earth as the Buddha and founded the false religion of Buddhism, to lead wicked men and evil demons astray and cause them to ensure their own doom by becoming Buddhists.

All Vishnu's other incarnations on earth occurred long, long ago in the distant mythological past (though there is one avatar which is still to come). The two most important were in human form as Krishna and Rama, and it is under these names that Vishnu is principally worshipped. In his avatar as Rama, according to mythology, he was a warrior-prince and the model of the good man, strong, brave, virtuous, a loyal son and a loving and faithful husband. His beautiful wife, Sita, is the model of the good woman, the loving and loyal wife and mother. Here the god and his consort represent an ideal of behaviour, not for the spiritual athlete but for the ordinary man and woman. At sophisticated levels the Hindi form of the god's name, Ram, came to mean God. Mahatma Gandhi, shot down by an assassin in 1948, died with the word Ram on his lips.

The cult of Krishna is far more widespread, and in fact Krishna is the most popular of all Hindu deities. Coming to earth to destroy evil demons, he was born as a human baby, and is often worshipped in this form, in which he naturally arouses deep emotions of love and protectiveness, not untinged with kindly amusement. The baby Krishna was brought up in a village among cowherds and, as he grew to manhood, the village women loved him. He teased them and played erotic tricks on them, dancing with them in the moonlight and stealing away when each of them believed that he loved her alone, withdrawing from them to give himself to them in the end. This sexual metaphor of withdrawal, heightened passion and fulfillment is interpreted in spiritual terms. The women's hunger for Krishna is every soul's longing for God.

The story of the god growing up among humble people and sharing their lives has a powerful human appeal. Whatever the sex of the worshipper, the god can be regarded in the light of a son, a lover, a husband, an elder brother, a father, a friend, and the emotions aroused by any and all of these relationships focus upon him. In the cult of Krishna there grew up something previously unknown in India, the worship of a god incarnate in human form who demands his follower's love.

The parallel with Christianity is obvious, but the question of possible Christian influence is again disputed and difficult. Christ too came to earth in human form, he too was both God and man, and he too was born as a human baby and grew up in obscurity among humble people. On the other hand, the stories of Krishna and Christ have an entirely different flavour, the erotic elements in Krishna's story are absent from Christ's, and there is no parallel in Indian religion to the death on the cross.

Another important difference is the Hindu belief that God has been partially incarnated quite frequently in human beings. There has been only one Christ, in Christian theology, but thousands of sages, teachers, ascetics and holy men, including some alive today, have been venerated by their followers in India as god-men, partial incarnations of the divine. This was a serious difficulty to Christian missionaries in India, who found many

Krishna as a child. He was born on earth as a human baby and grew up in a village among humble people, who did not realize that he was a god. The village boys swam in a pool, where a great snake lurked and devoured them, but Krishna danced on the snake's head until he pleaded for mercy and agreed to leave the pool for ever.

Hindus quite ready to accept that Jesus of Nazareth was divine, but quite unable to accept that he was a unique case.

Vaishnava, the worship of Vishnu, most often as Krishna, constitutes one of the three major sub-religions within Hinduism. Saiva, the worship of Siva, is the second. There are devotees of each god everywhere in India, but Vaishnava is stronger in the north and Saiva is stronger in the south. The two gods were rivals at first, but later achieved a peaceful coexistence, with each being regarded by his own worshippers as the true God of whom the other is a secondary form. Which god is worshipped as the true one very often depends on family tradition.

Siva is worshipped either directly or through an image of his *linga* (phallus) in stone, metal, wood or earth, standing on a platform which represents the *yoni* (vulva) of his consort. This does not imply any erotic element in his rites, or not amongst the great majority of his worshippers. It is said that the symbol has been a conventional image of the god for so long that most of his devotees do not realize that it has any sexual significance.

RIGHT Rama leading his army to battle, a 19th-century painting. Rama is another of the avatars of Vishnu, and the model of the ideal man.

ABOVE The linga (phallus) is the principal symbol of Siva, emblematic of his vast generative energy. The god is often represented in this form, the platform on which the linga stands symbolizing the vulva of his consort.

LEFT A Nepalese figure of Siva, from Katmandu. Since he unites opposites, Siva has a destructive and grim side to his character, but for his worshippers he is not a frightening deity but a god of love. The third eye in his forehead is the eye which purges away evil and pollution.

Siva has a grim and terrifying side to his nature, for he unites all opposite qualities. Loving and cruel, creative and destructive, sane and raving mad, he is eternally active and eternally at rest. He is the master of all generation, the source of all life, as his phallic emblem suggests, but he is also the lord of ascetics. The world is preserved in being by his meditations as he sits on the slopes of the Himalayas, smeared with ash, with the sacred River Ganges flowing from his matted hair. He is the god of life and yet also the god of death, the master of cemeteries, represented wearing a garland of skulls. In this form he personifies all the terror of colossal unbridled power, and he is often shown with a third eye in his forehead, the eye which burns and destroys. However for his worshippers he is not a frightening deity but a god of love, who cherishes his children and protects them from harm. When he punishes human beings he does so in love, to turn them from the wrong path.

Some Hindu thinkers conceived a trinity of gods, the Trimurti or triple form of the divine: Brahma the Creator, Vishnu the Preserver and Siva the Destroyer. This theoretical construct, however, has nothing to do with the actual practice of religion. For the two principal Hindu groups, either Vishnu or Siva is the supreme God who creates all things, preserves all things and destroys all things when their time runs out, and each rewards his faithful devotees in his heaven after death.

Exactly how and when these two gods rose to prominence is not known, but each evidently met a need for a powerful and protective deity, who rules the world and intervenes in it, who rewards and punishes, a god to love and be loved by. An order of Saivite monks, the Pasupatas, was in existence by the first Christian century. The early Gupta kings of the fourth century, who governed a northern empire from Pataliputra, declared themselves supreme devotees of Vishnu.

By this time the third major deity of medieval and modern Hinduism was beginning to emerge. Goddesses had undoubtedly been worshipped locally in India for untold centuries, but there now developed a widespread cult of a Goddess as the supreme power in the universe. She is principally worshipped now as Durga or Kali, and her cult is strongest in Bengal, where goats, sheep and buffalo are sacrificed to her, but many Hindus revere Devi, 'the Mother', as a secondary manifestation of the divine.

Hinduism is traditionally patriarchal in spirit and the goddesses are normally the subordinate and passive partners of the gods, but in the worship of the Goddess the position is reversed and the female is the active and dominant force. The Goddess is usually linked with Siva as his Sakti (Power), which means not merely his consort but his titanic energy. She is given his characteristics and worshipped in his place. Like Siva, she unites opposites. In one aspect she is beautiful, golden-skinned, loving and bountiful, the force behind all growth and plenty in nature. In another, as goddess of death, destruction and terror, she is black-skinned and hideous, her tongue lolling out and blood spilling from her mouth and running down her chin. For her devotees, however, she is not a goddess of whom to be terrified, but a merciful and gracious Mother, whose wrath, like Siva's, is reserved for the forces of evil.

ABOVE The Goddess, as Durga, killing the demon Mahisha, who took the form of a titanic bull buffalo. The gods were unable to vanquish Mahisha, who threatened to destroy the universe. In their fury waves of energy flowed from the bodies of the gods and formed the Goddess. She killed and beheaded Mahisha, so mercifully releasing his soul from the demonic body in which it was imprisoned.

RIGHT The Goddess is usually linked with Siva as his Sakti, his gigantic energy. Like him, she unites the opposites of life and death, creation and destruction, love and terror. For her worshippers, however, she is a merciful and bountiful mother and her wrath is reserved for the powers of evil. Figure of the goddess as Kali, from Madras, 18th or 19th century.

Many goddesses were linked with Siva and in mythology, by his consort Parvati, he was the father of two of the best known Hindu gods, Karttikeya and Ganesa. Karttikeya is a warlike deity with six heads, who in myth triumphantly slaughters armies of demons. He is also known as Skanda, which interestingly recalls Sikander, one form of the name of Alexander the Great. He is revered in southern India, where he is linked with fertility. His brother, Ganesa, is popular all over India as the elephant-headed god of good luck, to whom prayers are said for success in new ventures.

Temples, Cows and Caste

The Gupta Empire was overwhelmed by a new wave of foreign invasion, when the Huns and other tribes from Central Asia poured into northern India through the mountain passes. The empire fractured into numerous small kingdoms and, when the dust settled, the various Rajput princes and clans, many of them descended from the invaders, dominated the scene in the north and west.

The structure of Hinduism, as it remained down to modern times, was now virtually complete. The principal deities had emerged, and with them came images and temples. The first Hindu temples in stone and brick date from the Gupta period (though there were slightly earlier ones of wood) and at the same time the Hindu deities began to appear in art. Both developments may have drawn on Buddhist precedent.

The most important Hindu temples are staffed by thousands of priests and attendants. The god is treated in his temple as a king is treated in his palace. He and his consort, in the form of their images, are ceremonially wakened in the morning with lamps and music. They are washed, dressed and fed, and during the day their praises are sung in hymns and worshippers prostrate themselves before them and bring them gifts. They have a rest in the afternoon, and in the evening they are fed and undressed and put to bed. Down into the nineteenth century, troupes of girls, the *devadasis* or 'slaves of the god', entertained the god by dancing before him as a king's slave-girls would. In southern India, especially, they might also act as prostitutes, their earnings going to the upkeep of the temple.

On occasions, the god's image makes a royal progress through his city. Once a year, for example, the god Jagannatha, a form of Krishna, rides in procession through the town of Puri, south of Calcutta, on a massive chariot, drawn with ropes by his devotees. At one time, people used to throw themselves under the huge wheels of the chariot, in the belief that they would go straight to heaven.

Just as the god's statue is a representation of him in miniature, so his temple is a miniature replica of the world. Each part of it corresponds to some aspect of the life and structure of the universe, which may account for the erotic carvings on the walls of some Hindu temples. Until modern times, at least, Hinduism was not puritanical about sex, which was regarded as natural and enjoyable, and as much a part of the lives of gods as of men.

A Chinese Buddhist named Hsuan Tsang travelled in India in the 630s and 640s, in diligent search of Buddhist scriptures, and narrowly escaped

The elephant-headed god Ganesa, an 18th-century watercolour from Madras. Known as the Lord of Obstacles, he is prayed to for success in new ventures. The rat is his 'vehicle', and the god overcomes all obstacles for those who worship him aright as the elephant tramples down all barriers and the rat finds its way through all obstacles to the granary and the storehouse.

One of the elaborate and
magnificent monumental
gateways of the Great Temple
at Madurai, sacred to Siva and
his consort, here known as
Minakshi, 'the fish-eyed'. As
the worship of Siva gained
ground, the cults of many
local goddesses were
assimilated to it by marrying
the goddess to the great god.

being sacrificed to the goddess Durga by pirates on the Ganges. Hsuan Tsang saw many Hindu temples, including no less than twenty in the city of Varanasi (Benares), whose chief deity was Siva, then as now. He commented on the holiness of the Ganges, remarking that people came to drown themselves at the point where the Ganges and the Jumna join, near modern Allahabad, in the belief that they would be reborn in heaven.

Frequent washing and bathing is an important Hindu ritual requirement, and whatever water is used the Hindu should think of it as the water of the Ganges. Bathing places, the *ghats*, are provided along the banks of rivers and are regarded as sites at which heaven and earth intersect. The bodies of the dead are normally cremated in Hindu India, on a river bank close to a ghat, and often some of the ash is collected for later deposit in the Ganges. Pilgrimage to the Ganges and other sacred rivers is a way of coming closer to heaven in this life, and so of earning spiritual merit.

Another venerable Hindu institution is the sacred cow, and cows wandering placidly about the streets are a familiar sight in Indian cities. The origins of cow-worship in India are obscure, but the animal is closely linked

Puri in eastern India is the centre of the worship of Jagannatha, 'lord of the world', who is identified with Krishna. Staffed by thousands of priests and attendants, the god's temple contains shrines to Krishna, Vishnu, Siva and other gods. Once a year the image of Jagannatha is taken through the town on a wooden chariot, forty-five feet high and with sixteen massive wheels. People used to throw themselves under the wheels of the 'juggernaut' in the belief that they would go straight to heaven. The car on the right is that of Jagannatha.

A cremation ground on the edge of the Ganges at Varanasi (Benares). Except for holy men and babies, who are usually buried, cremation is the rule in Hindu India. The body is taken to the bank of a river, often near a ghat, to be close to heaven, and is burned there. The ashes and unburned bones are later buried or thrown into a river.

with the earth and the bounty of nature, and in poor country areas the local temple may be the cowshed. There is no cow-goddess of any importance; the animal itself is sacred. To kill or injure a cow, or to eat beef, came to be regarded as a profanation of the whole Hindu way of life. Down into this century the slaughter of cows by Muslims, who have no qualms about eating beef – it is pork which is taboo to them – has sparked off murderous riots. In some Hindu temples a cow is milked every morning before the image of the god. Cow dung, sometimes mixed with water, is used as a purifying agent and four other products of the cow – milk, curds, butter and urine – are also used in purification rituals. Gandhi, who said he yielded to no one in his worship of the cow, described the protection of cows as Hinduism's gift to the world, because it takes a human beyond his own species and enables him to realize his identity with all living things.

The ancient caste system, on the other hand, has been attacked over the centuries by many Hindu reformers and fierce arguments have raged over it in modern India, where public discrimination against the lower castes and the untouchables, who are at the bottom of the social pyramid, is now

illegal. (Traditionally, Europeans are untouchables.) There are some 3000 castes, with many sub-castes. The members of a caste may not share the same religious beliefs, but they do share rules intended to safeguard their purity, principally by regulating what they eat, who they eat with and whom they marry: an example of the Hindu instinct to control conduct rather than belief. The higher castes are vegetarian, but some of the lower are not. Eating with someone of a lower caste, and indeed any close contact, is contaminating and requires ritual purification. Marriage is allowed only within the caste, but this rule has frequently been ignored. Some castes traditionally follow a particular occupation.

Whether caste has any necessary place in Hindu religion is a hotly disputed point, but it is caste which is largely responsible for Hinduism's remarkable diversity. Indian society is racially extremely mixed and the caste system enabled people of different races, cultures, habits and traditions to preserve a separate identity within Hindu society. It is linked with the belief in rebirth and the wheel of existence, because being born into a higher or lower caste is a consequence of previous lives. From the orthodox conservative point of view, consequently, there is no injustice in the system, quite the contrary, for each person reaps what he has sown.

By the sixth century, developments in the cult of the Goddess, especially in Bengal and Assam, had started the Tantric movement (which also gained a foothold in Buddhism). Tantrism was not a sect but a current of religious and philosophical ideas, put into practice in small groups operating in secret. They believed in ritual sexual intercourse as a method of achieving liberation from the mortal state by enacting, and so entering into, the divine copulation of Siva and Sakti. Some groups, convinced that the way to escape from human limitations was to throw off all normal human restraints, religiously broke every conceivable taboo. The sect known as Kapaulikas, for instance, squatted on human corpses during their devotions and practised cannibalism and the ceremonial rape and slaughter of virgin girls.

Two systems more characteristic of Hindu spirituality are Yoga and Vedanta. Yoga is famed for its postures, breathing techniques and exercises. Its purpose is to achieve total self-understanding and self-mastery, and so attain union with the divine. It is supposed to have been founded far back in the distant past by the legendary sage Yajnavalkya, but the earliest systematic account of it is in the *Yoga Sutras* of the otherwise unknown author Patanjali, apparently dating from somewhere in the early centuries after Christ.

Sacred cows at a temple near Kanchipuram. The origins of Hindu veneration of the cow are obscure, but the animal is a symbol of the bounty of nature. Killing or injuring a cow, or eating beef, came to be regarded as a profanation of the Hindu way of life.

Vedanta, the most influential of all the Hindu schools of philosophy, is also descended from the *Upanishads* and centres on the doctrine of the identity of Brahman and Atman, the Absolute and the self. Its most famous figure is Sankara, a Brahmin from Malabar in the south-west, said to have spent his life as a wandering philosopher, visiting temples and discoursing with other learned sages. To the dismay of some later Vedantists, he insisted that liberation from the wheel of rebirths and union with the divine necessitates the total extinction of the individual personality.

Sankara was a devotee of Siva, but he also wrote hymns to Vishnu and

ABOVE 18th-century painting of the great Hindu god Siva, with his consort Parvati on the mythical Mount Kailasa in the Himalayas, the axis of the universe. With them are their children, the six-headed god Karttikeya and the elephant-headed Ganesa.

LEFT Cremation is the usual Hindu method of disposing of the dead, the traditional belief being that the dead person's spirit lingers near the body and cannot be reborn until the body is destroyed. Formerly a cow was sacrificed but the custom has been abandoned and at this cremation of a Brahmin in Bali the animal is represented by a wooden figure.

ABOVE LEFT Entrance of a temple of Vishnu near Madurai in southern India, guarded by figures of Garuda, the king of birds, and Hanuman, the chief of the monkey-people.

RIGHT The huge temple of Vishnu at Srirangam in southern India which contains the famous Horse Court with a colonnade of rearing war-horses.

Durga. He was a fierce opponent of Buddhism, but seems to have taken a leaf out of the Buddhist book in founding a Saivite monastic order, known as Dasnami, with four principal monasteries, in the north, south, west and east, at Badrinath, Sringeri, Dvaraka and Puri. The order and the abbots of the four monasteries are still extremely influential. It is said that on his deathbed Sankara asked God to forgive him for three things: for confining him who is formless in buildings, for venturing to describe him who is beyond description, and for implicitly denying his presence everywhere by visiting temples.

At a much more popular level, from perhaps the sixth or seventh century, there was a flourishing tradition of religious poetry, not in Sanskrit, the language of theologians, but in the languages of ordinary people, Tamil in the south, Hindi and others in the north. Little or nothing is known about the poets, but they wrote simple hymns in praise of Siva or Vishnu, expressing fervent and humble love of the deity in the bhakti spirit. Some of the hymns are still popular and are sung to this day.

The Muslim Conquest

According to a tradition which goes back to at least the third century, Christianity was first carried to India by the apostle Thomas, who was chosen by lot for the task. Though full of misgiving, Doubting Thomas made the long journey to India and won converts in the north-west, in Malabar (modern Kerala) and finally in the east, before being martyred by hostile Brahmins in AD 72. How much truth lies behind this story no one knows, but it may preserve a genuine memory of Christian missionary work in India very early on. Nestorian churches, of a Syrian and Persian brand of Christianity, were flourishing in southern India later, apparently from the sixth century or earlier.

A far more serious challenge to Hinduism came from Islam, which was not brought by missionaries and traders but by the sword. After the death of the prophet Muhammad in 632, Arab armies swarmed across Syria and Iran. They took Baluchistan, and in 712 an Arab force led by a twenty-year-old general, Muhammad ibn Kasim, seized the lower Indus valley. The Arabs pressed on northwards as far as Multan in the Punjab, with its famous shrine of Buddha. The north-west provinces were permanently captured for Islam, and emerged as Pakistan in 1947.

The area which is now Afghanistan also fell to Islam and the Turkish sultan of Ghazni, Mahmud the Great, built up a powerful Muslim state which loomed over India from the west. In the eleventh century he made repeated incursions into northern India. The Rajput armies of infantry and war-elephants were no match for his cavalry and he subdued most of the Punjab and bore off enormous quantities of treasure. In the following century a new power arose in Afghanistan, the Ghurid dynasty. Sultan Muhammad of Ghur took over the Punjab and pressed on east. Delhi fell in 1193 and by about 1200 Bihar and Bengal were in Muslim hands. In 1206 Muhammad of Ghur was murdered by one of his generals, Aibak, a slave who founded the romantically named Slave Dynasty of Delhi, and was

Muslim architecture is one of the glories of Indian civilization, but the Muslim conquest of northern India created the gulf between Hindus and Muslims which has existed ever since and which resulted in the creation of Pakistan in 1947. The Badshahi mosque in Lahore, Pakistan, was built by the Emperor Aurangzeb, a devout Muslim. Later, Lahore was the capital of Ranjit Singh's Sikh empire in the 19th century.

از رنگ و از سفیده و از سیاه و از رخت و از جنس ساحقه یا

فرمودم که در پیش من زیلوچه انداختند

LEFT Bathing ghat at Varanasi on the Ganges in northern India. Bathing places on the banks of rivers are regarded as sites at which heaven and earth intersect. There are thousands of sacred rivers, streams and pools in India, venerated as sources of fertility and life. The Ganges is considered the most sacred river in the world and bathing in it is believed to wash away all pollution, physical and moral.

RIGHT The Emperor Babar, or Babur, receiving envoys in his garden at Agra, a painting by Ram Das. Babar ('Tiger'), founder of the Mughal Empire, was a descendant of Genghis Khan. He defeated the sultan of Delhi in 1526 and made himself master of northern India. Under his successors, the Great Mughals (or Moguls), Muslim civilization in India reached its finest flowering.

killed playing polo four years later. The Delhi sultans extended their sway southwards. In the 1330s Sultan Muhammad ibn Tughluk briefly ruled most of India, but he could not hold the south, which broke up into a patchwork of Muslim and Hindu states. In the north too, the grip of later sultans weakened. Independent Muslim principalities sprang up and survived until absorbed into the Mughal Empire.

The Muslim conquest finally put paid to Buddhism in its own homeland, where it had long been in decline. The impact on Hinduism, though severe, was far less catastrophic. Large numbers of Hindus were converted to Islam, and the substantial Muslim population of the Indian sub-continent today is principally descended from Hindu converts, but the majority remained Hindu, even though they had to pay a special tax for the privilege. Hindu temples were pillaged. The great golden-domed temple of Siva at Somnath (near modern Patan, north of Bombay) was wrecked by Mahmud the Great in 1024. It is said to have been staffed by 1000 priests, 500 dancing girls and 200 musicians, and was famous for its image of the god's linga in polished stone, over seven feet high and adorned with jewels and gold. Mahmud took a mace to the linga with his own hands and it was smashed, but part of it was carried off to Ghazni and set in the threshold of a mosque, to be trodden under the feet of true believers. The story illustrates the Muslim hatred of idols.

Some temples were destroyed altogether and their materials used to build mosques. Those which survived in Muslim areas could no longer expect support from the ruling class, nor could the Brahmins. The Muslims held the Hindus in contempt as idolaters and worshippers of many gods, and had no use for some of the hallowed Hindu rules of behaviour, notably the taboo on beef. The long-term effect of the conquest was to create a gulf of hostility, suspicion and mutual incomprehension between Indians who were Hindus and Indians who were Muslims which has lasted ever since.

At sophisticated levels, however, the religious barrier could be crossed. Muslim potentates were patrons of learning and the arts, and Hindu scholars were welcome at many Muslim courts. Teachers in the Muslim Sufi and the Hindu bhakti traditions attracted followers from both camps.

An example is the poet and sage Kabir, whose followers today revere him as divine. He was brought up as a Muslim and seems to have been influenced by Sufi mysticism, but he taught a simplified Hinduism, a religion of love of God and love of man transcending creed and caste which drew both Hindu and Muslim disciples to him. He worshipped God as Rama, but said that it did not matter whether you called him Rama or Allah, it was the same God. He had no time for caste, priests or images, and held that God was not to be found in temples or mosques, in scriptures or rituals, in asceticism or Yoga, but in fields and workshops and at home.

In the main, however, the two religions kept their distance. One Hindu response to the challenge of Islam was to move away from austere theology and asceticism along easier and more popular paths. An important Vaishnava sect was founded by Vallabhacarya, a Brahmin from the south who taught at Varanasi and is regarded by his followers as an incarnation of Krishna. He preached the comfortable doctrine that the good things of life

Interior of Tirumalai's Hall, a large pillared hall outside the precinct of the Great Temple at Madurai. Madurai was one of the Hindu kingdoms in the south which remained independent of the Mughals. King Tirumalai rebuilt much of the temple in magnificent style in the 17th century.

RIGHT Krishna and the milkmaids. The youthful Krishna, loved by the village girls, teased them and played erotic tricks on them, hiding their clothes when they went swimming, dancing with them in the moonlight and stealing away when each of them believed that he loved her alone. These stories are interpreted in spiritual terms, with the women's longing for Krishna as the soul's hunger for God.

are provided by God and are there to be enjoyed. His followers at one time used to act out the loves of Krishna and the milkmaids as a way of entering intimately into the being of the god. They also surrendered their property and the use of their wives and daughters to the hereditary leaders of the movement, the Maharajahs or 'great kings', as incarnations of God on earth. The sect was purged of these scandals in the nineteenth century.

Caitanya, a Bengali Brahmin, was the inspiration of another leading Vaishnava sect, which now reveres him as divine. He put his trust in passionate love of Krishna, which he taught should induce in the devotee raptures of intense delight. Caitanya himself was subject to bouts of uncontrollable delight in which he would laugh, cry, sing, shout, dance, climb trees, run about and jump up and down. The sect has followed this ecstatic lead, dancing and singing hymns and chanting the god's name in mounting excitement, sometimes in procession through the streets. The Hare Krishna cult, founded in 1965 by Swami Prabhupada and now familiar in the West, is an offshoot of this movement.

LEFT An elaborate screen painting of the Buddha under the Bodhi-Tree. The halo is the mark of a divine or holy being in oriental art, as in Christianity.

ABOVE Monks in the interior of the Shwedagon Pagoda in Rangoon, the centre of Burmese religious life.

ABOVE RIGHT Gilt statue of the Buddha in the Shwedagon Pagoda. The figure is in the 'witness' position, in which the right hand touches the ground, calling the earth to witness his lordship of it.

RIGHT One of the stupas at Sanchi in central India. A stupa represents the Buddha's burial mound and enshrines a sacred relic.

The Mughal Empire

The ailing Sultanate of Delhi was given its quietus by yet another invasion from Afghanistan, led by a Turkish war-lord named Babar, who owned the first artillery train ever seen in India. He and his successors built up a Muslim empire which dominated northern and central India. The Emperor Aurargzeb, ruling in fabled splendour from the jewel-encrusted Peacock Throne in Agra, was briefly able to exact tribute even from the far south. At the same time, however, European powers were beginning to nibble at the Indian coastline and one of them would eventually swallow up the whole country.

When the greatest of the Great Mughals (or Moguls), the Emperor Akbar, came to the throne, Vasco de Gama had opened up the sea-route from Europe to India round the Cape and the Portuguese had planted themselves at Goa, Bombay and elsewhere on the west coast. A Christian mission had been established at Goa with the arrival of St Francis Xavier and two other Jesuits, though not many converts were made. Akbar was interested in Christianity and a succession of Jesuits laboured to convert him, but without success, for he proved to be equally interested in other

Late 16th-century painting of the Emperor Akbar, inspecting the building of Fathpur Sikri, one of his favourite residences, which he constructed near Agra and which contains one of the finest mosques in India. Akbar built it in thanksgiving for the birth of his son, subsequently the Emperor Jahangir. The birth had been foretold by a Muslim holy man, who was afterwards buried in the courtyard of the mosque.

LEFT The temple of the sun at Konarak, near Puri in eastern India, is also known as the Black Pagoda. Commenced in the 13th century, the temple is an architectural recreation of the chariot in which the Vedic sun god, Surya, traversed the sky, drawn by seven horses. The wheels of the 'chariot' stand ten feet high. Devout Muslims, who detested Hindu polytheism and idol-worship, disapproved of the temple's wealth of erotic statuary and regarded it as a peculiarly evil and ominous place.

The great ruined temple at
Angkor Wat in Cambodia.
Under the Khmer kings,
Buddhism and Hinduism
were blended together in
Cambodia. The temple was
surrounded by a moat and
was covered with carvings of
gods, men and animals.

religions as well. To the scandal of zealous Muslims, he hobnobbed not only with Jesuits but with Hindu holy men, Jains and Parsis (Indian Zoroastrians). He took Hindu wives, employed Hindu officials and did away with the special tax on non-Muslims.

Akbar was a man of enormous energy and intellectual curiosity, who tried to introduce the toleration of all religions into his empire, but to Muslims he seemed to tolerate all religions except his own. An epileptic, he had visions in which he believed that he received direct communications from God. These experiences persuaded him that he had better credentials as a messenger of the Almighty than the prophet Muhammad, and he founded a monotheistic religion of his own, the Divine Faith, in which he virtually took Muhammad's place. The new cult venerated the sun, fire and light – apparently as a result of Parsi influence – and the emperor saluted the sun in public every morning as the visible representative of the One God. Outside his own court, his religion won few followers. Most of Akbar's subjects clung to their own beliefs and their entrenched mutual hostilities.

Akbar's successors were less tolerant. The Emperor Aurangzeb, a devout Muslim, had large numbers of Hindu temples destroyed and reimposed the special tax on non-Muslims. His religious policy, which alienated many of his subjects, was a factor in the decline of the Mughal Empire. It also brought him into conflict with the Sikhs.

Guru Nanak, the first leader of the Sikhs, with the other nine Gurus and attendants. The Gurus are distinguished by their halos, like those of saints in Christian art. Nanak was a Hindu mystic, but the movement which he founded developed into a separate religion.

48

The Golden Temple at Amritsar, standing on an island in a sacred tank excavated by the fourth Sikh Guru, Ram Das, from which Amritsar takes its name, which means 'pool of immortality'. It replaced the earlier temple, which was destroyed in a war between the Sikhs and the Afghans.

The Sikhs

The founder and first Guru, or Teacher, of the Sikhs was a Hindu mystic from the Punjab named Nanak. He is said to have travelled widely in search of truth and to have visited Mecca, Baghdad, Tibet and Sri Lanka. Like Kabir, he believed in only one God, disapproved of images, rituals and priests, and taught love of God and love of man. He accepted, as Sikhs do today, the Hindu belief in successive lives and the operation of karma. He may have hoped to build a bridge between Hinduism and Islam, but under the Gurus who succeeded him the Sikhs developed into a separate religious community. The Golden Temple was built at Amritsar, in the Punjab, which became the Sikh headquarters. The Sikh holy book, the *Granth* (Collection), was compiled from the teachings and hymns of Nanak, his successors, Kabir and Hindu sages.

The ninth Guru, Tegh Bahadur, was summoned to Aurangzeb's court, where he refused to accept Islam and was executed, in 1675. His successor, Gobind Singh, built up Sikh fighting strength, and what had begun as a group of believers in brotherly love turned into a formidable military brotherhood which waged war against Muslims and which believed, as Muslims did, that death in battle was a passport to paradise. The Sikhs became an independent power, and under a famous leader in the nineteenth century, Maharajah Ranjit Singh, they dominated the whole Punjab. They fought two unsuccessful wars against the British in the 1840s, and subsequently many Sikhs entered the Indian Army, where they were renowned for their fighting qualities.

There are more than ten million Sikhs in India today, with flourishing Sikh communities abroad. Their most obvious outward marks are the turbans, beards and long hair of Sikh men, who believe in keeping whole and intact the bodies which God has given them, and so do not cut their hair. The turban is a symbol of this wholeness, and so of being a Sikh. Many Sikhs add the name Singh (Lion) to their family names, though not everyone named Singh is a Sikh. Sikhs worship the one God, who is called Sat (Truth) and sometimes Akal (Timeless). They do not believe that God has ever been incarnated on earth, and he is not represented by images. Since the death of Gobind Singh the *Granth* has been the Guru of the Sikhs. It has an honoured place in Sikh temples and homes, and devout Sikhs recite part of it every day.

The British Raj

The major threat to the Mughal Empire came not from the Sikhs but from the far more numerous Maratha tribes of central India. The Maratha war-leader Sivaji led Hindu resistance to Aurangzeb and laid the foundation of the Maratha Empire, which by 1700 had reduced the Great Mughal to a band of territory across the northern plains. By this time the Portuguese, Dutch, British and French all had enclaves of territory in India. The Europeans came originally to trade, but they were inevitably drawn into

Inside the Golden Temple musicians are playing. In front of them is a white cloth, on which is placed a copy of the *Granth*, the Sikh holy book. Worshippers drop coins on the cloth as offerings, equivalent to the 'collection' in Christian churches.

the tangles of Indian politics and to protect their trading interests they built up settlements and colonies. Over the next century and a half, the British, operating through the East India Company, first made themselves the dominant European power and then took control of more and more Indian states until eventually they were masters of all India. In 1858 the last of the Mughal emperors was deposed, the East India Company was wound up and India became a colony of the British crown.

The British regime exposed India to western science and technology, western notions of progress, western standards of efficiency and justice, western ideas about the value and purpose of human life. In the full flow of Victorian self-confidence and optimism, the British constructed railways and telegraphs, established hospitals, law courts and a postal service, and built schools and universities where western values were inculcated in the English language. The effect, at first, was inevitably to sap Indian self-confidence.

The East India Company had interfered in Indian customs as little as it could, refusing to let missionaries live in its territories and forbidding its Indian troops to turn Christian. In 1813, however, as a result of pressure from England, the rules were changed. The Nestorian churches in southern India, with their small congregations, had existed for many centuries, and a few Roman Catholic and Protestant missionaries from Europe had worked in India before 1813, but now the floodgates were opened. Thousands of missionaries and workers from all the principal Christian denominations poured into India from Britain, other European countries and North America. The largest numbers came from the Church of England, the Roman Catholic Church and the Methodist Episcopal Church of the United States.

Most of the newcomers regarded Indian religion as idolatrous, barbarous and morally repulsive. They considered it their duty to wean the Indians from the breasts of superstition, and being westerners themselves they naturally tried to win converts not only to one variety or another of the Christian faith but to western values in general. They busied themselves with schools, medical work, the relief of poverty and hunger, and the improvement of agricultural methods. They undoubtedly did an immense amount of good, but they frequently offended Indian sentiment. The immediate cause of the Indian Mutiny was the belief of many Indian soldiers that the new cartridges issued to them were greased with the fat of cows and pigs. Cow fat was profoundly offensive to Hindus and pig fat to Muslims, but in the background was the fear and resentment which had been aroused by the persistent preaching of Christianity by chaplains and commanding officers of some regiments.

In terms of conversions, the missionaries had far less success than had been hoped. By 1921 there were about five million Christians in the Indian subcontinent, less than two per cent of the total population, as against 215 million Hindus and 70 million Muslims. Five million people is a lot of people, certainly, but there had been no massive conversion to Christianity.

The authorities were more successful in either wiping out or at least rousing Indian opinion against objectionable features of Indian life.

LEFT A reading from the *Granth* in the Sikh temple at Chandigarh. The holy book is protected by a canopy. Since the death of the last Guru, the *Granth* has been regarded as the leader of the Sikhs.

Slavery was abolished. Temple prostitution was ended. A successful campaign was waged against the Thugs, a brotherhood of robbers and murderers, in existence since at least the thirteenth century, who strangled their victims as sacrifices to their goddess Bhavani. Suttee, the custom of burning a widow alive with her dead husband's corpse, so that she would go with him to the afterlife, was also suppressed. It went back at least to the sixth century and was particularly rife in the north. When the Sikh leader Ranjit Singh died in 1839, four of his wives and seven slave women were burned alive on his pyre.

Reforms of this kind and official disapproval of caste, polygamy and child marriage seriously offended conservative Hindu opinion, but support came from a growing number of Indian intellectuals, influenced by western education. It was on this moral front that Christianity had its most effective influence, and since the British withdrawal from India, Indian governments have introduced reforms which the British authorities did not dare to attempt.

Down to the nineteenth century, Hindus had lived within their religion as naturally as in the air they breathed, but the impact of the West weakened the confidence of Indians in their own traditions. Sophisticated Hindus became self-conscious and uncomfortable about their religion. Trying to justify it, as much to themselves as to anyone else, they rationalized and reformed it in conformity with western standards. Rammohan Roy was a Bengali Brahmin who saw his sister-in-law burned alive at her husband's funeral. She was forced up on to the pyre and her relatives held her there, struggling, with long poles while drums drowned her agonized screams. The horrified Roy became an influential opponent not only of suttee but of Hindu polytheism, image worship and the caste system. He made a careful study of Christianity, Islam and Buddhism, and approved of the Christian moral code, which he thought admirably fitted to regulate human behaviour. He did not become a Christian, however, but founded his own Hindu sect, the Brahmo Samaj (Society of God), which worshipped the Brahman of the *Upanishads*, with readings from the *Upanishads* and the singing of hymns.

Roy believed that he was purging Hinduism of a degenerate polytheism with which it had become infested. So did Dayananda Sarasvati, another Brahmin, who thought that the many deities of Hinduism were excrescences on the true monotheistic Hinduism of the four Vedas. He maintained that the Vedic hymns to different deities were really addressed to the same God under various names. Unlike Roy, he had no use for Christianity, Islam or any of the other religions of the world, which he said were corruptions of the pure Vedic monotheism from which they were all descended. For them to make converts from the parent faith was monstrous, and Dayananda vigorously attacked Christianity on this score. He founded the still flourishing Arya Samaj (Aryan Society or Noble Society) to promote his reformed Hinduism and win back converts from the other creeds.

That a westernizing reform impulse should lead to a fierce denunciation of Christianity and all non-Hindu religions shows how Hindu nationalism

Dayananda Sarasvati, who founded the Arya Samaj in 1875. After many years as a wandering ascetic, travelling all over India, Dayananda set out to purge Hinduism of what he regarded as polytheistic excrescences on an original monotheism. He believed that all the world's religions were corrupt descendants of Vedic monotheism and his movement is a striking example of the recovery of Hindu self-confidence, which had been shaken by the impact of the West.

had sprung up in reaction against the British regime. Nationalist intellectuals were encouraged by the Theosophical Society, which was founded in New York but in 1882 moved its headquarters to Adyar, near Madras, with some assistance from the Arya Samaj. The Theosophists, who claimed to be guided by mysterious Mahatmas or 'great souls' residing in the strongholds of the Himalayas, reversed the usual western attitude to India by telling Hindus that their spiritual heritage was far more valuable than that of the West.

Ramakrishna and Gandhi

Hinduism's recovery of its self-confidence was given a powerful impetus by a remarkable Bengali Brahmin, Ramakrishna. A devotee of Kali at a temple outside Calcutta, he saw visions of the Goddess and of Siva, Rama and Krishna. He engaged in Muslim and Christian devotions and saw visions of Muhammad and Christ as well. His experiences convinced him that all religions are essentially the same and essentially true, that they lead by different routes to the same goal, the realization of the oneness of all things in Brahman and the identity of the One and the self. Ramakrishna wrote little or nothing, but taught in sayings and parables. His teaching was Vedantist, but he was not a philosopher but a mystic in the bhakti tradition of heartfelt adoration of the divine, whose presence he sensed everywhere about him. An ascetic who refrained from sex, refused ever to touch money and cleaned out the temple latrines to purge himself of pride in his Brahmin caste, he was an inspiring personality. Healing miracles were attributed to him, many believed him divine, and his fame spread all over India.

Ramakrishna classed all religions, in effect, as variant forms of the Hinduism of the Vedanta school. This message was carried to the world by his leading disciple, Vivekananda, who made a great impression at the World Parliament of Religions in Chicago in 1893 with the pronouncement: 'All religions are one'. Vedanta Societies were founded in several American cities as a result of his visit. Returning to India, he set up the Ramakrishna Mission for the propagation of Vedanta, which now has more than a hundred branches in various countries. In India itself, the Mission has concentrated on education and the relief of poverty.

Hinduism had now moved from apologetic defensiveness to counterattack. It had developed a social conscience on the western liberal model, allied with nationalist fervour, and its claim to be the best of all religions had been carried abroad into the strongholds of the West. Though Vivekananda taught that all religions were at heart the same, he also taught that Hinduism was the oldest and purest of them all.

The new style of Hinduism was far more philosophical than popular and had scarcely touched the great masses of people in India. It was brought to them and employed as the inspiration of the political movement for Indian independence by Gandhi. Mohandas Karamchand Gandhi was born in 1869 at Porbandar, north-west of Bombay. He was educated in India and England, and spent many years as a lawyer in South Africa, where he fought for the rights of the Indian community. In his forties, in 1915, he

went back to India and became the commanding figure in the campaign to end British rule and gain independence. Ascetic by temperament and one of nature's vegetarians, the small, half-naked, bespectacled figure, with his loin cloth, spinning wheel and diet of goat's milk, was almost as famous in the West as in India. For many people in India he was an incarnation of Vishnu. For many others he was a Mahatma, a great holy man, divinely inspired.

Gandhi regarded himself as an orthodox Hindu. He defended image worship as an aid to approaching the divine and his veneration for the cow did him harm with Muslims. He carried the old principle of ahimsa, or non-violence, into politics with great effect, first in South Africa and then in India, as 'passive resistance'. But he was also a reformer. He disliked the Hindu preoccupation with pollution and waged what in the end was a successful campaign against the treatment of the untouchables. It was as a reformer that he was assassinated by an orthodox Hindu in 1948.

Mahatma Gandhi, the most famous Hindu of modern times and the leader of the independence movement.

A small group receive religious instruction by the Ganges at Varanasi. The personal master-pupil relationship is fundamental to the Indian religions. Traditionally, truth is not found in books but must be learned at first hand from those divinely appointed and inspired to receive it.

Gandhi believed in a personal and loving God, rather than in the impersonal Absolute of Vedanta. Like Vivekananda, however, he thought that all religions were essentially true, while also convinced of the superiority of Hinduism. He found much to admire in Christianity and Islam. His social philosophy was influenced by Christianity and by such western writers as Tolstoy and Ruskin, and he loved both the Bible and the Qur'an, but he loved the *Bhagavad Gita* more.

For all Gandhi's principle of non-violence, the movement which he led inflamed violent religious passions among both Hindus and Muslims because it was based on Hinduism: a religious rather than a geographical nationalism. There were fierce clashes between the two groups and in the last year before Partition 7000 people were killed in them. The British hoped to grant India independence as a unit, but what actually happened was decided by the religious issue. The Muslims believed they would be swamped. All efforts to reconcile the two communities failed and two separate states, India and Pakistan, were created in 1947. Millions of Muslims abandoned their homes in the new India for Pakistan, millions of Hindus, and the Sikhs, abandoned theirs in the new Pakistan for India. The migrations were accompanied by mob riots, massacres, pillage and human misery on an appalling scale.

There are still Muslim, Sikh, Christian, Buddhist and Jain minorities in the Republic of India, but eight out of every ten of its people are Hindus. The majority of them continue to practise their religion much as they always did. At sophisticated levels, where in one direction the influence of the West inspired a vigorous Hindu reaction, in the other it has prompted scepticism, agnosticism, religious apathy and impatience with tradition. Some educated and westernized Hindus are unbelievers, some are believers but have abandoned many of the traditional rites and rules. The irony is that the West was losing self-confidence while India was recovering it. Interest in Hindu mysticism has been mounting in the West. This development has been welcomed in some Hindu quarters. In others it has been greeted with the same contempt with which an educated Athenian of the fourth century BC might have viewed some barbarous foreigner expressing a passionate but naive interest in Plato.

3. Buddhism

Hinduism and Buddhism both grew up in India, but where Hinduism stayed at home, Buddhism emigrated and eventually had its greatest influence outside India, in China, Japan, Tibet, Sri Lanka and South-East Asia. Sharing the same background and developing cheek by jowl in India for 1500 years, the two religions naturally have much in common. They are both fundamentally gentle in spirit, peaceable and tolerant. They share the belief that human beings live many times on the earth, bound by karma to 'the sorrowful weary wheel' or 'the long long faring on' of earthly existence, from which they both desire to escape, but in both there is a gulf between the high register of abstruse and subtle speculation and the religion at its popular level. Popular Buddhism caters for the individual and his wants and needs in life. Deities are worshipped and prayed to because they have the good things of life in their gift and because they promise a happy life in heaven after death. High register Buddhism, by contrast, dismisses the individual as a delusion and his needs and wants as snares, and its aim is to escape from this world and from any popular concept of heaven.

In place of Hinduism's combination of polytheism and monotheism, Buddhism substitutes a combination of polytheism and atheism. There are two major sub-religions within Buddhism, Theravada and Mahayana, with their own sects and groups, but Buddhism is less varied, disparate and fragmented than Hinduism. It would be difficult to be more varied than Hinduism, and Buddhism unlike Hinduism does stem from a single founder whose teaching has been handed down by his followers ever since his own time. There is plenty of room for disagreement about the meaning of the teaching, but Buddhism has a central tradition, the tradition of the Buddha's own words. Since it preserves the doctrine of a single founder, it does not share the Hindu attitude that other people are best left to look after their own spiritual welfare and it has displayed a far greater zeal for missionary work.

Buddhism is a comparatively recent term, coined in the West. The Buddha's teachings are known to Buddhists as the *Dharma,* an

Scenes from the Buddha's life are carved on one of the four gateways of the principal stupa at Sanchi. One of them shows the Buddha's empty seat beneath the Bodhi-Tree. In early Buddhist art the Buddha himself was not represented and his presence in a scene was indicated by a symbol of this kind, apparently to prevent people from taking him as an object of worship. In popular Buddhism, however, the Buddha turned into a god.

untranslatable Sanskrit word embracing the ideas of truth, law, doctrine and 'what is right and proper'. The Buddha himself did not write books. He taught verbally, in lectures and discussion. His words were handed on from generation to generation of his disciples for about 400 years before they were written down, so that what is known of his teaching goes back to early Buddhist tradition, not directly to the Buddha himself.

The Path to Salvation

Early Buddhist teaching does not require a belief in gods and has no place for a God with a capital G. It sets out a path, the Aryan or Noble Path, to salvation gained by human effort alone, without divine aid. The early Buddhists seem to have accepted the traditional Indian deities, but they did not consider them important and treated them with gently sardonic humour. Early Buddhism was man-centred and its recipe for salvation had nothing to do with gods.

Although it has often been observed that Buddhism is a cheerful and good-humoured religion, the Buddhist attitude to life is intensely pessimistic. Life on earth is evil, painful and transitory. It is full of suffering and nothing lasts, nothing stays the same. Even what passes for pleasure passes away. Failing to realize the fundamental impermanence of things, human beings always want more. They demand more possessions, more sensations, fresh experiences, new ideas, and are never satisfied by any of them. This creates anxiety, an anxiety which can be the first step on the way to a solution.

Human nature is fundamentally good, in the Buddhist view, but the two things which are wrong with it, and which keep human beings tied to the world of successive births and deaths, are craving and the illusion of one's own individuality. Craving, or literally 'burning thirst', means wanting not only material things, prosperity and comfort, but longing for other people's love, people to love, children and a contented family life, success, fame, an enjoyable life after death, or the love of God. The whole web of needs and desires and affections in which we live is denounced as an entanglement in suffering and impermanence: hence the gulf between philosophical Buddhism and the popular religion, in which these things are the foundation of security and happiness.

Early Buddhism goes even further counter to popular assumptions, however, and this was regarded by contemporaries as its most startling and original point. Common sense tells us that at the centre of our experience is a separate identity, an I, a personality or a soul. This the Buddhists regard as an illusion. There is no such thing as a self, no reality behind such words as 'I' or 'mine' or 'owning' or 'belonging'. These concepts are imaginary, for we all change continuously and have no fixed underlying identity. A human being is a temporary and shifting agglomeration of a body, feelings, perceptions, impulses and consciousness, a succession of changing mental and physical states. It is the belief in a permanent self, whose interests must be safeguarded and promoted, that entangles us in the suffering of earthly life.

This view is not at all easy to accept, but it is put forward less as an

In this Indian carving of the 1st century BC the stupa symbolizes the Buddha's final entry into nirvana. It is surrounded by the Bodhi-Tree, referring to his attainment of enlightenment and flanked by winged spirits.

intellectual argument about reality than as an aid to living in the right way. The ideal Buddhist life is one which is 'selfless', and so Buddhist theory stresses the unreality of the self. For practical and moral purposes, early Buddhist teaching has to allow each of us a self which acts and is acted upon, which follows or fails to follow the Dharma.

It is obviously difficult to reconcile the teaching about the impermanence of the self with the belief that human beings live many lives, for if no 'I' exists, what is it that is reborn over and over again? The Buddhist answer is that what passes on from one life to the next is something as flickering and evanescent as a flame passing from one candle to another, which nevertheless is affected by the emotions and actions of previous existences.

Salvation lies in the cessation of craving and the dissolution of individuality. If you can extinguish your capacity to want anything, your attachment to the world and to experience in it, and the illusion of your own individuality, then you achieve the Buddhist ideal of perfect serenity. You 'become cool' and life ceases to be painful and impermanent. With the disappearance of the illusory individual, karma has nothing on which to operate and the succession of rebirths comes to an end. Life becomes an ideal and eternal state, which is called *nirvana*, 'coolness' or 'going out', as of a flame.

It is no good asking what nirvana is, the Buddhists say, or whether someone who has attained it survives death or not. The meaning of nirvana cannot be conveyed in words, but can only be experienced, as the Buddha himself experienced it. The Buddha is quoted describing what it is not, rather than what it is (and the same is true of Hindu writers on Brahman, the Absolute). Nirvana is something 'unborn, unbecome, unmade, unconditioned'. It is compared to coolness after a fever, and Buddhists have called it the cool cave, the harbour of refuge, the holy city, the further shore. It is a condition in which the individual personality is snuffed out, as it were, and thereby experiences perfect peace. Its nearest parallel in human life, and this is presumably the experience on which the concept is based, is a state sometimes reached in trance, of total absorption in which the external world ceases to impinge on the mind and in which there is a sense of freedom and tranquillity.

A state of contented non-being seems highly paradoxical, but the Buddhists delighted in paradox because by stultifying reason one was set free. Buddhists say that their Way cannot be taught in books or intellectually appreciated, but has to be lived. It must be taken on trust to begin with and then, by living it, its truth becomes plain.

The foundation of the Way, without which no progress can be made, is a moral code. The minimal requirements are to refrain from harming living things, from stealing, from illicit sex, from lying and from the use of alcohol and drugs. There is nothing in these rules to prevent an ordinary Buddhist from pursuing a secular career and accumulating money and property, though if he does he is entangling himself in suffering and illusion. Buddhist monks, however, are required to lead lives of strict poverty, chastity and harmlessness.

A moral life, in the Buddhist view, is the only basis for true understanding. Its purpose is partly to acquire good karma, so as to move up the ladder of lives, but more importantly to erode away craving and egocentricity. Given the moral basis, understanding is developed through meditation. This again cannot be learned from books, but must be taught personally by an instructor. Meditation inculcates the right attitude of mind and leads on beyond thinking and reasoning to experiences in which the meditator is believed to escape from the physical body and to acquire supernatural powers, including the ability to fly, to change shape, to read minds, to see and hear things at a great distance: the abilities of the shaman, in effect. Eventually the final 'enlightenment' or 'awakening' is achieved and with it entry into nirvana.

In the early teaching there are different stages of progress. The 'stream-winner' has gone far enough on the path to be sure of a good rebirth in his next earthly life and of enlightenment after not more than seven earthly lives. The 'once-returner' will have only one more earthly life. The 'non-returner' will be reborn in a heaven and there will attain nirvana. The *arhat*, or saint, achieves nirvana in his present life on earth and when he dies he will not be reborn.

Early Buddhism shares with the *Upanishads* the longing to lose the individual self, the belief that meditation is the way to the goal, and the view that the traditional gods are unimportant, but it denies the equation of the self with the Absolute because it denies the self. That no belief in gods is necessary does not mean, as is sometimes suggested, that it is a rationalist system suitable to the modern scientific and sceptical age. On the contrary, Buddhism rejects reason as a way to truth; salvation is attained through meditative experience in which reason is confounded and transcended, and it is here that the secret of Buddhism's appeal to the modern West mainly lies.

The Buddha

Buddha is not the name of a person but of a spiritual category. The founder of Buddhism is called 'the Buddha' as a title, meaning the Enlightened or Awakened One. There are said to have been many Buddhas before him, though there is no historical evidence of their existence, and a Buddha appears on earth whenever man's spiritual condition requires it. Traditions about the founder's life were handed down orally by his followers for centuries and the details of his career are inextricably mixed with legend. The earliest written biography is the anonymous *Mahavastu* (the Great Event) in Sanskrit, of the second century BC or later, and the great poet Asvaghosha wrote the *Buddhacarita* (Acts of the Buddha), also in Sanskrit, in the second century AD.

Siddhartha Gautama, the future Buddha, was born in about 563 BC at Kapilavastu, a town in the Himalayan foothills of what is now Nepal. His father was a chief of the Sakya people, though legend later pictured him as a great king, and the Buddha was afterwards often called Sakyamuni, the Sage of the Sakyas. He grew up in Kapilavastu, where he married and had a son. As a young man, he was troubled by the question which has tormented

The birth of the Buddha, who emerged from the side of his mother, Queen Maya. According to legend, she gave birth to him painlessly, standing up in the gardens of Lumbini outside Kapilavastu. Gandhara stone carving, about AD 150.

so many human beings, why it is that man is born into the world only to endure suffering and death. Like others of his time, he was not satisfied by the Vedic religion with its gods and sacrifices and priests, and like others he tried to find the answer by leaving his accustomed milieu and searching for wisdom outside it. He left his home and family, joined a group of ascetics and for six years subjected himself to austerities which are said to have reduced him almost to a skeleton. He still found no answer which satisfied him and at the age of thirty-five he abandoned asceticism. He went to a place on the bank of the Neranjara river near Gaya (in Bihar province) and sat down under a tree, later to be famous as the Bodhi-Tree or Bo-tree, the Tree of Awakening. There he meditated, cross-legged and motionless, for many days and nights until, one night towards dawn, he achieved enlightenment and entered nirvana.

The Buddha had attained nirvana by himself, without the assistance of any god. He could have disappeared from the mortal sphere altogether, but out of his great compassion for all living things he stayed in the mortal world to teach what he had learned.

Tradition has it that the Buddha first proclaimed the Dharma at a deer-park at Sarnath, near Varanasi, to an audience of five, the five ascetics with whom he had previously lived. They were profoundly impressed, by his glowing personality as well as by his teaching, and they became his first disciples. For the rest of his life he remained in the central Ganges area, going from place to place teaching and gathering followers. He spent much of his time in the cities of Sravasti and Rajagriha, the capitals of the kingdoms of Kosala and Magadha. King Pasenadi of Kosala and King

Bimbisara of Magadha were his devoted supporters. Gaya, where the Buddha attained enlightenment, was in the kingdom of Magadha, which became the heartland of Buddhism in India for several centuries.

The Buddha died at the age of eighty at the village of Kusinagara (modern Kasia), not far from his birthplace. He passed away in a grove of trees, surrounded by sorrowing disciples.

Numerous miracles were credited to the Buddha and legends grew up about him which have been depicted in art all over the East. It was said that his conception and birth were immaculate. His virgin mother, Queen Maya, dreamed that a snow-white elephant entered her body through her right side, without causing her pain. After a pregnancy of ten months she gave birth to the child in the gardens of Lumbini, outside Kapilavastu. He emerged painlessly from her right side. He could speak and walk as soon as he was born and his body shone like gold.

This fresco from Ajanta depicts the popular story of how Mara, the Evil One and Lord of Death, tried to prevent the Buddha's enlightenment. Mara first sent his daughters to seduce the Buddha and then attacked him with an army of evil spirits, but in vain.

Another popular story was that when the Buddha-to-be was meditating under the Bodhi-Tree he was assailed by Mara, the Evil One, who tried to prevent his enlightenment. Mara sent his three lovely daughters to seduce Gautama, but he took no notice of them. Then Mara attacked him with an army of evil spirits and hideous monsters, but when they surrounded the tree they suddenly found themselves paralyzed. Later, when the Buddha had achieved enlightenment, Mara tempted him to abandon the human world. He hesitated for a moment, but the god Brahma came and implored him to teach the Dharma, and the Buddha agreed.

Mara is the Buddhist equivalent of Satan in Christianity, drawn from the earlier Indian concept of Death as the Evil One. There were innumerable demons, monsters and harmful ghosts in popular belief, but Mara is much bigger game, the lord of this world, a great power hostile to man and a personification of all the evil in human experience. It is ironic that a system which denied God should have created the Devil, but like so much else in Buddhist teaching Mara was less a philosophical concept than a practical tool. He was used as a bridge leading from popular fears of assorted sinister powers to the belief that all the suffering of life had a single source. The point was that Mara had been defeated. His power had been broken by the Buddha's enlightenment, and so Buddhists could feel confident that their spiritual progress could not be prevented by hostile forces from outside themselves.

The Buddhist Community

The Buddha lived at a time when the Vedic religion was under severe criticism, and he was one of its most forceful opponents. He rejected its scriptures, its sacrifices and its priests, and he either did not believe in its gods or did not take them seriously. His own experience also made him recoil from the contemporary enthusiasm for asceticism. He taught a middle way between futile self-torture at one extreme and futile self-indulgence at the other.

His teaching clearly fell on fertile ground. It was delivered openly in public, unlike the *Upanishads*, which were meant for a spiritual elite. It must presumably have been clear from an early stage that the Dharma was too difficult for the majority of mortals, and that nirvana could be won only by the few, but the Buddha's moral ideals for ordinary people could be put into practice without imposing an intolerable strain on flesh and blood. For any new movement a simple moral code has the advantage of providing a share in the movement for those who are not athletes of the spirit. Followers, male and female, were welcomed from any caste or walk of life.

Social and political conditions were also propitious. The tribal republics and smaller kingdoms were being swallowed up by the larger kingdoms of Kosala and Magadha. Familiar, small-scale institutions were being replaced by new and larger ones in which authority was more remote and impersonal, a state of affairs which, as in the modern West, creates anxiety and a search for spiritual security in a disturbed and hostile world. This security Buddhism offered in the life of the Buddhist community.

The traditional formula of Buddhist allegiance, known as 'the three jewels', is: 'To the Buddha I go for refuge, to the Dharma I go for refuge, to the Sangha I go for refuge.' The *Sangha* (Assembly) is the whole community of Buddhists. In a more restricted sense it is the order of Buddhist monks, which the Buddha himself founded and to which he entrusted the continuation of the movement, for he named no successor. Denying the validity of the individual soul, Buddhism regards individualism as a delusion and a disease. It is through the community, and especially in the order of monks (in the early days there were also groups of nuns), that the Buddhist learns to destroy self-centredness and the craving for personal possessions and satisfactions in a life shared with others.

The order of monks was something new in India. Buddhist monks, who are called 'sharers' (*bhikkus*), abandon their homes and possessions, and live together in communities where the individual monk owns little or nothing. The laity provide the monks with their monasteries, their food, their yellow robes and other necessities, in this way earning merit which brings a good rebirth in the next earthly life. The monks in turn supply the laity with spiritual and social services. The local monastery is the school where the children are taught. The monks officiate at ceremonies and festivals, and are frequently the leaders of their local communities. Membership of the order may or may not last for life, for a monk can return to lay life when he chooses. It is also an old Buddhist tradition that to preserve peace and harmony in a monastery any group of monks who find themselves seriously at odds with the majority should secede and set up their own community. This has enabled numerous sects and groups to coexist within Buddhism with few of the internal religious wars which mark the history of Christianity and Islam.

LEFT Buddhist monks eat a simple meal in the Temple of the Reclining Buddha in Bangkok, Thailand. The galleries contain 394 gilded statues of the Buddha. The figures seen here are in the 'witness' position.

The fundamental rule of Buddhist morality is that no action should be taken which will harm yourself or anyone else. Buddhist morality in practice is often more positive than this negative principle suggests, and it is another paradox of Buddhism that although it denies the individual's reality, it believes strongly in compassionate treatment of other people.

Mahavira and the Jains

While Buddhism was developing in eastern India, another movement was gathering strength, in the same area and aided by the same factors. Its leader, Vardhamana, was called 'the naked ascetic' by the Buddhists, but his own followers called him Mahavira, 'Great Hero', and Jina, 'Victor'. They took their name, *Jainas*, from the second of these titles. The Jains maintain that theirs is the oldest of all Indian religions, going far back beyond the Aryan invasions, and just as there are supposed to have been many Buddhas before Gautama, so the Jains believe in many Jinas before Mahavira.

The Jain account of Mahavira's life closely resembles the early Buddhist tradition about Gautama. Mahavira was the son of a tribal chieftain and was born near modern Patna. When he was thirty, he left his home and family, and for thirteen years he subjected himself to rigorous austerities, going about completely naked, remaining silent and meditating. At length, while meditating beneath a tree, he achieved perfection and omniscience, which freed him from the bonds of karma and rebirth. He spent the rest of his life teaching and gathering followers, finally starving himself to death at the age of seventy-two at Pava, a village near Patna, which has ever since been a place of Jain pilgrimage.

Like the Buddhists, the Jains accepted that all life is trapped in the cycle of birth and rebirth, rejected the Vedic religion and did not believe in a God. However, they did not accept the Buddhist denial of anything eternal in human nature. In Jainism the soul is eternal and travels on from one existence to another unless it can find release. Life is regarded as fraught with suffering, as in Buddhism, but the Jains discern souls not only in human beings and animals, but in plants, stones and metals, in the earth and in water, in the air and in fire, in the wind and the rain. The whole world is a prison-house of misery and torment in which life is held captive in matter.

The human predicament is expressed in a Jain story about a traveller who was suddenly charged by a wild elephant. In desperation he jumped into an old well beneath a tree, caught hold of a clump of reeds growing from the wall and hung there, halfway down the well. Looking down, he saw snakes, hissing and waiting for him to fall. Looking up, he saw two mice, busily engaged in gnawing through the reeds to which he was clinging. Then the elephant, mad with rage, charged the tree, from which a honeycomb fell on the traveller's head. Bees swarmed round him and stung him fiercely, but a single drop of honey trickled down over his face to his mouth, and at once he forgot his danger and thought only of getting another drop of honey.

ABOVE A monk walks among the ruins of Anuradhapura, the capital city of King Devanampiya Tissa in the 3rd century BC and the earliest centre of Buddhism in Sri Lanka. Ruined and abandoned, the city was rediscovered in the 19th century and is now visited by thousands of pilgrims every year.

Since incarceration in matter is the cause of the soul's suffering, the way to escape is to free oneself of all material entanglements and bodily desires. Unlike the Buddha, Mahavira did not reject extreme asceticism as worthless. On the contrary, according to tradition, he attained perfection at the end of a protracted course of severe austerity, and Jainism gives self-denial an important place in its regime of salvation. Jain monks lead extremely austere lives of poverty, chastity, study of the scriptures and self-discipline by meditation, fasting and silence. Devout monks and laymen, when they feel the end of life drawing near, sometimes follow Mahavira's example and starve themselves to death in the ultimate detachment from matter of which the human frame is capable.

The Jains have also carried further than Hindus and Buddhists the principle of ahimsa, or not harming living things. A Jain monk carries a whisk with which he brushes insects gently out of his way, so as not to tread on them, and wears a cloth over his mouth so as not to harm insects or minute organisms by breathing them in. He should never light a lamp at night, walk about in the dark, put out a fire, or harm water and the vermin on his body by bathing. All this is not only a matter of respect for life, but of refraining from actions, since actions enmesh the soul in matter. Gandhi

ABOVE LEFT Ornate interior of one of the famous Jain temples on Mount Abu in central India, built by the Solanki dynasty in the 11th to 13th centuries. The mountain is regarded as sacred by the Jains.

Tree-spirit, from a Jain building at Mathura in northern India, 2nd century AD. Traditionally, these spirits guard treasures buried among the roots of trees. The Jains accepted the gods and spirits of popular Indian belief, but regarded them as subordinate to their founder, Mahavira, and the other Jinas.

met and was impressed by Jain holy men in his youth, and his doctrine of non-violence owes something to Jain teaching.

The rules for laymen are naturally less demanding. Their minimal code is not to harm living things, not to lie, not to steal, to be faithful in marriage, and not to be attached to material objects and worldly goods. Despite this last rule, there is a contrast between the poverty of Jain monks and the prosperity of the Jain laity, many of whom are occupied in commerce and finance. It is this prosperity which has given the Jains an influence in India out of all proportion to their numbers – now perhaps about three million – and it is connected with the principle of ahimsa, for Jains may not engage in agriculture and farming, which hurt the earth, animals and plants, or in crafts, which torture metal, wood and other materials. The Jains are much respected for their charitable works, their schools and their hospitals for human beings and animals.

Bronze image of a Jina, from western India, 9th or 10th century. Jina means 'victor' or 'conqueror' and the Jains believe that many of these great souls appeared on earth before Mahavira. The name Jain means 'follower of the Jinas'.

As in Buddhism, the early converts to Jainism brought their accustomed gods with them. There is no Supreme Being in Jainism, but images of the Hindu deities are venerated in Jain temples. They are ranked below Mahavira and the other Jinas, who are treated as gods. Hymns of devotion are sung to them and their images are ceremonially washed and honoured with the waving of lamps.

The Emperor Asoka

Jainism has never attracted a large following or penetrated the world outside India. Its own rules make it impossible for the great mass of working people to be Jains, but in its earlier days Mahavira's movement gained support from powerful kings. Chandragupta 1 Maurya, king of Magadha and founder of the Maurya dynasty, is said to have turned away from his wars and his amply stocked harem to become a pious Jain. Tradition has it that he abdicated his throne and committed suicide in the Jain manner by starving himself to death. His grandson, however, the great Emperor Asoka, was a Buddhist and with his encouragement Buddhism not only spread all through India but was carried to the outside world.

Asoka's decision to become a Buddhist layman was apparently precipitated by the bloodshed and suffering caused by his conquest of Kalinga, on the eastern seaboard, in the early years of his reign. He himself recorded that 100,000 people were killed in the campaign. Appalled, he set himself to become an ideal king on Buddhist lines, ruling with justice, mercy and consideration for the welfare of his subjects. He was less interested in Buddhist philosophy than in Buddhism as a moral code, which he enthusiastically commended to his people in notices carved on pillars and rocks. The principles he inculcated were kindness and generosity, fulfilling one's obligations to others and, above all, refraining from killing living creatures. He himself abandoned war, gave up hunting, became a vegetarian and announced that he no longer had great numbers of animals slaughtered to make curries for his court. He strongly disapproved of animal sacrifices and had little use for religious rituals in general.

Asoka not only promoted Buddhism within his realm, but sent missionaries to carry it abroad, to Sri Lanka, Central Asia and as far afield as Syria, Egypt and Greece. He made no attempt to impose Buddhism on all his subjects, but the fact that the ruler of most of India was an ardent Buddhist naturally brought Buddhism a substantial increase of converts, not all of whom necessarily adopted it for the purest motives. With an increase of numbers, it inevitably became more popular in its beliefs and practices, and it was this which began to turn Buddhism from a fundamentally atheistic movement into a world religion.

In early Buddhist teaching, salvation depended on one's own efforts. The Buddha was not a god or a superhuman saviour, and could not be, for he had passed out of the world altogether with his death and final entry into nirvana. It seems likely, however, that many of his followers believed him to be something more than a man, and in time he became a divine figure. The tendency to deify great men has always been strong in India and the

The Emperor Asoka was an enthusiastic convert to Buddhism and commended the religion to his subjects in notices carved on rocks and pillars. The top of one of the pillars is preserved in the museum at Sarnath in northern India, where the Buddha first revealed his teaching.

simple human need for something to worship built on a foundation of reverence for the Buddha's memory and preservation of his words. The bhakti attitude of passionate devotion to a personal, saving God, which so powerfully influenced Indian religion in general, focused on the Buddha, as on Vishnu and Siva.

Another factor was the early Buddhist policy of tolerating the gods and spirits of popular belief. Many Buddhists continued to believe in the Devas, the traditional Indian deities, as Asoka himself did. Gods and spirits survived within Buddhism and the Buddha himself became one of them. He can be seen turning into a superhuman figure in the legends which grew up about him. In the tale of Brahma urging him to teach the Dharma, and in other stories, the gods are represented as subordinate to the Buddha, who towers above them.

Large numbers of *stupas*, the earliest form of Buddhist shrine, were built during Asoka's reign. A stupa is a mound of brick or stone erected to house a relic of the Buddha, a sacred text or a relic of a Buddhist saint or king. According to tradition, the Buddha was cremated and his remains were divided between various towns, where stupas were built over them. The multiplication of stupas shows respect for the Buddha's memory turning into worship. Some Buddhist monks opposed the popular cult of the Buddha and the belief, which was already current, that he had not been a man but a heavenly being, who had descended to earth for a time to make known the Dharma.

Prayer flags stream from the Bodnath stupa in Nepal, and the eyes of a Buddha gaze out to the four directions of space. In Mahayana Buddhism the four directions and the centre are associated with the cult of the Five Cosmic or Celestial Buddhas.

Buddhism in Sri Lanka

Sri Lanka has the oldest continuous Buddhist tradition of any country in the world. Buddhism was introduced there in Asoka's time, and one of its schools, Theravada, 'the doctrine of the elders', has been for centuries the dominant religion of Sri Lanka, Burma, Thailand, Laos, Cambodia and southern Vietnam.

The first mission to Sri Lanka, according to tradition, was led by one of Asoka's sons, Mahinda (or Mahendra), who was a Buddhist monk. He was welcomed by the king, Devanampiya Tissa, who became a Buddhist layman and founded the Great Monastery at his capital of Anuradhapura, which was the headquarters of Buddhism in Sri Lanka. The first stupa, enshrining one of the Buddha's collar-bones and venerated to this day by pilgrims, was built at Anuradhapura and a shoot of the Bodhi-Tree was brought from Gaya and planted near the city. As elsewhere, the adoption of the new religion by the ruling authority was crucial to its success with the populace, and as elsewhere the Buddhists took a tolerant attitude to the local gods and spirits. Indra and the other Vedic and local deities who were worshipped in Sri Lanka were said to have been converted to Buddhism and were ranked below the Buddha. Theravada became the state religion, supported by generations of Sinhalese kings, and in time the principle grew up that only a Buddhist could be the rightful king.

It was in Sri Lanka, in the first century BC, that the Buddhist scriptures were first written down, in Pali, an Indian language which died out in India. The philosopher Buddhaghosa, a Brahmin convert, emigrated to Sri Lanka from Gaya in the fifth century AD and wrote what became accepted as the definitive Theravadin commentary on the scriptures and an authoritative summary of Buddhist teaching, the *Visuddhi-magga* (the Path of Purification).

As in India, respect for the Buddha's memory could turn into worship. A legend grew up that the Buddha had visited Sri Lanka, flying there through the air, and Fa-hsien, a Chinese pilgrim to Sri Lanka in the fifth century, saw the great pagoda (an architectural development of the stupa), magnificently ornamented with gold and silver, which had been built over a footprint left by the Buddha in the ground. A tooth of the Buddha had been brought to the country earlier, and is treated with reverence at the Temple of the Tooth in Kandy. Each year the relic is carried through the town in procession every night for a week, on the back of an elephant.

The pattern of Buddhist worship in Sri Lanka probably preserves much that was typical of Buddhism in its early days in India. Images or pictures of the Buddha are venerated in the home, and though they are officially regarded as mere reminders of the founder and his teaching, it is likely that the veneration often amounts to worship. The procedure on visiting a stupa is to walk round it, keeping it to one's right, and then to offer flowers and perhaps a lamp or incense. The same offerings are made to the image of the Buddha in the shrine or temple, but the temple compound may also contain a temple to a Sinhalese or Hindu Indian deity or deities, who are honoured in a similar way. The Buddha ranks above the other deities and it seems that veneration of his image is intended primarily to gain merit, so as

ABOVE At the Shwedagon temple in Rangoon pagodas surround the main stupa, which the faithful circle round on a large platform. The whole temple is covered with gold.

LEFT The great 9th-century temple of Borobudur ('many Buddhas') in Java is surmounted by seventy-two stupas, each containing a Buddha-image. The temple is a hill clothed with stone and its carvings of scenes from the life of the Buddha total almost three miles in length.

LEFT The Bodhi-Tree at Anuradhapura in Sri Lanka is the oldest tree in the world of which there is any historical account. It is said to have grown from a shoot of the original tree beneath which the Buddha achieved enlightenment.

BELOW Gigantic reclining Buddha at the ruined city of Polonnaruwa, which was the capital of Sri Lanka from the 8th to the 13th centuries. The statue represents the Buddha's *parinirvana* or final deliverance from life into the peace and security of nirvana.

ABOVE Immense statues of
the Buddha convey the idea
of his colossal spiritual
stature. This one near
Anuradhapura stands forty-
two feet high.

RIGHT The Kelaniya temple,
near Colombo. Sri Lanka has
the oldest continuous
Buddhist tradition of any
country in the world.

to earn a better life on earth the next time round, while it is the other deities to whom prayers and offerings are made for help in specific worldly matters, for a son or a good crop, for recovery from illness, for promotion or success in business. On the other hand, at times of crisis a Buddhist monk is called in to read appropriate verses which are believed to give protection against disease, enemies, snakebite and other dangers.

It is not only Buddhists who combine different religions, deities and sacred places in a single system. The annual festival at the shrine of the Sinhalese deity Kataragama, for example, is attended by thousands of pilgrims from Sri Lanka and the south of India who are technically Buddhists, Hindus, Muslims or Christians.

The Buddha's footprints symbolize the impress which he made on the world. At this shrine in Bodh Gaya, where the Buddha achieved enlightenment, the footprints are venerated with offerings of flowers.

Mahayana: the Divine Saviours

There was no one of Asoka's stature to succeed him in India and his patronage of Buddhism had aroused opposition from the Brahmins, who were by tradition the rightful advisers of Indian kings. Fifty years after his death the Maurya dynasty fell, partly in consequence of Brahmin intrigues. The last of the Mauryas, the Buddhist Brihadratha, was murdered by one of his generals, Pushyamitra Sunga, who seized the throne, persecuted Buddhists and had a number of Buddhist monasteries destroyed.

Buddhism continued to thrive at the popular level, however, and its popularity drove it along the road to the split between Mahayana Buddhism and Hinayana Buddhism which has lasted ever since; though the split was not so sharp as to prevent Mahayana and Hinayana monks from frequently living amicably together in the same monasteries. Mahayana, the 'great vehicle' or 'great method', was so named by its adherents to emphasize that it had a broader appeal than the older and more austere form of Buddhism, which they called 'little vehicle', Hinayana, a term which the supporters of the latter naturally disliked. The Theravada Buddhism of Sri Lanka and South-East Asia today is the surviving representative of Hinayana, descended from one of its early sects.

Hinayana was the tradition that maintained that salvation was won only through one's own efforts, not with the aid of any divine being, and which either did not believe in the gods at all or wrote them off as unimportant spirits. This meant that it was only the Buddhist monk, following the correct discipline of meditation, who could attain nirvana. The ordinary laity had no such prospect.

The Hinayana case was weakened by the lack of evidence that any of the monks succeeded in attaining nirvana. In earlier days, tradition had it, there had been many saintly arhats who experienced full enlightenment, but this seemed no longer to be true. Nor was the extinction of the personality in nirvana a goal which large numbers of people in practice found attractive. Mahayana took up a much more popular stance. It believed in divine saviours, through whom any believer, monk or layman, could win salvation as a result of earnest faith rather than by the arduous meditation of the earlier discipline. These saviours were deities who had power in this world, and who could be loved in the bhakti spirit.

Among them, of course, was the Buddha himself, who was now depicted as a god in images intended to be worshipped. The earliest examples date from the first century AD and come from Mathura, in northern India, and Gandhara, a kingdom in the north-west, covering parts of modern Pakistan and Afghanistan, where Indian culture mingled with influences from Greece and Rome. Before this in Buddhist art the Buddha's presence in a scene was represented by a symbol, such as his footprints or an empty throne or the wheel of the Dharma, apparently as a safeguard against people taking him as an object of worship. In Gandhara, however, he was represented as a standing figure in the manner of the Greek gods, sometimes with the head of an Apollo and wearing a robe like a Roman toga.

Mathura and Gandhara became part of the Kushana Empire, which stretched from northern India westward to the frontiers of Iran. Its most famous ruler, Kanishka, was a Buddhist and built a colossal stupa at his capital, modern Peshawar, to house a casket containing some of the ashes of the Buddha. Asvaghosha, the biographer of the Buddha, lived at Kanishka's court. The variety of gods venerated in Kanishka's territories can be seen from his coins, on which Siva, Mithra and various Greek deities appear, as well as the Buddha. Iranian influences left their mark on the development of Mahayana Buddhism and it was from this stronghold between northern India and Iran that Mahayana and the Graeco-Buddhist art style spread through Central Asia to China and eventually to Japan.

The south of India, which was also open to western influence through its flourishing trade with the Roman Empire, was apparently another early centre of Mahayana. According to tradition, the first Mahayana scriptures, which date from the early centuries of the Christian era, were written in the south. The most important scriptures are the *Sutras*, which are believed to preserve the words of the Buddha himself, as memorized by his cousin and faithful disciple Ananda, and handed down to subsequent generations.

The historical Buddha was only one of the Mahayana deities. He was the temporary earthly vehicle of the Absolute, the Supreme Reality, which had been manifested in numerous other Buddhas as well. Even more important, for many Buddhists, were the Bodhisattvas. They were beings who through many arduous lives had ascended the steps of spiritual progress to the exalted point of almost becoming a Buddha, but out of their compassion for all living things had postponed entry into nirvana and remained in this universe of suffering to help others.

The greatest Bodhisattvas became saviour-gods. Each was believed to exist in a spiritual magnetic field, as it were, into which he could draw those who faithfully relied on him. From the ideal of the infinitely compassionate and surpassingly wise being who helps others along the road he himself has trodden – for in Mahayana everything that lives, in however humble and mean a form, has the capacity to become a Buddha – there developed the popular belief in a divine saviour who transfers part of his own spiritual merit to each believer and so sets aside the consequences of karma, opens up a short cut to salvation and takes his devotees to himself in a paradise of bliss after death: not because they have laboured along the path of meditation, but simply because they have faith in him. It is there, in paradise, that they will complete their journey to perfection.

In Mahayana the ideal of the Bodhisattva who lives for the salvation of others replaced the older ideal of the arhat, who was accused by the Mahayanists of selfishly living only for his own salvation. Where the early tradition had demanded right living and meditation, Mahayana developed forms of devotion on the Hindu model. Some of the Buddhas and Bodhisattvas had specialized fields of activity and some acquired entire cults of their own. There is Bhaisajyaguru, for example, the Buddha of healing, and Kshitigarbha, the Bodhisattva who rescues souls from hell. The cult of Amitabha or Amitayus (Infinite Light or Infinite Duration), who presides over a paradise in the west, probably had its beginnings in the Kushana Empire under the influence of Iranian sun-worship and was later extremely popular in China and Japan. Avalokitesvara helped those who called him to mind and spoke his name in need or distress, giving women sons or daughters as required, protecting sailors from shipwreck, merchants from robbers, and robbers in their turn from prison and execution. He saved those who thought earnestly of him from fire, wild beasts, hostile magic and the malice of enemies, and by the seventh century he was the most popular Buddhist deity in India.

There is also Maitreya (the Loving One), the reincarnation of the Buddha who is still to come in the future, to whose advent many Mahayana Buddhists look forward with longing and hope. His name comes from *mitra*, 'friend', and there is probably a link with the Iranian god Mithra. The world of his time will be far more beautiful and fruitful than it is now, covered with fresh green grass and with soil in which crops will grow by themselves without labour. Every good Buddhist will be reborn then and the human race will be much taller and stronger than it is today and will live much longer. Everyone will be honest and good, happy and prosperous, and there will be no crime or wrongdoing. Then Maitreya will be born and everyone will attain nirvana through his teaching.

The famous Lotus Sutra or 'Lotus of the Good Law' (*Saddharma-pundarika*), which was later very influential in the East, contradicts the older tradition by saying that the Buddha did not disappear into nirvana but remains present and active in the universe, as the great teacher and helper of all living things. He is the glorious lord of the universe and the saviour of the world. All creatures have an inherent Buddha-nature at the centre of their being and all can be saved.

As in the case of Hinduism, the question of possible Christian influence on Mahayana is difficult and disputed. Both Christianity and Mahayana emphasize the love and compassion of self-sacrificing divine saviours, who take to themselves in heaven those who believe in them. Both conceive of a divine world-ruler who is also the world-saviour, and both look forward to a future golden age on earth with the return of the saviour. Mahayana was certainly receptive to influences from the Mediterranean world and it may be that Christian ideas had some effect on it.

Mahayana philosophy, however, as distinct from the popular religion, did not regard its Buddhas and Bodhisattvas as real and had no belief in the

ABOVE Bronze figure of Maitreya, from India, 10th or 11th century. Mahayana Buddhists look forward to the coming of Maitreya, the Loving One, who will preside over a golden age in the future. He is shown about to step down and descend into the world.

RIGHT 17th-century Tibetan image of Avalokitesvara, enthroned and holding the lotus, symbol of spiritual flowering and wisdom, in his left hand. The most popular Buddhist deity in India when Buddhism was exported to Tibet, Avalokitesvara became the national god of Tibet.

individual. It preserved the early Buddhist view of the separate individual self as an illusion and the ultimate goal as the destruction of this illusion and the 'going out' of personality. The philosopher Nagarjuna and his school maintained that everything in the observable world was an illusion, including all the Buddhas and Bodhisattvas of popular belief. These deities were part of the 'method', the 'vehicle' which would carry the mass of ignorant believers to salvation, then to be discarded, as the ferry is no longer needed when the river has been safely crossed. An opposing school, led by two brothers, Asanga and Vasubandhu, held that this was going too far and that the individual consciousness is real as a partial manifestation of the Absolute. Salvation is gained when consciousness is purified by meditation to the point when it exists without being aware of anything other than itself. It has then merged with the Absolute.

These rarefied and abstruse cogitations had little to do with popular Mahayana, which had developed gods and now added goddesses, in the form of female Buddhas and Bodhisattvas. A great mother goddess appeared, Tara the Saviouress, who was sometimes identified with the abstract concept of Prajnaparamita, the Supreme Wisdom. She was also the Mother of all Buddhas, of whom Maya, the virgin mother of the historical Buddha, was regarded as the principal manifestation.

Tantric Buddhism

Some Tantric groups provided all the Buddhas and Bodhisattvas with female consorts, corresponding to the Hindu concept of Sakti. The Tantric movement came to the surface in Buddhism in the sixth century. The *Tantras*, the scriptures of Hindu and Buddhist Tantrism, are couched in a mysterious code-language of symbols and allusions, many of them erotic. They are based on the belief in great opposite forces pervading the universe, which are personified as male and female deities. In some Buddhist *Tantras*, for example, the reconciliation of opposite forces which keeps the universe in being is pictured as the sexual union of the Buddha and the goddess Tara: corresponding to the embrace of Siva and Sakti in Hindu Tantrism. In 'right-handed' Tantrism the male is the dominant force of the two, in 'left-handed' Tantrism the female.

Tantrism was a quest for spiritual perfection and magical power. Its purpose was to achieve complete control of oneself and all the forces of nature, so as to attain union with the cosmos and the divine. Long training was required to master Tantric methods, into which the pupil had to be initiated by a guru. The methods of Yoga, including breathing techniques and postures, were employed to subject the body to the control of the will. *Mudras* or gestures, *mantras* or syllables, words and phrases, and *mandalas* and *yantras*, symbolic diagrams of the forces at work in the universe, were used as aids to meditation and the achievement of spiritual and magical power. In meditation the initiate identified himself with various gods and goddesses representing cosmic forces. He visualized them and took them into his mind so that he became one with them, a process likened to sexual courtship and consummation.

Gateway at Angkor Thom, the ruined city and temple complex which was the capital of the Khmer kings in Cambodia, built about 1200 as an image of heaven on earth. In an example of the use of religion to support the political regime, the king is shown as Avalokitesvara, the god who helps all who call on him in time of need.

This was not always in the mind only, for some Tantric monks used female partners to represent the goddesses. In left-handed Tantrism, ritual sexual intercourse was employed, not for pleasure but as a way of entering into the underlying processes and structure of the universe.

The Decline of Buddhism in India

Gradually, over many centuries and for reasons that are not at all clear, Buddhism declined in India. Popular Mahayana and popular Hinduism were so similar that Mahayana may have lost its distinctive attraction, while the Buddhist monasteries grew larger, richer, laxer and fewer, so that fewer areas had a local community of monks to keep the religion alive. Some monasteries were rich enough to own slaves and to hire labourers to tend their estates. Most of the Indian ruling families were Hindu, which denied Buddhism the steady support of authority.

Harsha, who ruled a northern empire from Kanauj in the seventh century, was a Buddhist, but his empire broke up when he was murdered. Many of the famous Buddhist paintings from Ajanta, where the monks lived in caves, date from his time. They often illustrate episodes from the Buddha's life. Even at this period, however, the Chinese pilgrim Hsuan Tsang, travelling through northern India, found monasteries abandoned and stupas crumbling with neglect, while Hindu temples were flourishing.

From the eighth century to the twelfth the Pala dynasty in Bengal and Bihar were Buddhists. They founded monasteries and universities which were seats of Tantric philosophy and learning, but were finally overthrown by a new dynasty which was Vaishnavite. The last blow came with the Muslim invasions, when the wealth of the surviving Buddhist monasteries and the pacifism of the Buddhist monks made them desirable targets for plunder. They were destroyed, the monks were driven out and Buddhism became virtually extinct in the land of its birth. Only in the last hundred years or so has Buddhism revived a little in India, but there are fewer Buddhists in India, Pakistan and Bangladesh today than there are Christians.

Buddhism in Tibet

The Buddhist tradition in Tibet was well over a thousand years old when the Chinese invaded and occupied the country in 1950. Nine years later a revolt against Chinese rule was suppressed and the Dalai Lama, the spiritual head of the country, fled into exile in India. Many other Tibetans followed him or have escaped since. There are said to have been close to 2500 monasteries in Tibet in the 1950s. According to press reports in 1979, most of them have been closed down and only a handful are still in existence, each with a few elderly monks. The status of the remaining monasteries is indicated by the fact that they are administered by the Office for the Preservation of Cultural Relics.

The official Communist line is that Tibetan 'backwardness' is due to centuries of Buddhist rule and that 'progress' can only be made by eliminating religion from the lives of the people. All the same, journalists noticed many signs that religion has not yet withered away in Tibet. It was reported, for example, that 3000 to 4000 people worship every week at the Jokhang temple in Lhasa. This temple was founded in the seventh century AD and its image of Sakyamuni, the historical Buddha, was considered the most sacred in the country.

Mahayana Buddhism gained ground slowly in Tibet from the seventh century on, with the encouragement of kings and powerful families. It came to Tibet from India and China, but the Indian influence was the dominant one. The first monastery was built in the eighth century. Later, Tibetan monks went to study in India and Nepal, and Indian texts were brought back and translated. Various religious orders were founded, each with its own monasteries. Safe from Muslim invasion, Buddhism continued to thrive, and by the thirteenth century it was firmly in the saddle.

As elsewhere, the Buddhists were tolerant of already established cults and much of the native religion blended with Buddhism in popular Tibetan belief. Before the coming of Buddhism gods of the sky, the earth and mountains were worshipped, and there were shamans who became possessed by these deities in trance. Tibetan kings were believed to be manifestations of the sky-god, each of them coming down to earth as a baby and returning to the sky at the end of his earthly life.

The pre-Buddhist gods were absorbed into the Buddhist system. They

The Dalai Lama as a boy in 1950, when the Chinese invaded Tibet. His predecessors had ruled Tibet for centuries as manifestations of Avalokitesvara. When each Dalai Lama died, a search was mounted to find the child in whom he had been reincarnated.

LEFT The caves at Ajanta, north-east of Bombay, were carved out of the rock as Buddhist monasteries and temples. Famous for their sculptures and wall paintings, which include scenes from the Buddha's life, they were abandoned by the 8th century as Buddhism declined in India.

ABOVE Monks sound midday from the roof of the Potala Palace, the residence of the Dalai Lama in Lhasa.

LEFT Figures of giants and animals guard the approach to the Nyatapola temple in Nepal. The pagoda is a development of the stupa and a symbol of spiritual aspiration and achievement.

were said to have been converted to the new religion, which they henceforth protected. The principal deities, however, were the great Mahayana Buddhas and Bodhisattvas, especially Avalokitesvara, who was virtually the national god of Tibet. The Mahayana goddesses were also worshipped, including the mother goddess Tara, and the whole apparatus of Indian Tantric Buddhism, with its magic, its sexual symbolism and its rarer sexual practices, was preserved in Tibet long after it had died out in India.

The principal distinguishing feature of Tibetan Buddhism is belief in reincarnating lamas. Lama, 'superior', is a title given to abbots of Buddhist monasteries and senior monks. The purpose of the monastic life is to achieve nirvana and it came to be believed that certain heads of monasteries and particularly saintly monks were living Bodhisattvas, born on earth as men over and over again to help others. When such a lama died, a search was made to find the child in whom he had been reincarnated. The main test was whether the child recognized various objects which he had used in his previous life. He was then trained in his monastery until he was a young man and old enough to take over his duties. If he found monastic life intolerable, however, he was allowed to resign.

The most famous example is the line of Dalai Lamas, the heads of the Gelugpa Order. The first of them died in 1475 and was reborn in a child who was duly installed as the second Dalai Lama. In 1642 the fifth Dalai Lama became the ruler of Tibet and from that time until the 1950s the succession to the highest political and ecclesiastical office in the land was by reincarnation. The Manchu emperors of China established a protectorate over Tibet in the eighteenth century, but the Dalai Lama and his advisers continued to rule the country. Each Dalai Lama was believed to be a manifestation of Avalokitesvara and a reincarnation of all his predecessors.

In the same way, each of the Panchen Lamas, the second most important figures in the state, was regarded as a manifestation of the Buddha Amitabha. The present Panchen Lama was taken away to China in 1964 and subjected to a course of 'thought reform' which turned him into a Communist mouthpiece.

ABOVE Gilt bronze figure of an arhat holding a book of Buddhist scriptures, late 15th century, with an inscription in Tibetan Chinese. The long ear-lobes are a mark of spiritual achievement and authority.

ABOVE LEFT An elderly Tibetan exile in India, turning a prayer wheel, an aid to meditation which at popular levels is often believed to put the prayer into effect.

4. China & Japan

Though Buddhism died out in India, it flourished in China and Japan, where Mahayana blended with native religions. Buddhism was for centuries the state religion of Japan, and it is one of the 'three doctrines' of Chinese tradition, the other two being Confucianism and Taoism. A fourth doctrine should now be added, Communism, which despite its disapproval of religion has a religious hold on its adherents.

China is a huge country, larger than Europe or the United States, containing about a fifth of the human race. The Chinese name for the country is 'the Middle Kingdom', implying that it is the centre of the world. For most of the last 2000 years it has been a single unit, ruled by one central government, and religion has been one of the principal tools employed by Chinese regimes to maintain order and unity among millions of people of different racial origins, speaking mutually unintelligible languages and dialects. During most of Chinese history after the second century BC Confucianism was the philosophical and ethical system which commanded the allegiance of the mandarins, the high-ranking bureaucrats who ran the country under a succession of ruling dynasties. The unusual stability and distinctive flavour of Chinese civilization owed much to the mandarins and their adoption of the Confucian values of order, harmony, serenity and decorum. The complexity of Chinese writing with its multitude of ideograms made it far more difficult to learn to read and write than it has been in the West and gave the small literate class a peculiarly powerful position in society.

From time immemorial, Chinese peasants have worshipped local deities, gods of nature and fertility and spirits of rivers and hills. Remarkably little is known about these cults, because Chinese intellectuals have despised them, but they go back beyond the distant beginnings of Chinese recorded history in the days of the Shang dynasty, who ruled in northern China. The Shang kings may have been regarded as divine during their lives and were treated as gods after death. Large numbers of human beings were killed and buried with the dead kings, presumably to serve them beyond the grave.

The sacred mountain of Mai-chi-shan in Kansu province, northern China. The colossal figures represent Mi-lo (Maitreya), the future Buddha, flanked by two Bodhisattvas. The Mahayana deities from India became naturalized in China, and worshippers prayed to be reborn in Mi-lo's heaven, where they would see him face to face.

85

The royal house and the aristocratic families venerated their ancestors, who were believed to guide and protect their descendants, and to whom each family owed its social position. Common people, who had no position of importance, were not thought to have any ancestors worth recalling.

The good will of the royal ancestors ensured the prosperity of the king and the kingdom. Above them was a supreme deity, Shang-ti, who seems to have been the original ancestor of the Shang dynasty itself. He governed the world from the sky, controlling the weather and the growth of crops, and his descendant, the ruling king, offered him sacrifices and asked for his guidance and help in all important matters. Shang-ti was assisted by lesser deities, including those of the sun, the moon, thunder and rain, rivers and mountains, and the directions. Offerings were made to many of these deities, who were thought of in human form and were sometimes seen in dreams. There are also accounts of fertility festivals involving orgiastic eating, drinking and sex.

The king was the chief priest of the state religion and sacrificed prisoners of war to his ancestors. The cults of the lesser deities were largely in the hands of male and female shamans, the *wu*. The shamans were responsible for making rain, treating disease and communicating with the divine powers and the ancestors. By wild dancing they worked themselves into states of ecstasy in which the gods and the ancestors seemed to speak through their mouths.

Some of the concepts which influenced Chinese religion for centuries are already visible at this early stage. One is reverence for the family and respect for one's elders, even after death. Another is the idea of a harmonious natural order which depends on various deities, responsible for different departments of nature, who are subordinates of a supreme divine power. This supreme god is linked with the sky, and the king, who is his descendant and his counterpart on earth, has a close and special relationship with him. The safety and prosperity of society depends on this relationship, so that political power and good government rest on the maintenance of harmonious relations with the order of nature.

The strength of this concept was demonstrated when the last king of the Shang dynasty, Ti Hsin, was overthrown and driven to burn himself to death by Wu Wang, founder of the Chou dynasty. The Chou family identified Shang-ti with their own concept of T'ien, Heaven, as the supreme power in the universe. Heaven's deputy on earth was the Son of Heaven, the Chou king himself. To justify the successful rebellion against the long-established Shang dynasty, the new dynasty maintained that Ti Hsin by his wickedness had forfeited the approval of Heaven, which had taken the mandate to rule on earth away from him and bestowed it on the virtuous house of Chou instead.

This concept of the mandate of Heaven became an important element of the state religion. It meant that whichever dynasty actually ruled China had been invested with the right to do so by Heaven, and consequently had a right to support. If a family attempted to seize power, as sometimes happened, and failed, that was because it lacked the approval of Heaven, and if it succeeded then plainly it did so in accordance with Heaven's will. This

Yen-lo, the Chinese equivalent of Yama, the Buddhist ruler of the dead, looks on while punishments are meted out to offenders in hell.

is a belief which makes for stability by investing actual power with moral authority, and which safeguards the infallibility of Heaven by making sure that whatever happens is ascribed to Heaven's decision. (The Christian concept of providence, similarly, ascribes whatever happens to the will of God.) It leads on to the belief that government and society must be virtuous or risk the disapproval of Heaven, and 'virtuous' means in conformity with the order of nature. Disruptions of the natural order consequently indicate that there is something seriously wrong in human affairs. Not only the fall of a dynasty or defeat in war but natural catastrophes such as floods, drought or pestilence were later put down to a lack of 'virtue' in society (and again there is a parallel in Christianity).

Confucius and Confucianism

K'ung Fu-tzu, or Master K'ung, known in the West as Confucius, was a contemporary of the Buddha and Mahavira in India. Like them, he lived at a time when the social order was breaking down – in this case in fierce struggles among the feudal lords who had gradually reduced the Chou king to a cipher. Unlike them, he was not much interested in religion and it is a shade ironic that he was later honoured with temples in every district of China. Confucianism was less a religion than an attitude to life and a code of conduct which has been called 'Chinese humanism'.

Confucius seems to have accepted the concept of Heaven as the supreme power, of which men should stand in awe, and the associated idea of the mandate of Heaven. He also approved of the veneration of ancestors, as part of the ideal of the family and respect for one's elders, but he did not look to religion for a solution to the turmoil of his time. Instead he asserted that every human being and every creature and object has an appointed place in the order of nature and should behave as his or its station requires. Like many self-educated men, he attached an importance to education seldom granted it by those who have been educated by others. He looked to education to produce an elite of 'superior men', virtuous and capable, to whom government and administration should be entrusted for the benefit of all. This principle could hardly fail to appeal to the powerful bureaucracy of later China, but in his own time Confucius could find few people to take any interest in his ideas. He did gather a small group of disciples and the pithy sayings attributed to him were written down long afterwards as his *Analects* or *Conversations*. By tradition he was also the author of some of the other classic works of Confucianism.

Like Confucius, the second great figure of early Confucianism, Mencius (Meng Tzu, or Master Meng), who believed in Heaven as a personal and moral deity, failed to persuade anyone in power to put his principles into practice. Nor did the philosopher Hsun Tzu, who regarded Heaven as the impersonal order of nature and the nature deities and ancestral spirits not as supernatural beings but as types of moral excellence.

In the later centuries of the Chou dynasty, the Chinese feudal system collapsed in incessant civil war, until the Ch'in dynasty, from which the name China comes, united northern and central China in an organized

empire run by a civil service. The Han dynasty, which followed on, extended the empire until it held at least nominal sway over the whole of what we now call China. Early in the Han period, Confucianism gained the upper hand inside the bureaucracy and the approval of the emperors, who preferred a meritocracy of 'superior men' to a hereditary feudal nobility who were thought to be more difficult to control.

Under the Emperor Wu Ti, Confucianism became the official orthodoxy of the court. Places in the imperial civil service were opened to entry by examination. In time the Confucian classics became the basis of the Chinese education system and a thorough knowledge of them a prerequisite for a successful career in the civil service. In AD 59 the Emperor Ming ordered sacrifices to be offered to Confucius in the public schools. The great sage had become a kind of patron saint of education, and numerous temples were later built in his honour, where sacrifices were decorously offered with music and dancing in the spring.

Confucianism, like Buddhism, is a western term. Confucians called it 'the way (*tao*) of the sages' or 'the way of the ancients'. The Confucian social and moral code was the accepted ideal of the Chinese upper classes down to the Revolution of 1911 and still has a powerful influence in Chinese communities outside mainland China. It was intended to promote good order and social harmony. It did not rest on the authority of a God and its psychological sanction was not a sense of sin, at offending a deity, but a sense of shame at falling below the standards expected of one. Confucianism had a strong sense of duty and was prudish about sex. It put much stress on benevolence, politeness and formality in all dealings, family loyalty and respect for one's elders and betters, respect for precedent and tradition, good faith and trustworthiness, calmness of spirit, a detached and fatalistic view of the ups and downs of life, and a cultivated distaste for vulgarity. 'The superior man understands what is right,' Confucius said, 'the inferior man understands what will sell.' He also said: 'Do not do to others what you would not wish them to do to you.' His ideal of human conduct was to be a good son, a good brother and a good friend.

On its religious or semi-religious side, the central concept of Confucianism was the old belief that to ensure security and prosperity, government and society must be in tune with the order of nature. This was achieved by good moral behaviour by all classes, by everyone keeping to his station in life, and through the performance of rituals. The emperor himself, the Son of Heaven, offered the customary sacrifices to Heaven on behalf of the whole empire, the chief officials in each district offered them to the subordinate deities on behalf of the district, and the head of each family offered them at home to the ancestors. It was a very old belief that sacrifice was the correct expression of the right reciprocal relationship between the powers of nature and human beings. The emperor offered four great sacrifices in person every year, to Heaven, to Earth, to the royal ancestors, and to the gods of soil and grain. In addition, to secure a good harvest, the emperor went each year to the temple of Shen Nung, the god of agriculture, where he ploughed six furrows in the sacred field. The rest of the field was then ploughed by his attendants, in order of rank.

Figure, probably of an official, from a tomb of the T'ang dynasty. China was governed by a powerful civil service, under the emperor, and in time the same system was translated into the sky, where a celestial bureaucracy administered every detail of life in the world.

LEFT Idealized portrait of Confucius, founder of the philosophical school which dominated Chinese political and intellectual life for centuries and which devised its own religion.

Confucian thinkers generally did not regard the gods as personal beings, but as impersonal phenomena of nature. Their attitude to the ancestors was similarly matter of fact. Veneration of ancestors implies that people survive death, but many Confucians did not believe in survival, and many more were agnostic about it. What mattered was the conduct of life. Ordinary people firmly believed in the spirits of the dead and their power to help or harm, but to Confucians the offerings to ancestors were socially desirable regardless of whether the dead survived or not. They upheld the ideal of filial piety, which was the keystone of the harmony of society at large, viewed as one great family, with the emperor as the father of his people and his senior officials as respected elders. The whole apparatus of the state religion, in fact, was intended to express and support the unity and cohesion of the empire.

The Rise of Taoism

Religious fervour had no place in the Confucian system. It made no provision for private worship. It took no stock in asceticism or in the indecorous and ungentlemanly pursuit of ecstasy and trance. Anyone who looked for a close personal relationship with the divine turned to Taoism or Buddhism.

The traditional founder of Taoism was Lao Tzu (Old Master), an older contemporary of Confucius. Nothing is known about his life, but according to legend his mother carried him in her womb for sixty years or more before his birth, so that when he at last came into the world his hair was white with age. The classic exposition of Taoist mysticism, the *Tao Te Ching* (the Way and Its Power) is attributed to him, but Taoism has its roots further back among the early shamans who in states of ecstasy were believed to be possessed by the gods. Through meditation and trance the Taoists attained a state in which, as they put it, 'I lose me'. In this state came the full realization and experience of the One, the single unchanging principle which lies behind surface appearances, a unity of which all phenomena are part. This great all-embracing One or Absolute was called Tao, which is the Chinese character for 'way', meaning both a path or road and figuratively a method or course.

Like the Confucians, the Taoists adopted the Yin-Yang theory of the universe, as formulated in the fourth century BC by Tsou Yen. Yin and Yang are two great opposite forces which permeate the entire universe and on whose interplay everything depends: Yang being the male, active and positive force, Yin the female, passive and negative one. In Taoism the two opposites are reconciled and transcended in Tao. Wisdom for the Taoist consists in being in harmony with the rhythms of nature, and consequently, the right principle of behaviour is to leave things be, and desist from vainly struggling to change and improve things. The only appropriate attitude to nature and Tao is one of humble non-interference. 'Do nothing,' as a famous Taoist saying has it, 'and there is nothing that is not done.' Government, politics, war, commerce and all the products of striving and self-assertion are impertinent and self-defeating attempts to interfere with

Lacquer panel showing the Yin-Yang symbol. Yin and Yang, in Chinese theory, were two great opposite and complementary principles, on whose interplay everything in the universe depended.

RIGHT Lao Tzu, the traditional founder of Taoism, with disciples.

the operations of Tao. Confucianism and Taoism were both reactions to the anarchy in China in the later Chou period, but where the former recommended involvement in society, the other chose non-involvement.

The fundamental paradox of the *Tao Te Ching* is that union with Tao is not achieved by trying to achieve it. On the contrary, it is attained by not trying to achieve anything, by ridding oneself of all desires. This quietist attitude did not prevent Taoists from recommending asceticism, cleanliness, and postures and breathing techniques like those of Yoga as aids to meditation and the trance-experiences in which union with the One was achieved. Since Tao is eternal, it was believed that those who attained union with it became immortal and lived on for ever in a body of finer consistency than the normal one, either in this world or in a paradise. The Taoists used magic and alchemy in attempts to prolong life indefinitely. The first Ch'in emperor made determined efforts to become immortal; he gathered a small army of magicians to help him, forbade any mention of death in his presence and sent an expedition in a vain search for the herb of immortality on an island in the eastern sea.

Like other religions, Taoism had a high and a low register. Some Taoists retired to secluded hermitages, where they practised the simple and quiet life, and engaged in meditation, prayer and study. Taoism as a popular religion had an entirely different flavour. It had developed by the second century AD with a sizeable following among the peasantry. It was not a solitary but a communal faith, concerned with the worship of numerous gods and goddesses, with securing good fortune and happiness on earth, with the acquisition of spiritual merit and with entry into the eternal delight of paradise after death.

This miniature pagoda is a reliquary, believed to contain a tooth of the Buddha, in the Kuang Chi temple, Peking. Relics are treated with the same veneration in Buddhism as in Roman Catholic Christianity.

The most famous figure of early popular Taoism was Chang Ling, who dominated a community in Szechuan in the west. He was a formidable magician, who was believed to have brought all spirits and demons under his control and to protect his followers from supernatural evil. His power was thought to have descended to his grandson, Chang Lu, who ruled his own small Taoist state in the Szechuan area at the turn of the second and third centuries AD. Popular Taoism had a strong sense of sin and the necessity for repentance. Worshippers confessed to stealing, lust, drunkenness and other offences, and paid in rice for their sins to be lifted. All disease was believed to be caused by sin. The priests chanted incantations over water, which was then given to the repentant patient to drink. If no cure resulted, this was put down to the patient's lack of faith. There were also rites in which repentant sinners rolled about in mud and engaged in orgiastic sex. This type of Taoism spread to peasant communities all over China in the third and fourth centuries. By this time, however, a rival for popular favour had appeared on the scene, for Buddhism had been exported to China.

Buddhism and Taoism

Buddhist monks entered China along the trade route from Central Asia and by the end of the first century AD there was a Buddhist community at the Han emperor's capital of Loyang. More missionaries came in during the following centuries, Chinese converts were made, monasteries and temples were established and the laborious work began of translating Buddhist scriptures, largely Mahayana scriptures, into Chinese. There was a long period of disorder after the fall of the Han dynasty, when China was splintered into rival kingdoms and invaded by Huns and Turks, until the Sui dynasty reunited the empire. Both Buddhism and Taoism made headway in a troubled world, by offering a remedy for anxiety which the Chinese state religion was too divorced from any personal, individual relationship with the spiritual to provide.

Scornful Chinese intellectuals regarded the foreign religion as an inferior variety of Taoism. Lao Tzu was said to have gone to the west and taught Taoism to the barbarians – in a simplified form appropriate to their limited intelligence – and from them it had now returned. Taoists claimed that Lao Tzu and the Buddha were the same person. In fact, Buddhism was in many ways distinctly un-Chinese. The Indian belief that human beings live over and over again on earth was entirely unknown in China. The Chinese reverence for the family clashed with the Buddha's teaching that family ties were a hindrance to enlightenment, and with the celibacy required of Buddhist monks. Where Buddhism saw life as suffering, Chinese tradition regarded the order of nature as fundamentally good and the right life as one lived in harmony with nature. Far from wanting to escape from the body and individual personality, most Taoists wanted to prolong their individual existence indefinitely.

On the other hand, both the Buddhists and the *Tao Te Ching* identified wanting and striving as crucial faults of human nature. Both Buddhism and

Kuan Ti, god of war, a popular deity as preventer of war and protector against harm, 19th-century watercolour. Originally a general of the 3rd century AD, he was believed to have joined the celestial bureaucracy after death and was promoted in rank by subsequent emperors until in 1594 he was proclaimed Faithful and Loyal Great Deity, Supporter of Heaven, Protector of the Realm.

Taoism believed that salvation was gained through meditation and trance, and both employed similar techniques. At the popular level, Mahayana and Taoism were both polytheistic religions which catered for people's needs in life and promised happiness in paradise after death. The two religions influenced each other, Chinese versions of the Buddhist scriptures were adapted to Chinese ideas, and Buddhism and Taoism were often mingled together in popular belief.

Buddhism gained converts and support among the ruling families and the intellectuals as well as the peasantry, and the Buddhist monasteries grew prosperous. The belief in a succession of earthly lives was successfully transplanted to Chinese soil and so were the principal Mahayana Buddhas and Bodhisattvas, who became naturalized Chinese deities. They included the historical Buddha himself, the future Buddha Maitreya, Amitabha and Avalokitesvara, a male Bodhisattva who turned into a popular Chinese goddess as Kuan Yin, the merciful protector of women and helper of people in trouble.

The first of the Sui emperors, Wen Ti, was a Buddhist, but as emperor he gave official encouragement to the Confucians and Taoists as well. He founded a Taoist institute for the study of astrology and other methods of divination, through which he intended to control the Taoist priests. Claiming to rule with the mandate of Heaven, and needing the Confucian bureaucrats to run the empire, he carried out his duties as head of the state religion and promoted Confucian education. In the last few years of his reign, however, he tried to make Buddhism the common religion of China and built numerous pagodas (the equivalents of stupas). Buddhist writers hailed him as the Chinese Asoka. However, his son and successor, Yang Ti, though a Buddhist by upbringing and education, found it necessary to conciliate the powerful Confucian civil servants.

A Chinese Buddhist might revere all the major Buddhas and Bodhisattvas or might focus his devotion on whichever of them most appealed to him. From the sixth century on, separate organized sects emerged, taking their stand on the translated texts of different Buddhist groups and schools of thought in India. One of the most influential was the T'ien T'ai sect, with the Lotus Sutra as its principal scripture, which worshipped the historical Buddha as the eternal saviour and lord of the universe. In the seventh century the Ch'ing T'u (Pure Land) sect came to the fore, the Pure Land being the paradise of Amitabha in the west, to which the deity's followers would win entry by faith in him, loving devotion to him and earnest repetition of his name in the formula 'Namo Amit'o Fo' (Glory to Amitabha Buddha). This was the only outward observance demanded of the Pure Land believer. The cult of Amitabha spread all through Chinese Buddhism and the sect soon ceased to be a separate entity.

Another group, the Ch'an sect, is better known in the West under its Japanese name, Zen. The name means 'meditation', which is misleading, because the sect rejected the gradual method of approach to enlightenment through meditation. In Ch'an enlightenment is attained suddenly in a flash of intuition. Unlike the Pure Land cult, which required no training and

Porcelain figure of Kuan Yin. The personification of compassion, she was much loved and her cult was not confined to Buddhist families.

RIGHT The Indian Buddhist deity Avalokitesvara turned in China into the merciful goddess Kuan Yin. She may have been a Chinese goddess who was adopted by Buddhists.

The Ch'i-yin pagoda at the White Horse temple in Loyang, built in the 6th or 7th century. Loyang was earlier the capital of the Han dynasty and a Buddhist community was established there by the end of the 1st century AD.

little self-discipline, and was extremely popular with laymen, Ch'an was confined largely to monks, personally trained by a master. A long period of preparation was needed, during which the pupil practised disciplining himself by remaining silent and emptying his mind of all ideas, while waiting attentively for the enlightenment which would come with the sudden manifestation of his own inward Buddha-nature. His master set him to consider baffling paradoxes called *koans*, intended to undermine reason and common sense, which hinder spiritual progress. While contemplating these, he was expected to work with his hands in the monastery or in the fields, unlike the more conventional Buddhist monks.

Taoism, meanwhile, was also flourishing, with its own temples, monasteries and voluminous scriptures to rival those of Buddhism. Local Taoist communities were in charge of married priests whose position was hereditary, so that a temple might remain in the hands of the same priestly family for many generations. Taoism had been purged of its crude and orgiastic rituals (though they survived in corners here and there) and at the popular level Taoism and Buddhism tended to coalesce. Each provided rites, prayers and magic spells to obtain good fortune, success and help in trouble from the gods, whose images were venerated in their temples with respectful bows and offerings of incense. Each gave the faithful the opportunity to acquire spiritual merit, by adherence to the religion, making gifts to temples and monasteries, and good moral behaviour, including charity to the poor. This merit would stand the believer in good stead after death. The Buddhist belief in rebirth was accepted in popular Taoism, and in both religions it was widely accepted that after death the individual would go to the underworld or hell. There he would be painfully punished for any serious misdeeds, but if his stock of merit was adequate he would be reborn on earth in a better condition of life. Alternatively he might have enough merit to leave the wheel of earthly lives and be reborn in a paradise. Buddhists and Taoists both held services for the dead to secure their speedy release from the underworld through the merits of the living.

The greatest of the Taoist deities was the sky god, who came to be known as Yu Huang (the Pure August). He personified Tao as the One, the unity underlying all diversity, and was the equivalent of Heaven in the state religion. There were numerous other Taoist deities, including many of the nature gods of the state religion, legendary emperors and sages, and Lao Tzu himself. Buddhist deities were taken into Taoism, and Amitabha was sometimes identified with Yu Huang.

The attitude of governments to Buddhism and Taoism varied with the personal beliefs of different emperors, but most of them found it necessary to support Confucianism for the security and efficient administration of the state. Several of the T'ang emperors were fervent Taoists and the dynasty claimed descent from Lao Tzu. Some of the emperors were believed to have achieved immortality – or to have poisoned themselves, depending on the point of view – by drinking Taoist elixirs. On the other hand, the formidable Empress Wu in the late seventh century was an ardent Buddhist, hailed by Buddhist propagandists as an incarnation of the Buddha Maitreya.

RIGHT Taoist temple in Hong Kong, with incense burners. The sweet smell of incense is offered to deities in many religions.

The immortals visit Hsi Wang Mu's garden, 17th-century painting. Hsi Wang Mu, the Royal Mother of the Western Paradise, was a beautiful and gracious Taoist goddess, who lived on a mythical mountain in the west. Once every 6000 years the peaches in her garden ripened and all the immortals gathered to eat the magic fruit which renewed their immortality.

LEFT Tibetan thang-ka, or painted scroll, 19th century, showing Mara, the Lord of Death, who holds the wheel of life. In Buddhism, as in Hinduism, all creatures live and die again and again unless they can gain liberation from the 'sorrowful, weary wheel' of existence.

ABOVE Sages with the Yin-Yang, a Chinese painting.

RIGHT The so-called Temple of Heaven in Peking, with its dragon pavement. A miniature image of Heaven, built in the late 19th century.

In the ninth century there was an unsuccessful attempt to suppress Buddhism, mainly on the ground that the country's resources were going to waste on lavish temples and economically unproductive monasteries. The same government persecuted the tiny groups of Christians and Manichaeans (followers of the Persian prophet Mani). Christianity reached China in the seventh century, but made little impression. Zoroastrianism, Judaism and Islam also penetrated into China in the T'ang period, but only as the religions of foreign traders.

The Celestial Civil Service

The Sung dynasty saw a Confucian revival movement, known as Neo-Confucianism, whose greatest figure was the philosopher Chu Hsi. Directed to strengthening the civil service and against Buddhism, this movement proclaimed the order of nature as a rational and moral order with which man should live in harmony. Rejecting the Buddhist and Taoist concentration on meditation, the inner life and salvation, the Neo-Confucians believed in active participation in society.

Neo-Confucianism restored the self-confidence and improved the quality of the civil service. Backed by the vigorous policies of the early Sung emperors, the mandarins took so firm a grip on the Middle Kingdom that a bureaucratic system was imposed on the gods. Just as the Son of Heaven ruled China through his officials, so Heaven, personified as the Jade Emperor, ruled the universe through a divine bureaucracy. His chief ministers and their departments supervised all the forces of nature and every facet of life.

A particularly important figure in the celestial administration was the Great Emperor of the Eastern Peak, at the head of seventy-five departments which decided the course of life and date of death of all creatures, human and animal. City gods and village gods, corresponding to human district officials, formed another ministry. All activities, businesses, shops, crafts and occupations, including thieves and prostitutes, had their supervisory gods. In the home were the household gods, whose figurines or paper images were venerated with incense. The tablets of the ancestors were also kept in the household shrine. All the family news was told to them and they could be asked to intercede with the divine bureaucrats in time of need. The kitchen god went to Heaven once a year to report on the behaviour of every member of the family. Just before the time of his departure, at New Year, he was given honey, to sweeten his utterance or sometimes to stick his lips together so that he could not report at all.

An enormous array of gods and godlings were involved, drawn from the traditional state religion, Buddhism, Taoism and local cults. According to their rank, they had temples, shrines or inscribed tablets, at which they were honoured. There was no clear line between the human and the divine bureaucracy, which were part of the same administration. Honest and hard-working officials in the imperial civil service were believed to join the celestial civil service after death. People thought that the emperor's officials would be punished by the appropriate divine departments if they did

Figure of an official, Ch'ing dynasty, typifying the ideals of calmness of spirit, formality, courtesy and respect for tradition which inspired the Confucian civil service.

ABOVE LEFT The Four Kings of Hell, in Chinese Buddhism, who are subordinates of Yen-lo, the ruler of the dead. Their celestial counterparts are the Four Diamond Kings of Heaven.

LEFT Temple of Inari, the Shinto rice god, at Kyoto in Japan. Shinto is the old pre-Buddhist religion of Japan.

ABOVE Shou-lao, the Chinese Taoist god of longevity, holding a peach, the symbol of long life and immortality, associated with the vulva. The god was believed to decide the length of each person's life.

RIGHT Colossal seated figure of Amida Buddha, in the posture of meditation, at Kamakura, Japan, 13th century. Devotees of Amida believe that through loving faith in him and earnest repetition of his name they will go to his heaven in the west.

wrong, but on the other hand the higher imperial bureaucrats outranked the lower levels of the celestial civil service and punished gods who were negligent or incompetent: one who failed to bring rain to his district, for instance, or neglected to halt an epidemic. The offending god's image might be given a thrashing, or he could be demoted and another god appointed in his place to see if he could do better. He probably could, since rain does come and epidemics do stop eventually.

This eminently sensible and highly successful system was well adapted to the administration of a huge empire and the control of a teeming population. Psychologically, it satisfied the instinct for order, gave human officials a cautionary sense of being invisibly as well as visibly overseen, explained disasters and failures as divine bureaucratic mistakes, and provided for their punishment. It also gave ordinary citizens gods who could be appealed to for help. Just as the favour of mortal officials might be won by appropriate gifts, so could the assistance of the gods, and more cheaply, by giving them mock paper money or paper clothes.

As a result, the religion of the celestial bureaucracy took and kept a firm hold on Chinese loyalty, into the twentieth century, and Buddhism and Taoism went into a long, slow decline. Some emperors had Buddhist leanings, Buddhist and Taoist monasteries survived, some families remained Buddhist or Taoist, and there were occasional local rebellions by groups with Buddhist or Taoist sympathies, but for most Chinese Buddhism and Taoism merged into the Confucian state religion. In villages there might be a Confucian temple, a Buddhist or Taoist temple and shrines of local deities and ancestors, but more often temples in which all these elements were amalgamated.

China and the West

In the thirteenth century the great Mongol leader Genghis Khan, who believed in a supreme God who had commissioned him to conquer the whole world, built up an immense empire stretching from Mongolia and northern China across Tibet and Central Asia to the Black Sea. After his death the empire was divided between his four sons. His grandson, Kublai Khan, conquered all China and founded the Yuan dynasty, with its capital at Peking. The Yuan emperors were generally tolerant in religious matters, but took their responsibilities as Sons of Heaven seriously. Islam flourished in the army. Christianity of both the Roman Catholic and the Eastern Orthodox branches made a little headway.

The Yuan dynasty was overthrown by the native Chinese Ming dynasty, and it in turn by a Manchurian dynasty. Both claimed to have the mandate of Heaven and under both the Confucian state religion remained dominant. The European powers began to nibble at China's edges, the Portuguese establishing a trading post at Macao in 1557. The Italian Matteo Ricci, the first Jesuit missionary to establish himself in China, reached Macao in 1582 and went on to Peking where he stayed for the rest of his life. Dominican and Franciscan missionaries came later, but European pressure for concessions stiffened the resistance of the Chinese upper classes, most of

Chinese Buddhist monk and nuns at the entrance of a cave-temple at Ipoh, Malaysia. They are wearing rosaries, which are used in Buddhism, as in Christianity, as aids to meditation. The circle of the rosary represents the wheel of the Buddhist law and the endless wheel of existence, with the individual beads as individual existences.

LEFT Grottoes with Buddha images in the hill behind the Chi Hsia monastery and temple, north of Nanking. The great Buddhas and Bodhisattvas of popular Mahayana are saviour gods. In philosophical Mahayana they are regarded as illusions, but belief in them helps the ordinary worshipper to make spiritual progress.

ABOVE Fire temple at Isfahan, Iran. Reverence for fire, which keeps darkness and cold at bay, is an old characteristic of Iranian religion and survives in modern Zoroastrianism.

LEFT The miraculous crossing of the Red Sea, from the Sarajevo Haggadah, 13th century, an illuminated Hebrew manuscript containing tales from the Bible. Below, the figure on the left is Miriam, who took a timbrel and sang to the glory of God, who drowned the pursuing Egyptians.

RIGHT The Israelites leaving Egypt, from the Kaufman Haggadah. The exodus from Egypt, the escape from captivity and oppression to the Promised Land, is celebrated every year at Passover.

עֲקֶרֶת הַבַּיִת אֵם הַבָּנִים

שְׂמֵחָה הַלְלוּיָהּ

בְּצֵאת

יִשְׂרָאֵל מִמִּצְרַיִם

בֵּית יַעֲקֹב מֵעַם לֹעֵז הָיְתָה

יְהוּדָה לְקָדְשׁוֹ יִשְׂרָאֵל

whom regarded westerners with contempt as savages and barbarians. The Emperor Ch'ien Lung, a zealous Confucian, banned all Christian missionary work and confined foreign trade, except with Russia, to the single port of Canton.

It was not until the nineteenth century that the western powers forced their way into China and smashed an orderly society to pieces. The Opium War, fought to enable the British to go on bringing the Chinese the blessings of opium, demonstrated China's weakness against European arms. Treaties with European powers and the United States laid China open to the West. The lesson was not lost on the Chinese; it was Mao Tse-tung, a century later, who remarked that political power grows out of the barrel of a gun.

Roman Catholic and Protestant missionaries flocked into China. As in India, they were less successful in making converts than in welfare work, the founding of schools and hospitals, and the importation of western ideas. Young Chinese intellectuals lost confidence in China's traditions and decided that the country needed modernizing and westernizing, while the majority of Chinese, humiliated and resentful, remained hostile to the foreigners and their ways.

A curious by-product of Christian missionary efforts was the T'ai P'ing rebellion, which threatened to bring down the Manchu dynasty. The rebels took Nanking in 1853 and for some years controlled the Yangtze valley. Their leader, Hung Hsiu-ch'uan, was a school teacher who had failed the civil service examinations. He had been taught for a time by a Protestant missionary. He saw visions which convinced him that it was his mission to wipe out the worship of idols. Calling himself the younger brother of Christ, he hoped to establish the Heavenly Kingdom of Peace on earth. His followers, who went into battle singing Christian hymns, were required to attend services on Sundays at which they were publicly praised or reproved, a foretaste of Communist methods. There were also Muslim rebellions in China in the 1860s and '70s, but these too were ultimately suppressed.

With the barbarians not just at the gates but inside the stronghold, the traditional Chinese system crumbled. The Boxer Rising, in which Christians were massacred, was a desperate attempt to expel the 'foreign devils' from China. In Peking the Empress Tzu Hsi ordered the killing of all foreigners. The rising was put down by the armies of the European powers, which proceeded to treat China as a conquered country.

A revolutionary movement now developed, spearheaded by the Kuomintang (National People's Party), whose founder and leader was Sun Yat-sen, a Protestant convert who had been educated at a mission school in Hawaii. The revolution itself came in 1911 and the last of the Manchu emperors, a small boy of six, abdicated in the following year. The new regime abandoned Confucianism and embraced western culture. Although a good many Confucian bureaucrats remained in positions of power, the revolutionaries were bitterly hostile to the popular religion, as to everything traditional, and there were officially sponsored campaigns in which temples and images were destroyed.

Genghis Khan's invasion of China. The Mongol war-leader, who was convinced he had a divine mission to conquer the world, believed that man's greatest pleasure was to defeat his enemies, seize their possessions and hold their women in his arms. His descendants ruled all China for a century.

LEFT King David leads the Ark into Jerusalem, a painting by Pesellino, 15th century. The Ark was the portable shrine in which God travelled with the Israelites when they invaded Palestine. David captured the hill-fortress of Jerusalem, made it his capital, and had the Ark brought there in joyous procession.

BELOW Two heroic figures from the Old Testament, Caleb and Joshua, 15th-century stained glass in the church of St Lawrence, Nuremberg.

RIGHT German Jewish Haggadah, 15th century, showing the Passover festival.

In the 1920s, '30s and '40s China was torn by civil war, in struggles be-tween rival war-lords, and parts of the country were occupied by the Japanese. In this new time of troubles Buddhism and Taoism revived. The numbers of Christians increased, in the face of attacks on them by the Communists as imperialist lackeys and running-dogs of foreign powers. The Kuomintang regime under Chiang Kai-shek did an about turn in 1943 and attempted to bring back Confucian principles, to subordinate the individual to the state, and restore order.

It was too late. Order was restored and individualism suppressed, but by the Communists, whose triumph was greeted with widespread relief in China at the end of a long period of anarchy. The new government officially tolerated all religions, but what this meant in practice was that all religions were required to teach Communist principles. Religion was once again to serve the purposes of the state. Foreign missionaries were imprisoned or more often expelled. In 1960 there were said to be about four million Chinese Christians, the bulk of them Roman Catholics, in a total population of almost 700 million. The Muslim population was much bigger, about 50 million. It was Communism, however, which took the place of Confucianism as the ideology employed by the masters of China to maintain order and unity.

Shinto in Japan

Japan is a tiny country compared with China, only as large as Great Britain and Ireland together, but with a population of over 100 million. Very little is known of its history before the sixth century AD, by which time the Yamato clan had emerged as rulers. The Japanese name for the country is Nihon or Nippon, 'sun origin', and as in China, the Japanese and their rulers long claimed a special relationship with a great divine power in the sky. Until the end of the Second World War, Japanese children were taught at school as a matter of historical fact that the emperors of Japan from time immemorial were descended from the sun-goddess Amaterasu, who had entrusted the imperial house with the right to rule. For many centuries, in reality, the emperors were figureheads, but government was carried on in the emperor's name and claimed through him a divine right to the obedience of his subjects. This doctrine was repudiated by the Emperor Hirohito in a radio broadcast to his people in 1946.

In early times the Japanese worshipped the powers of nature and venerated their ancestors. The principal gods were those concerned with fertility. There was no supreme divine power, but the most important deity was the sun-goddess, and the emperors, her descendants, were the chief priests of her cult. Second to her was the storm-god, Susano. Besides the nature gods, there were also clan gods, each the ancestor of a particular clan, with the clan chief as high priest. Deities were called *kami*, 'superior ones', but anything which inspired wonder, awe and dread was a kami and was treated as sacred. The sea, mountains, trees, rivers and streams, animals, ancestors, great chiefs and warriors, weapons and other man-made objects were paid the respect due to the numinous. The fact that there was

The torii of a Shinto shrine stands in the water of Lake Ashi at Hakonen, Japan. The origin and significance of these gateways is uncertain, but they are characteristic of Shinto shrines.

no dividing line between divine and human, so that living men as well as ancestors could have a sacred mystique, particularly shocked Christian missionaries and has been important in many of the religious cults of modern Japan.

This old native religion, which is still flourishing, is called Shinto, 'the way of the kami'. The name was probably coined to distinguish it from the way of the Buddha when Mahayana Buddhism was introduced into Japan. As part of the everyday life of the clan, it had at first no name, no separate organization and no buildings. The kami were worshipped at natural sanctuaries, on top of a hill, by a tree or a rock, in any place felt to have a sacred atmosphere. Direct communications from them came through male and female shamans, who danced themselves into ecstatic states in which they were believed to be the mouthpieces of the gods.

In time 'houses', simple shrines, were built for the more important gods, served by married priests who often had another occupation as well. By the tenth century there were close to 3000 shrines, the most important being the imperial shrine of the goddess Amaterasu at Ise. With rare exceptions, there were no images of the kami, who were represented by symbols – a mirror, for example, or a sword.

Like Hinduism, Shinto had a strong sense of pollution, which occurred through contact with death, disease, excrement, menstruation or spilled blood. The worshipper was purified by washing and the waving of a wand above his head by a priest. It was correct ceremonial, rather than repentance, which would purify a man who had, for example, committed a murder. In early times the capital was moved when an emperor died, because the old capital was polluted. Stringent precautions are still taken to keep the sacred island of Itsukushima free of pollution. No one is allowed to die or be buried on the island and any woman who becomes pregnant is taken over to the mainland.

Apart from purification, the purposes of the rites at the shrines were to honour and thank the deity for blessings received, persuade the deity not to do any harm, and obtain help in practical matters. Correct ritual was expected to secure the desired result. The major concern of the religion was with fertility, and until recent times prostitutes were attached to some Shinto shrines. Worshippers bowed their heads in obeisance to the kami and brought gifts of rice, fish, fruit, vegetables, wine and cloth. Nowadays money is frequently given and the cloth is symbolized by strips of paper. Twigs of the sacred sakaki tree, which stands in the shrine compound, are offered as symbols of the first fruits of the harvest. At festivals, often linked with the agricultural year, there is singing and dancing at the local shrines to entertain the kami, who may also be carried around the district in a portable shrine borne on long poles.

At home, traditionally, a shelf served as an altar for the kami, where cooked rice, fruit and water were offered. Food and drink were also given to the family's ancestors, at their graves or more often at home. These household shrines have become much rarer in Japan since 1945.

Shinto was, and remains, essentially directed to making the best of life, the religion of people who live in rapport with nature, who respect the

Deities are carried round the district in portable shrines, borne on long poles, at Shinto festivals, to bring the area the blessings of the deity's presence. The same custom occurs in Hinduism and in Roman Catholic Christianity.

natural order and the traditional social order which is regarded as part of it, and whose overriding priorities are prosperity and social harmony. Highly conservative and uninterested in philosophical speculation, it is more concerned with the interests of the group – the family, the clan or the nation – than with the individual. It has little to say about life after death, but the individual hopes to become a kami and be honoured by his family when he is dead.

Buddhism and Shinto

In marked contrast with Shinto, Buddhism saw life as shot through with suffering and offered liberation from it. Mahayana Buddhism came to Japan from China by way of Korea in the sixth century AD and was taken up at court and in aristocratic circles, where expectations were no doubt higher and there was more opportunity for a concern with individual salvation than among the peasantry. Under Prince Shotoku and a succession of pro-Buddhist rulers, Buddhism became the state religion. Temples were built, monasteries were founded, hospitals and homes for orphans and the old were established. Buddhist monks came in from China and Korea, Japanese monks went to study in China and Chinese Buddhist sects took root in Japan.

After 645 the old clan system, with which Shinto was closely bound up, was weakened by the introduction of a bureaucracy of imperial officials on the Chinese model. Buddhism flourished among the upper classes and the Shinto priests had to come to terms with it. The Buddhists on their side were tolerant, as usual, and despite their fundamental differences the two religions began to blend. This development was approved at the highest level, presumably for political as well as religious reasons, to promote harmony and good order in the state. In the 740s the imperial shrine at Ise sanctioned the building of the Todai-ji temple at the capital, Nara. Though this was a Buddhist temple, its compound contained a shrine to a Shinto deity, the war-god Hachiman. Correspondingly, an image of the Buddha was given an honoured home in the precincts of the Ise shrine itself.

Through this blending with Shinto, Buddhism became naturalized in Japan during the Nara and Heian periods, so called because the capital was first at Nara and then at Heian (modern Kyoto). The process was given an impetus by two Buddhist sects which are still very much alive, Tendai and Shingon. Both were founded by Japanese monks who studied in China and each made room for the Shinto kami in its system. Tendai, the Japanese form of the Chinese T'ien T'ai sect, was founded by a monk named Saicho, who was posthumously given the honorific title of Dengyo Daishi (Propagator of the True Religion). Shingon was founded by Kukai, or Kobo Daishi (Propagator of the Law). In Shingon the Shinto kami were regarded as Japanese manifestations of the great Mahayana Buddhas and Bodhisattvas. The sun-goddess Amaterasu, for instance, was identified with Vairocana Buddha as 'the Great Sun'.

A worshipper praying in the Hall of the Second Month, part of the Todai-ji temple in Nara, which was founded by the Emperor Shomu in the 8th century.

RIGHT A Buddhist monk at a temple in South Korea. Buddhism spread from China, by way of Korea, to Japan in the 6th century.

The tendency of the two religions to coalesce produced what is called Ryobu Shinto, or Dual Aspect Shinto. The Shinto and Buddhist deities were linked together and Buddhist sanctuaries were built in Shinto shrines where Buddhist rites were conducted. Shinto acquired the Buddhist moral code and the kami acquired images in Buddhist style. Opinions differed as to whether the kami were junior to the Buddhas and Bodhisattvas or the other way round, but the combination of both religions was popular and it was in this form that Buddhism made its first major impact on the Japanese masses. Buddhist altars were installed alongside Shinto altars in many houses and people appealed to Buddhist and Shinto deities alike for fertility, good fortune, recovery from disease and help in trouble. The majority of Japanese today are, at least nominally, adherents of both Shinto and one or other of the main Buddhist groups, many temples and shrines combine Buddhist and Shinto features, and it is still the custom to have a Shinto wedding and a Buddhist funeral.

After 1192 a succession of war-lords held power in Japan with the title of Shogun (Commander-in-Chief) or Shikken (Regent) and ruled the country in the emperor's name but from a separate court at Kamakura. New Buddhist sects now emerged, all of which have a large following in modern Japan. Unlike Tendai and Shingon, each of these new movements was exclusive and separatist, rejecting all other forms of Buddhism.

The Buddha Hall in the Todai-ji temple. Rebuilt in the 17th century, it was constructed to house a colossal bronze image of Vairocana Buddha, the Mahayana sun-deity. Known as the Daibutsu, more than 50 feet high and weighing over 500 tons, the statue is said to be the largest bronze image in the world.

Wooden figure of Jizo Bosatsu, the Japanese form of the Indian Bodhisattva Kshitigarbha, 15th to 16th century. He delivers souls from hell and protects pregnant women, children and travellers.

RIGHT The Buddhist deity Fudu, with his attendants, bronze, 18th century. He carries the sword with which he subdues wrongdoers and enemies of Buddhism, and the rope with which he binds them.

Pure Land Buddhism came to Japan from China. The Jodo (Pure Land) sect traces its origin to a monk named Honen, who believed that faith in Amida Buddha (the Indian Amitabha) and earnest repetition of his name would bring the believer to safe refuge after death in the Pure Land, Amida's western paradise. One of Honen's disciples, Shinran, went further than his master by insisting that good moral behaviour had nothing to do with salvation and that Amida's boundless compassion would bring the wicked as surely to paradise as the good. This principle had great popular appeal and the Jodo Shinshu (True Pure Land) sect is today the largest of the traditional Buddhist organizations in Japan.

Zen Buddhism first became a separate movement in Japan in 1191, when a monk named Eisai returned from studying Ch'an methods in China and founded the Rinzai school of Zen. Rinzai makes extensive use of the koans, or riddles, intended as the Zen masters said, 'to make the calculating mind die'. It is this type of Zen which recently had a vogue in the West, where one of the koans became famous: 'What is the sound made by one hand clapping?' Another example is the story of the monk who asked his master, 'Who is the Buddha?' The answer was, 'Three measures of flax.'

Figure of Kannon, the Japanese form of the Chinese goddess Kuan Yin, in a temple in Kamakura.

LEFT The influence of Zen Buddhism is seen in the simplicity and purity of this garden of raked white sand and rocks in Kyoto.

The more popular form of Zen in Japan, the Soto school founded by Dogen, does not use koans and employs meditation in a cross-legged position to attain *satori*, or enlightenment. Unlike Pure Land, which relies on a divine saviour, Zen believes in achieving enlightenment through one's own efforts. Although it takes years of training in a monastery to become a Zen master, Zen is popular with laymen, who spend periods of retreat in Zen monasteries. In the past it appealed to many of the samurai, the warrior class, equivalent to the knights of medieval Europe. They valued its training in calming the mind among the dangers of the soldier's life, and the ability to transcend slow reasoned reactions was found especially valuable in learning the art of swordsmanship. Zen also influenced the gentler arts, including landscape gardening and the tea ceremony, which originated as a ritual of rest and refreshment after the strain of Zen meditation.

Another major movement, the only one not imported from China, was founded by Nichiren, a pugnacious fanatic who was expelled from his Tendai monastery for his intolerance. He believed in the Lotus Sutra as the only true scripture and his followers chanted 'Adoration to the Lotus

The Buddha's death and final passing to nirvana, clay model in the Horyu-ji pagoda in Nara, one of the oldest Buddhist temples in Japan. The Buddha's passing is witnessed by disciples, monks and gods.

Sutra' as a means to enlightenment. Nichiren ascribed everything that was wong in Japan, including all natural disasters, to the refusal of other people to recognize that his brand of Buddhism was the right one. He wanted the Kamakura government to impose it by force as the single national religion and suppress all the other sects, which he fiercely attacked, denouncing Zen devotees as 'demons' and the Pure Land as 'the everlasting hell'. He was persecuted and exiled for his pains, but his militant movement lives on.

The Closed Country

Under the Ashikaga Shogunate there was a long period of turmoil, civil war and anarchy. Buddhist monasteries became fortified nests of armed monks, at first for defence against marauders, but later the sects used their military power to build up large estates, take over entire provinces and fight each other. There were violent clashes, especially between the Jodo Shinshu and Nichiren factions. Towards the end of this period St Francis Xavier and two other Jesuits arrived in Japan. The missionaries and their Jesuit, Franciscan and Dominican successors had considerable success, although or perhaps because the Japanese tended to think that Christianity was a new form of Buddhism imported from India.

Order was restored by the war-lord Oda Nobunaga, who deposed the last Ashikaga shogun. He and his ally Tokugawa Ieyasu put down the armed Buddhist sects, destroying monasteries and slaughtering monks. The Christians were sometimes officially favoured and sometimes persecuted. In 1597, for example, six missionaries and twenty Japanese Christians were crucified at Nagasaki. Tokugawa Ieyasu became shogun in 1603, and eleven years later issued a law suppressing Christianity, apparently because he feared Christians as a fifth column, potential allies of the European powers which might attempt to dominate Japan. Only a few small groups of Christians survived in secret, camouflaging their religion behind a veil of Shinto and Buddhism.

The Tokugawa shoguns were deeply suspicious of European imperialism, with good reason. They closed the ports to foreign trade and kept Japan sealed off from the outside world for more than 200 years of peace and order. Under a rigidly conservative regime, its face set against all change, Buddhism was the officially favoured religion, but the sects were forbidden to proselytize and Shinto was left alone. Confucian principles, long known in Japan, were much in vogue, for the Confucian emphasis on keeping one's appointed place in society and being obedient to authority was congenial to a benevolent tyranny. At the same time, however, an anti-Confucian, anti-Buddhist, anti-Chinese movement developed among intellectuals who were determined to purge Shinto of foreign accretions. The effect was to encourage Japanese nationalism. Shinto was now presented not as the junior partner of Buddhism but as the fount and origin of Buddhism, Confucianism and all other religions. Such writers as Moto-ori Norinaga and Hirata Atsutane maintained that Japan was the land of the gods, ruled by sovereigns descended from the sun-goddess, and that the Japanese needed no foreign lessons in what they ought to do. The seeds of the aggressive, emperor-revering Japanese nationalism of the 1930s were already being sown.

In 1853 an American naval squadron under a rock-ribbed veteran, Commodore Perry, appeared in Tokyo Bay demanding the opening of trade relations. Prayers for the destruction of the barbarians, offered at seven shrines at the emperor's command, were unavailing. As in China, the superiority of western weapons was obvious, and the Americans forced a reluctant Japan open to foreign trade and influence. The European powers came shouldering in, with Christian missionaries in their train – Roman Catholic, Protestant and Eastern Orthodox. The shogunate was abolished and power was restored at long last to the imperial house in the person of the forceful fifteen-year-old Emperor Meiji.

Modern Japan

Under the Meiji government Japan was rapidly and efficiently westernized and industrialized. The government's religious policy was to allow Buddhists and Christians freedom of worship under state supervision, to disentangle Shinto from Buddhism and use a new organization, State Shinto, to focus the loyalty of all Japanese on the emperor and the nation. Officially, State Shinto was not a religion but a moral institution, inculcating patriotic values, and its priests were civil servants.

Nationalist fervour waxed steadily, as Japan grew stronger and China weaker. By the 1930s Japan was firmly in the grip of an aggressive policy, with State Shinto as its ideological support, stressing loyalty to the emperor's sacred person, Japanese superiority to all other peoples and the divine destiny of Japan as the land of the gods to rule the world. All citizens, including Buddhists and Christians, were required to take part in the patriotic ceremonies of State Shinto. Most of the foreign missionaries left the country. During the Second World War unquestioning obedience to orders and loyalty to the emperor to the death had much to do with the success of Japanese arms. When defeat loomed, the *kamikaze* pilots who crashed their planes suicidally on enemy warships were told that after a glorious death they would become kami. In the end defeat could not be staved off and the Japanese were forced to surrender. The American military authorities dissolved the link between Shinto and the state, and the old belief in the divinity of the emperor was repudiated.

Since 1945 numerous new sects have blossomed. Most of them were founded before the Second World War and some in the nineteenth century, when small cults formed around latter-day shamans who believed they were the physical vehicles of deities. Though compelled to conform to State Shinto until 1945, these cults expressed a hunger for direct contact with the divine in the person of the founder and a need for religio-magical assistance in coping with the troubles of life. The Kurozomikyo movement, for example, grew up around a Shinto priest, Kurozumi Munetada, who claimed to have attained union with the sun-goddess, the source of all life, and who was revered as a living kami. Tenrikyo (Divine Teaching), which now has followers in Korea and South America, as well as

The story of the forty-seven samurai who, in the 18th century, took revenge on a feudal lord responsible for their master's disgrace and then committed suicide is re-enacted in the temple in Tokyo where they are buried. Incense is burned in front of their tombs every year. The samurai, the warrior class of Japan, were strongly influenced by Zen. Their code of honour was revived in the interests of Japanese imperialism in the 1930s and '40s.

three million adherents in Japan and its own university, was founded by Nakayama Miki, a farmer's wife. She was a Pure Land Buddhist until the 1830s, when she was possessed by a succession of Shinto kami, culminating in an experience of union with the supreme god, whom she called Tenri O no Mikoto. She devoted herself to faith healing and helping the poor, gathered followers and wrote extensive scriptures. She is believed to live on invisibly at the sect's headquarters in Tenri City. There is a television set in her room, meals are served to her and a bath is made ready for her in the evening. Fertility and purification rites have an important role in the religion, whose members believe that their bodies have been lent to them by God and that they should use them to lead harmonious and joyful lives, help others and strive to rid themselves of evil thoughts.

The most influential of the new movements is Soka Gakkai (Value Creating Society), which with more than sixteen million members claims the allegiance of one in every seven Japanese. Soka Gakkai was started in 1930 by Makiguchi Tsunesaburo and Toda Josei, who were strongly influenced by Nichiren Shoshu, a small, fiercely intolerant and nationalistic sect which identified Nichiren as the Eternal Buddha. Worshippers could achieve unity with him through adoration of a mandala, ascribed to Nichiren himself, on which is written a formula of homage to the Lotus Sutra. Soka Gakkai, which has its own political party, the Clean Government Party, does not regard itself as a religion but as the lay bastion of Nichiren Shoshu. Members are told that all the misfortunes and troubles of life disappear for the worshipper of the Nichiren mandala, which Toda Josei called 'the happiness machine'.

The bewilderment of defeat in 1945, the horror of the atomic bombing of Hiroshima and Nagasaki, the sudden demolition of old loyalties and accepted traditions, and the pressure to adopt quite different values drove Japanese in millions to the new movements. The traditional religions seemed to be outworn and the new groups offered a personal approach to the divine and a happiness machine of some kind, with simple rules for self-improvement and putting the world to rights. Many promised a better future to look forward to. Both Soka Gakkai and Tenrikyo, for instance, look forward to a coming, destined time of peace and happiness on earth, towards which members must work.

The statistics of religious affiliation in contemporary Japan are confusing. Although many Japanese no longer believe in any religion at all, so many are real or nominal adherents of both Shinto and Buddhism that when the figures for all the religions are added up there appear to be more believers in the country than there are people. Christians number less than one per cent of the population, and Islam and Judaism have never made any headway in Japan. Among those who cleave to a single religion, Buddhism in one form or another seems to have rather more support than Shinto.

5. Zoroastrianism

The principal religions of the world count their adherents in the millions, and on this scale it almost needs a microscope to see Zoroastrianism at all. There are about 100,000 Zoroastrians in India and Pakistan, where they are called Parsis. They do not accept converts and their numbers are steadily diminishing. There are also a few thousand Zoroastrians in Iran, and smaller communities in North America, Britain, East Africa and Hong Kong. Despite its comparative poverty in numbers, however, Zoroastrianism is enormously rich in ideas, which have had an influence far beyond its own ranks.

The Parsi community in Bombay is the centre of Zoroastrianism today, but the religion grew up in Iran, or Persia as it used to be called. In the ancient world Iran was a bridge between Mesopotamia and the Mediterranean world to the west and India to the east. From this central position Iranian beliefs influenced Judaism, Christianity and Islam in one direction, and Mahayana Buddhism in the other.

The early history of Zoroastrianism is much in dispute. The religion was founded by Zoroaster (the Greek form of his name, which is Zarathushtra in Persian), but it is not certain when he lived, where he lived or how much of later Zoroastrianism came from him. Tradition puts him in western Iran in the sixth century BC, a little earlier than the Buddha in India, but it is now thought that he lived in north-eastern Iran, in the area on the borders of modern Afghanistan and Turkmenistan. An alternative theory dates him much earlier, somewhere in the period from 1700 to 1500 BC, and places him in the plains of Central Asia, perhaps before the first groups of Aryans moved south from the plains into Iran and India.

The Aryans who settled in Iran, 'the land of the Aryans', were the ancestors of the Medes and Persians, who became the dominant peoples of western Iran. In the sixth century BC the Achaemenid dynasty of Persia subdued the Medes and built up a huge empire, which at its peak held sway over Egypt, Palestine, Syria, most of Asia Minor, Mesopotamia, Iran and the country to the east as far as the Jaxartes and Indus rivers. Alexander the

Roman head of Mithras, found in London. The ancient Aryan deity Mithra, or Mitra, was believed to cross the sky with the sun every day, looking down with his thousand eyes to watch men and punish those who broke their word. He survived in Zoroastrianism as a warrior god. The cult of Mithras spread all over the Roman world and he was especially popular with soldiers.

Great conquered this first Iranian empire, but the Parthians from north-eastern Iran built up another, and the Persian Sasanid dynasty a third, which lasted until the Arabs conquered Iran in the seventh century AD.

The Roots of Zoroastrianism

The Aryans who occupied India and Iran shared the same religion. As in India, the Iranian gods were the great powers of nature. They had no temples or images, but were worshipped in the open air, where animals were slaughtered and burned on fires in sacrifice to them. The fire which carried the offerings up to the gods in smoke was the god Atar (Agni in India) and fire was venerated as the intermediary between gods and men, and the protector against cold and darkness. Reverence for fire is one of modern Zoroastrianism's inheritances from the past. The sacred fire in each temple is approached only by priests who have been ritually purified and whose mouths are veiled to prevent them from defiling it with their breath. The worshipper, who brings an offering of money and sandalwood for the fire, is not allowed into the fire-chamber itself, but stands barefoot on the threshold, bows to the fire and prays to God. The fire is a semi-divine symbol of the presence of God and the conquest of darkness and evil.

The Aryans in Iran also deified an intoxicating drink called *haoma* (soma in India), under whose exhilarating influence man was thought to ascend to the plane of the gods. Whether Zoroaster himself approved of this is uncertain, but the drinking of haoma became a central rite of later Zoroastrianism. The haoma was addressed as the son of God. It was offered to God and was then drunk by the priest and the worshippers as an anticipation of eternal life with God. The parallel with the Christian Mass is obvious.

As in India again, Iranian religion was much concerned with pollution and ritual cleansing, and elaborate purification rites developed in Zoroastrianism, as in Hinduism. It is to avoid polluting fire or earth that the Zoroastrians do not cremate or bury their dead, but expose them to be eaten by vultures in special buildings known as Towers of Silence. A decline in the number of vultures in Bombay has caused difficulties for the Parsis in recent years, but the custom is still observed.

In Iran, however, no belief in rebirth and karma developed, as in India. Under Zoroaster's influence a quite different set of ideas grew up about rewards and punishments, the afterlife and the destiny of man. Zoroaster was a priest of the traditional Iranian religion, but he reacted against it. Unlike the Buddha, who claimed to have discovered the truth by himself, Zoroaster claimed that the truth had been revealed to him by God. According to tradition, he was thirty when he went to a river at dawn one day to fetch water. On the river bank he saw a being radiant with light, who conducted him into the presence of God. Zoroaster later had other visions of God, heard his voice and was aware of his presence. These experiences left him in no doubt that he had a message for man, a message that must be true because it came by direct revelation from God. His duty was to wean his countrymen away from the worship of many deities and win them to the service of the only true God, Ahura Mazda, the Wise Lord.

The building on the hill is a Tower of Silence. Zoroastrians do not bury or cremate their dead, which would pollute the earth or fire, but expose them to be eaten by vultures in Towers of Silence. Nearby are buildings where the funeral service is conducted and where a sacred fire burns.

LEFT King Vishtaspa entertaining another monarch, a Muslim version of a Zoroastrian tradition. The figure behind the throne may be meant to be Zoroaster. Bodleian MS Elliot 325, fol. 328r.

Zoroaster's contemporaries flatly rejected his message at first, but he succeeded in converting a king named Vishtaspa, and with Vishtaspa's backing the new religion was taken seriously and began to spread. The prophet's own teaching is believed to be preserved in the Gathas, seventeen hymns which are included in the Avesta, the Zoroastrian holy book. The Avesta was written down in the Sasanian period in an archaic and otherwise unknown language, called Avestan. The bulk of it did not survive the Muslim conquest of Iran.

Ohrmazd and Ahriman

Zoroastrianism is a mixture, in varying proportions at different periods, of monotheism, polytheism and dualism. It is monotheistic in that Ahura Mazda or Ohrmazd (the later form of the name) is the only true God. It is polytheistic because other spiritual beings, including some of the ancient Iranian deities, are regarded as worthy of worship, though subordinate to Ohrmazd. The fundamental Zoroastrian doctrine, however, is dualistic.

Ohrmazd, who dwells on high in eternal light, is entirely good, but unlike the God of Judaism, Christianity and Islam, he is not all-powerful. On the contrary, he has a great enemy, Ahriman (earlier Angra Mainyu, the Destructive Spirit), who is entirely evil. The whole world, all through time, is the battleground on which these titanic forces contend. Ohrmazd is the principle of good, light, order, virtue and truth. Ahriman is the opposite principle of evil, darkness, chaos, wickedness and falsehood – sometimes called simply 'the Lie'. All the goodness of life, all happiness, all beauty, all health, all fruitfulness, belongs to Ohrmazd. All evil belongs to Ahriman, all suffering, death, disease, destruction, ugliness and malevolence. Although Ohrmazd created the world, he is not responsible for the evil in it. Ahriman is responsible, because long ago in the mythical past he deliberately chose evil in preference to good. Ahriman is not a god, however, he is not on the same level as Ohrmazd, and he is doomed to defeat in the distant future – 12,000 years from Zoroaster's time – when the world will return to the purity and goodness of its first creation.

This belief goes back to Zoroaster himself. How he arrived at it, and whether it developed from the old Aryan idea of the gods battling against cosmic forces of disorder and infertility, is not known. As he was a visionary, he may not have reached it by deliberate thought, but it has substantial practical advantages. Unlike the Buddha's teaching that all earthly experience is suffering and that it is better not to live, Zoroastrianism recognizes a good side and a bad side to life, which accords with common sense, and teaches that human beings have an important spiritual purpose in living. It is to expand the realm of good and diminish the empire of evil. In this task man is a co-worker with God, a warrior in God's cause.

At the same time, Zoroastrianism avoids the fundamental problem of monotheism, which is how to explain the existence of evil and undeserved suffering in a world made and ruled by a God who is good and all-powerful. Zoroastrians disapprove of Hindu attempts to find the One, the Absolute, in which good and evil are reconciled and transcended. They similarly disapprove of Christianity, because they maintain that it finds the root of evil in God and teaches that God condemned even his own son to suffer, which they consider an abominable notion.

They also disapprove of Islam, which they say makes man virtually God's slave. Zoroastrians believe strongly in human free will. Each of us has a free choice, to support good or support evil. By good thoughts, words and actions we extend the territory of good. The material world and the body are not evil in Zoroastrianism. They can be used for evil, of course, but they can and should be used for good. It is the Zoroastrian's duty to be both good and happy. Asceticism is as wrong as a life dedicated to greed and lust. Traditionally, agriculture and the raising of children in marriage are religious activities, through which the cause of good is advanced. In nineteenth-century India the Parsis extended this principle to business and the development of technology, and the Parsi community became noted for its wealth, its enthusiasm for western ways and its charitable generosity.

Muslim version of the Zoroastrian story of the first human couple, Mashya and Mashyoi, who told the first lie, saying that the Evil Spirit had created the earth. Here Ahriman is shown disguised as a saintly old man and tempting them with an apple, a motif taken over from the story of Adam and Eve in the Old Testament.

There is no question in Zoroastrianism, as in the Indian religions, of the consequences of past actions working themselves out in present and future lives on earth, which leaves each human being something less than a free agent. At death each person is judged by his thoughts, words and actions, and is sent either to heaven, to live in light and bliss with Ohrmazd, or to hell, to be punished in darkness and torment in the House of the Lie. At first the damned were to remain damned for ever, but in later Zoroastrianism an eternal hell was considered an immoral concept and the belief emerged that when Ahriman is finally overthrown the wicked would be purged of their evil and share in the happiness of the pure and perfect world.

In later Zoroastrianism the last days of the present world are pictured as a time when Ahriman and his lieutenants of darkness mount a tremendous final attack on good. The natural order will be disrupted, a fierce winter will hold the world in an icy grip and a terrible monster, Dahak, will be let loose to wreak havoc. Then a virgin will bathe in a lake in which the seed of Zoroaster is miraculously preserved. Impregnated by it, she will give birth to Saoshyant, the Saviour. Saoshyant will raise all the dead, in reconstituted physical bodies, for the Last Judgement, the good like white sheep and the wicked like black sheep. The wicked will be purged and in a last great battle the powers of evil will be annihilated. Exactly what will happen to Ahriman himself is not clear from the texts, but the world will be made perfect and all human beings who have ever existed will live for ever with Ohrmazd in happiness and peace.

This Zoroastrian picture of the last days strikingly resembles Christian concepts. It may have influenced the Buddhist belief in the coming of Maitreya to inaugurate the perfect world of the future.

Zenith and Decline

The rulers of the Achaemenian Empire were tolerant of the various religions of their subject peoples, but they themselves were Zoroastrians of a sort. Darius the Great, for example, proclaimed in inscriptions that he ruled by the grace of Ahura Mazda, and castigated all who opposed him as partisans of the Lie. The Magi, the powerful pre-Zoroastrian priesthood of the Medes and Persians, retained a dominating position at court and presided over a variety of Zoroastrianism in which, contrary to the prophet's principles, the cults of other deities besides Ahura Mazda were encouraged. Artaxerxes II and later Iranian kings honoured three deities, Ahura Mazda, Anahita and Mithra. Temples and images of the gods were now introduced, and fire-temples where the sacred fires were kept burning perpetually.

Anahita was the goddess of water and fertility. Mithra was an old Aryan deity, known as Mitra in India, who watched over agreements. He was believed to travel across the sky with the sun every day, looking down with his thousand eyes to see who kept his word and who broke it. The belief that Mithra sees everything which happens on earth is still alive in Zoroastrianism. He developed into a warrior-god, fighting the powers of darkness, and Zoroastrian priests (the priesthood is hereditary) are invested with the bull-headed mace of Mithra as a symbol of their duty to contend against evil. In the Roman Empire, as Mithras, the god acquired many worshippers and Mithraism was a rival to emerging Christianity.

Mithra and other deities, including Anahita, Atar and Haoma, survive in Zoroastrianism as the Yazatas, worshipful beings. Ohrmazd is thought to be too important to be pestered with incessant requests for help in everyday matters, and believers choose one of the Yazatas as a helper, protector and object of special affection, in much the same way that a Roman Catholic may venerate and ask the help of a favourite saint.

Anahita, goddess of the waters and fertility, cups her breasts in a gesture of bounty. The statue has a certain resemblance to the prehistoric 'Venus' figures. Like Mithra, Anahita has survived in modern Zoroastrianism as one of the 'worshipful beings'.

RIGHT Fire temple in front of the burial place of Xerxes at Naqsh-i Rustam, near Persepolis, where the Achaemenid kings were buried in rock-cut tombs. Temples in which the sacred fires were never allowed to go out were introduced by the later Achaemenid rulers.

Figure of a royal personage of the Sasanid dynasty under the symbol of Ahura Mazda.

Zoroastrianism reached its zenith in the Sasanian period, when the local Zoroastrian communities were organized into a single Church, controlled by the state through a Chief Magus. The Sasanids disapproved of image-worship and statues were removed from the temples and replaced by sacred fires, which has been the rule ever since. The emperor himself, the King of Kings, was treated as a god, the representative of Ohrmazd on earth, and depicted with a halo, a divine glory of light. It was the custom to prostrate oneself before him as before a god, and the common people were not allowed to see his face, which was masked.

The Zoroastrian state religion was strong enough to stand off the challenges of Manichaeism and Christianity, but eventually Islam dealt Zoroastrianism the death-blow in its own homeland. The Arab armies invaded Mesopotamia in 636 and took Ctesiphon, the Sasanid capital. By 652 the Arabs were in control of most of Iran. Temples were turned into mosques and many Zoroastrians were converted to Islam, reluctantly or otherwise. From the early tenth century on, small groups of Zoroastrians emigrated to India, where they were known as Parsis (Persians), and the religion's centre of gravity shifted to India, where it has remained ever since.

6. Judaism

There are said to be fifteen million Jews in the world today, of whom six million live in America and three million in Israel. The figure refers to people of Jewish family, not all of whom are Jewish by religion, and it is staggeringly small in relation to the influence which Jewry has exerted on the world. One of the ironies of history is that three of the world's major religions – Judaism, Christianity and Islam – are descended from the beliefs of an insignificant people of minimal political and cultural importance in their own time. While great empires rose and fell in the ancient world – Egypt, Assyria, Babylonia, Persia, Rome – the Jews remained a tiny, obscure nation, regarded by outsiders as backward, eccentric and strangely devoted to their peculiar practices and their odd, irritable deity. The ancient empires crumbled to dust, but the religion of the Jews has influenced the lives of millions. It is as if we were told that in 2000 years time half the world will have fallen heir to some currently disregarded cult in southern California, and it is a fact in which the believers see the hand of God.

Another, this time tragic, irony is that a religion of such influence should have suffered incessant persecution, especially at the hands of its own unwanted daughter, Christianity. The fundamental reason is that Judaism is a racial as well as a religious phenomenon, which Christianity and Islam are not. A Jew is anyone born of Jewish stock or anyone who professes the Jewish religion. Converts have been few and the majority of Jews have always been born Jews, though in the modern world there are many Jews who have abandoned their ancestral faith and customs. Judaism is the religion of a single people and has permeated every aspect of Jewish life. Hence the difficulty of making converts, for those attracted by the religion may feel it impossible to adopt a whole way of life in which they have not been reared. Jews have been shunned and persecuted, not only for their religion but as outsiders, strangers, a people of foreign ways.

A contributory factor to the long history of anti-semitism is what a distinguished Jewish scholar has called 'national self-centredness', the

Scene outside a synagogue in Jerusalem on the eighth day of the feast of Sukkoth, when the reading of the Torah has been completed for the year and the scrolls are rewound, ready to begin again. The complete Torah – the first five books of the Bible, attributed to Moses – is read in the synagogues on the sabbath in the course of a year.

belief that the Jews are the chosen people of God, born to carry out the mission of bringing the whole world to his service. On the Day of Atonement, one of the great Jewish festivals, prayers are offered for the ultimate conversion of all mankind. There have been times when Jewish missionaries were active, as in the Roman world, but since the rise of Christianity and Islam the Jews have not been vigorous proselytizers. This has been in sheer self-preservation, but also with the feeling that although the daughter religions do not properly understand God, they at least recognize the right God and inculcate the right moral code, which is a good deal better than nothing. Any progress beyond this must be left to God.

Judaism is strictly monotheistic. There is only one God, and all other 'gods' are either fictions or evil powers. As soon as they can speak, Jewish children are taught the declaration of faith called the Shema, a verse from the book of Deuteronomy (chapter 6): 'Hear O Israel; the Lord is our God, the Lord is One.' The devout repeat this verse every morning and evening, and it is spoken in the last moments of consciousness by the dying. Judaism disapproves of the Christian worship of Christ and the Trinity as departures from monotheism.

Another fundamental characteristic of the religion is respect for the holy scripture, the Hebrew Bible, or Old Testament as Christians call it, and especially for the Pentateuch, the first five books, which are attributed to Moses and known as the Torah, or Teaching (though the word can also be used for the whole body of Jewish teaching). The Bible is 'the word of God', written down by human beings inspired by God. The Torah contains the history of the world from its creation by God to the death of Moses in sight of the Promised Land. It also contains the detailed prescriptions of Jewish law delivered to Moses by God, including the Ten Commandments and other moral rules, dietary regulations – the best known of which outside Jewry is the prohibition of pork – rules for animal sacrifices, offerings and rituals, laws to do with the appointments and duties of priests, with the observance of the sabbath and with the administration of justice, rules for ritual purification and laws about sexual behaviour.

These laws come from a time when morals, rituals and custom were not separated. 'Thou shalt not kill' and, in effect, 'Thou shalt not eat shellfish' have the same divine backing and are both part of the proper behaviour of God's people. 'Love thy neighbour' is a rule. It is also a rule that a menstruating woman is unclean and may not enter a holy place until she has offered a lamb, a pigeon or a dove to God. For all its traditional inheritance of customs and rites, however, there is no question that Judaism is an ethical religion. Prophets and teachers have repeatedly stressed that good moral behaviour and genuine repentance of wrongdoing are more important than correct performance of ritual or strict observance of customs. The essential moral rules of Judaism have for centuries formed the basic moral code of the entire western world. There is a famous story about the great teacher Hillel, who lived in the first century BC. He was asked by a prospective convert to teach him the whole Torah while he stood on one leg. Hillel said: 'That which is hateful unto thee do not do unto thy neighbour. This is the whole of the Torah.'

Title page of a Bible printed in Amsterdam. At the top is the scene on Mount Sinai, when God came down upon the mountain in fire, lightning and thunder, and Moses went up to the summit alone to receive the commandments and the law. The words in Hebrew refer to the three divisions of the Jewish scripture, the Torah, the Prophets (including the historical books), and the Writings (including Psalms, Proverbs and Job).

Out of Egypt

It is not certain where the history of the Jews and the Jewish religion begins. The principal source is the Bible, but the Old Testament is history seen through Jewish spectacles and intended to trace the working out of a divine plan, stretching back to the beginning of the world. Something like a thousand years separates the earliest sections of the Old Testament from the latest and the material is not in chronological order of composition; the opening chapters of Genesis are not the oldest part of the Bible.

One of the oldest passages, in Deuteronomy (chapter 26), begins the history of Israel with a few nomadic Semitic tribesmen who went to Egypt, settled there and in time increased in numbers. The Egyptians enslaved them and treated them harshly. They appealed to their god, who rescued them from Egypt, 'with a mighty hand and an outstretched arm, with great terror, with signs and wonders', and brought them into the land of Canaan, or Palestine, 'a land flowing with milk and honey'. Two themes already present here are the tremendous, terrifying power of Israel's god and the belief that Palestine is the god-given Jewish homeland.

This tradition of the escape from oppression in Egypt was firmly established early on. Traditions which were written down later went back before the period in Egypt to an ancestor who lived in Canaan, named Jacob or Israel (Champion of God). The Old Testament often personifies groups of people as individuals. Jacob himself personifies the Jewish nation and he is said to have had twelve sons, from whom were descended the twelve tribes which afterwards made up the Jewish confederation in Palestine. One of them was Yehudi (Judah), from whose name the word Jew derives.

Further back still, Jacob was said to be descended from Abraham, who lived in the city of Ur in Mesopotamia. He left Ur with his family and migrated to Canaan, settling near Hebron. According to Genesis, he did this on the instructions of God, who intended Canaan for his descendants, and the origin of circumcision, the mark distinguishing Jews from other people (and also an Egyptian custom), is traced back to Abraham. It is known that Semitic tribesmen from Arabia had settled in Mesopotamia well before 2000 BC, and the story of Abraham may represent the migration of a group from Ur to Canaan, perhaps in 1960 BC, when Ur was sacked by raiders from the east.

Though the traditions of Abraham and Jacob probably have some foundation in fact, the first Jewish figure who is undisputedly historical is Moses, the leader of the exodus from Egypt and the first and greatest of the prophets. His date is uncertain. One theory places him in Egypt in about 1250 BC, in the time of Pharaoh Ramses II. Another dates him earlier, to the time of Pharaoh Thothmes III, and puts the exodus in 1447 BC, early in the reign of Amenophis II, the son of Thothmes.

Legend grew up about Moses, as about other great figures of the past. According to the Bible, Pharaoh gave orders that all the male babies of the Jews were to be thrown into the Nile. When Moses was born, his mother hid him for as long as she could and then put him in a basket which she placed among the rushes at the edge of the Nile. Pharaoh's daughter –

This carving at the Knesset in Jerusalem illustrates a story about the famous teacher Hillel, who was asked by a prospective convert to teach him the whole of the Torah while he stood on one leg. Hillel summed up the teaching of the Torah as 'That which is hateful unto thee do not do unto thy neighbour.'

identified with Hatshepsut, the sister of Thothmes III by some historians –
came to the river to bathe, found the baby, took pity on him and brought
him up.

When Moses grew up, he felt intense sympathy for his oppressed people,
so much so that he was forced to escape from Egypt to the desert, among
the nomads of Midian, where he married the daughter of a priest. On a
mountain there he saw a burning bush, and God spoke to him out of the
bush, saying that he was the ancestral god of Israel and that Moses was to
lead the people out of Egypt to Canaan. Moses asked God his name, and
God replied, 'I am who I am.' This phrase in Hebrew is a form of the divine
name apparently meaning 'He who is', which used to be rendered Jehovah
and is now usually spelled Yahweh.

There follows the celebrated story of how Moses asked Pharaoh to let
the people go, how Pharaoh refused, how God brought plagues and disasters upon the Egyptians and how the fleeing Israelites came to the Red Sea,
where God parted the waters for them to cross. Pharaoh's chariots and horse-
men, in hot pursuit, were all drowned when the waters joined again.

Moses led the Israelites to Mount Sinai, traditionally identified as Jebel
Musa, a high peak in the south of the Sinai peninsula. God came down
upon the mountain in fire, with thunder and lightning and the huge blast of
a trumpet and a great cloud of smoke, while the mountain quaked and the
people, warned not to go too close or they would be killed, trembled with
fear. Moses went up to the summit, where he received the Ten Commandments and the law, and God made the covenant, the agreement by which
he committed himself to Israel as his holy nation, his kingdom of priests.

Moses receiving the law on
Mount Sinai and, below,
expounding the law to the
Israelites, Carolingian
manuscript, 9th century.

The Israelites spent many years in the desert, persistently forsaking Yahweh for other gods, but brought back to Yahweh by Moses. He died in sight of the River Jordan and the people wept for him. Under his successor as leader, Joshua, the Israelites crossed the Jordan, carrying with them the Ark, the portable wooden shrine in which God was present among them. Forcing their way in among the Canaanites, the Semitic peoples already living in Palestine, they settled down in the country. The Ark was taken to Shiloh, which became the centre of Yahweh's worship.

This magnificent story can be taken as a fundamentally accurate account of what happened, with whatever embellishments are credited to piety. Alternatively, it can be seen as a successful rewriting of history by later enthusiasts for Yahweh, intended to persuade other Jews that Yahweh was their ancestral god and the god whom alone they should worship. What may have happened is that the tribes who left Egypt took as their patron, under Moses's influence, a god of storm and war, Yahweh, whose presence was sensed in lightning and in storm-clouds on the mountains, and who was perhaps worshipped by nomads in Midian, where Moses had his first experience of the god. The Israelites were joined by other desert tribes for the invasion of Canaan, still under Yahweh's patronage, but after they had settled in the country many of them returned to their own tribal gods and were also attracted to the native Canaanite deities, the gods of the land. This horrified the Yahwists, who urged them to cleave to the god who had saved them from oppression in Egypt, given them the Promised Land and appointed them – improbable as it might rationally seem – for a special role in history.

Certainly the pattern of the following years, as told in the Bible, is of the Israelites forgetting Yahweh, being defeated by the Canaanites, returning to their Yahwist allegiance, winning a victory and then relapsing again. This is described in Yahwist terms, with each defeat explained as God's punishment of his faithless people.

God in the Old Testament is fundamentally a deity of gigantic and terrifying force, which is interpreted as his all-consuming 'wrath'. This is vividly brought out in the description of his colossal manifestation on Mount Sinai and in the story of the fearful plagues which he visited on the Egyptians to display his power. The Ark in which he travelled was as dangerous as a massive charge of electricity and could be touched only by priests. When one of the people put a hand to it, to steady it when it was in danger of falling, the Bible records that he was struck dead on the spot. God's power is a fact of nature beyond moral considerations. To be exposed to it is as lethal, however good one's motives, as exposure to lightning.

This huge destructive force is unleashed in war, when God goes invincibly into battle against his people's enemies, which no doubt reflects the fact that the Israelites were more likely to win battles when they fought as a single religious unit, confident in their war-god. The consequence was that loyalty to Yahweh was linked with the preservation of Israel as a nation, and the Jewish concept of holy war – war as a sacred duty for God's purposes – was inherited by Christians and Muslims, who fought holy wars against each other.

ABOVE Scene at a well outside Haran, in Turkey. According to tradition, it was here that the beautiful Rebecca came to the well and was seen by Abraham's servants. She married Abraham's son, Isaac, and was the mother of Jacob, the immediate ancestor of the twelve tribes of Israel. Jacob personifies the Jewish nation in the Bible, which also calls him Israel, meaning 'Champion of God'. In the Bible's view of history the Jews are God's chosen people, with the mission of bringing the whole world to his service.

If a god is to take a firm hold on men's minds, the one attribute which he needs above all others is power. This does not mean that human beings do not want to be loved and supported by the divine. They do, because they are helpless and need loving, but because they are weak they need the love of a god who is strong, just as children need strength in their parents as well as affection. Yahweh in the Old Testament is not only a deity of violence and cataclysmic rage. The other side of his nature is merciful and benevolent, and he makes his presence known as a still small voice as well as in fire and storm. He is the Father of his people, which involves discipline as well as love. Over and over again his children stray from his service and he punishes them by exposing them to foreign aggression, but when they cry for help he loyally and patiently saves them once more.

The most admired figure in Jewish history as leader, law-giver and prophet is Moses. In the East great religious teachers have often been considered divine, but Judaism has no place for god-men. A prophet in the Jewish tradition is a man who meets God face to face, as it were, in visionary and ecstatic experiences and becomes God's appointed spokesman. He reveals what God is like and what God commands men to do, interprets events in the light of God's purposes and explains what is to happen in the future. Moses is the earliest in the long line of Jewish prophets, a succession which has no parallel in other religions and which gave Judaism its distinctive character as a blend of monotheism, nationalism and a moral code.

TOP Imaginative 19th-century reconstruction of the setting up of the tabernacle, the sanctuary erected in the wilderness, following the instructions of God on Mount Sinai.

ABOVE The best-known symbol of Judaism is the six-pointed Shield of David (or Star of David).

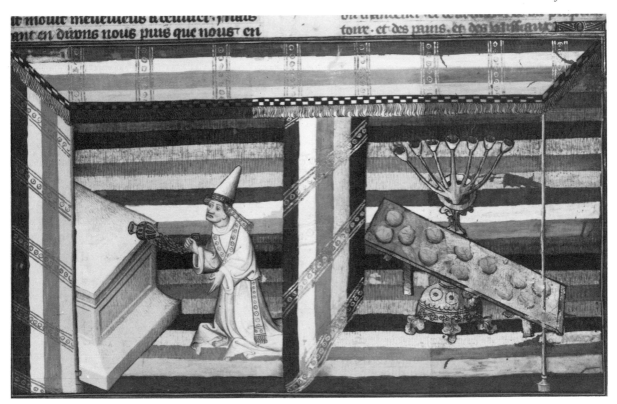

The tabernacle, from a 14th-century French manuscript. In the Holy of Holies is the high priest, with a censer of incense. In the Holy Place is the table bearing twelve loaves of bread and the seven-branched lamp, the Menorah.

OVERLEAF Engraving of a 17th-century reconstruction of Solomon's Temple, which reproduced the features of the tabernacle. The magnificence and elaborate decoration of the building are described in detail in the Bible, but at its heart was a simple shrine, the Holy of Holies, the dwelling-place of God on earth, which only the high priest was allowed to enter, once a year on the Day of Atonement.

From David to the Exile

Late in the eleventh century, the Israelite leaders decided that unity against their neighbours required a monarchy. The first king, Saul, was killed in battle. His successor was David, a formidable warrior who established a kingdom covering most of Palestine. Storming the Canaanite hill-fortress of Jerusalem, he made it his capital and the Ark was brought there from Shiloh in ceremonial procession, with the king himself dancing before it. Later generations looked back to David as the greatest national hero after Moses, the king who fastened the Israelite grip securely on Palestine and who was, correspondingly, most signally favoured by God. David's son Solomon, famed for his wisdom, his wealth and his harem of foreign women, built a magnificent temple for Yahweh at Jerusalem, with the Holy of Holies, the innermost shrine, as the dwelling-place of God on earth. As the political and religious capital, and with the building of the Temple, Jerusalem began to acquire a sacred mystique. It became in Jewish eyes a uniquely holy place, God's chosen home, the focus of national loyalty, the geographical and spiritual centre of the world.

It was probably in Solomon's time that the bulk of Genesis was written, compiled from earlier traditions, with its accounts of God's creation and planning of the world. The concept of God as Creator and Planner is one of the things which broadly distinguish the Judaic religions from the eastern religions. Creation myths play no great role in Hinduism and Buddhism, where the world spins for ever in recurrent cycles of infinite time, but in the

139

SAL

K

I

I

western tradition time is linear, not cyclical. The world had a beginning, and will also have an end. It was made by a Maker, who saw that his creations were good, as Genesis says. The moral is that life is not evil or pointless, but has a divine origin and purpose. Life is good, or should be, and asceticism has played no significant role in Judaism.

After Solomon's death the northern tribes rebelled against his son Rehoboam and set up their own kingdom under Jeroboam. There were now two kingdoms, Israel in the north, and Judah, formed of the tribes of Judah and Benjamin, in the south. The existence of each was precarious for great powers were on the move. The northern kingdom was finally dispatched by Sargon II of Assyria, who annexed it and deported thousands of Israelites to Mesopotamia and Iran. The deportees vanished into a limbo of history as 'the lost tribes of Israel'. They were replaced in Palestine by Assyrian settlers, who intermarried with the surviving northerners to form a people to whom the southern Jews remained fiercely hostile for centuries, the Samaritans. The southern kingdom, Judah, was dominated at different times by Assyria, Egypt and Babylonia, until in 587 BC Nebuchadnezzar II of Babylon besieged Jerusalem, sacked the city and destroyed the Temple. Many of the citizens were carried off into exile in Babylonia.

From the Yahwist standpoint the troubled history of both kingdoms was due to the persistent lapses from monotheism of too many of the kings and the people, who went 'whoring' after foreign gods, worshipping them as well as Yahweh. Solomon himself imported Egyptian and Canaanite gods into Jerusalem along with his foreign women. Once the Israelites had settled down in Palestine as agriculturalists, they inevitably became preoccupied with the fertility of the land and so with the local gods in whose gift fertility was believed to lie. Kings of both Israel and Judah paid honours to the Canaanite god Baal, the lord of storm and the winter rain which brought the crops to life in the spring, and his consort, the goddess Asherah, whose cult involved erotic rites and sacred prostitution, intended to promote fertility by imitative magic. At Mizpeh, north of Jerusalem, in the ninth century temples of Asherah and Yahweh stood side by side.

Yahwist prophets rose up to assail these deviations. Elijah, whose name means 'Yahweh is God', denounced King Ahab of Israel and his wife Jezebel for supporting the cults of Baal and Asherah, with such ferocity that Jezebel passed into history as an archetype of female evil. The prophet won a famous victory over the priests of Baal on Mount Carmel by succeeding in calling down lightning from the sky when they could not, but Jezebel's fury against him was such that he had to flee for his life.

With the menace of Assyria looming up in the north, Amos, Hosea, Isaiah and Micah called for a return to the one true God. In their own time, it seems, the prophets had little effect on events, but their words were written down by their admirers and so preserved, in language of thrilling beauty and power, and in the long run they profoundly influenced Judaism and the world. The heart of the prophetic message is the sense of God as not only enormously powerful, the heavenly king who rules the world, but as a holy and moral being, the God of righteousness, of justice, of compassion, of decent dealings with one's fellow men. The prophets

Elijah calling down fire from heaven, from the *Biblia Pauperum*, Flemish, about 1400. Elijah undertook his famous ritual contest against the priests of Baal on Mount Carmel to demonstrate that Yahweh was the true God and Baal a false god.

The creation, from the Sarajevo Haggadah. The pages, each of which has to be read from right to left, show the Spirit of God hovering over the waters of chaos, followed by the seven days of creation: the making of light and darkness; the sky; the earth, seas and plants; the sun, moon and stars; fish, birds and animals; mankind; and finally the seventh day of rest. The tradition in Genesis of God creating the world in seven days was accepted as literally true in the West until the 19th century, when it was challenged by scientific discoveries and the theory of evolution.

attacked not only the worship of foreign gods but the secularization, materialism, luxury and exploitation of the poor which they believed had infected Israel as a consequence of a settled life in Palestine and wealth from foreign trade.

The prophets had a sharp sense of 'sin', which does not mean merely crime, offending against a human code, but breaking rules that have a supernatural sanction, in this case the rules of God. Sinning may mean ritual or moral transgression, but the prophets put their emphasis on morals. What God requires of men, the prophet Micah said (chapter 6), is not sacrifices and offerings, thousands of rams and rivers of oil, but good moral behaviour. 'He has showed you, O man, what is good; and what does the Lord require of you but to do justice, and to love kindness, and to walk humbly with your God?'

This prophetic insistence on God's righteousness and his demand for righteousness in man has struck a chord in the human conscience over many centuries, and also a chord in the human need to feel guilty. Although the Indian religions certainly do not condone immorality, the Judaic religions put a far stronger emphasis on sin as a barrier between man and God, between man and salvation. An enduring element of this emphasis is the importance of sexual morality in the Judaic religions. One of the strangest characteristics of the Jewish god, in foreign eyes, was that he had no wife, no beautiful goddess as his queen. (He also had no family, no biography and no visible representations, the making of images of God being strictly forbidden in Jewish law.) God could not have a consort because Yahwism was monotheistic. The fact that God was above sex gave human sexuality a certain taint of ungodliness. Sex was necessary for the purpose for which God had created it, the continuation of humankind through the mutual love of husband and wife, but outside this limit it was an abuse of man's God-given body. The prophets were horrified by the promiscuous eroticism of the Canaanite fertility cults and their condemnation of defection from Yahweh in terms of whoring and harlotry gave a powerful impetus to the puritanical strand in the western religions.

Another enduring consequence of the prophets' impact on the Judaic religions is their intolerance. Those who believe themselves to be the appointed spokesmen of God are inevitably confident of their own rightness and of the wrongness of all who oppose or ignore them. The western religions do not share the Indian tradition of many paths to the truth. For them there is only one path, their own, and everyone should follow it.

The Abomination of Desolation

The 'Babylonian captivity' lasted about fifty years for some of the families deported from Judah to Mesopotamia, and considerably more for others. Many prospered in exile and some never returned to Palestine at all. The Jews were not prevented from practising their religion and although some of them presumably blended into their new surroundings, others preserved their Jewish identity. In doing this, instead of taking to the worship of Babylonian gods and abandoning Yahweh, who might be thought to have failed them, they became more zealous for him than before. Psalm 137, which begins 'By the waters of Babylon there we sat down and wept', expresses a fierce hatred of Babylonia and a determination not to be absorbed in a foreign culture: 'If I forget you, O Jerusalem, let my right hand wither!'

The exiles were comforted by the prophet Ezekiel, who held out the hope of a return to the Promised Land. Another prophet, now known as the second Isaiah (Deutero-Isaiah), spoke of the Suffering Servant of Yahweh – 'He was despised and rejected by men; a man of sorrows, and acquainted with grief' (Isaiah, chapter 53) – in an enigmatic passage which Christians later believed to be a prophecy of Christ. It is not clear whether the prophet was thinking of an individual, or Israel as a whole, or a movement or ideal within Judaism, but he encouraged Jewish hopes and Jewish nationalism by stressing the goodness, mercy and overwhelming power of Yahweh, who had forgiven his people's failings and would gloriously vindicate them in the end, when all nations would bow before them.

Without a king, with Jerusalem lost and the Temple destroyed, the exiles found a centre for their religion in the scriptures, though how much of the Old Testament was now in existence is not known. The seventh day of the week, the sabbath, which had long been a day of rest, now turned into a day of religious devotion, when people met to hear the scriptures read and expounded, prayers were offered and, possibly, psalms were sung. Special 'assembly-houses' were built for the meetings and these were the first synagogues.

When Babylon fell to a Persian conqueror, Cyrus the Great, Palestine became part of the Achaemenian Empire. Cyrus allowed some of the exiles

Miniature from a 13th-century Hebrew manuscript, showing the high priest who wears the 'breastplate of judgement'.

BELOW The death of Jezebel, an engraving by Gustave Doré. Jezebel, a priestess of Asherah, encouraged the Canaanite fertility cults. Elijah, as the spokesman of God, cursed her and she was duly thrown from her window and eaten by dogs.

to return to devastated Jerusalem and over the following years the city was reconstructed and the Temple rebuilt. Other groups of exiles returned later. Yahweh had come back to his earthly home, but for 200 years Judea, the region around Jerusalem, was a Persian province and Judaism came under the influence of Zoroastrian ideas. The monarchy was not restored under Persian imperial rule and immediate political and religious authority was in the hands of the high priest at Jerusalem, supported by aristocratic priestly families. The institution of the local synagogue had taken firm root and flourished everywhere in Jewry. Outside Judea there was still an important Jewish community in Babylonia and another grew up in Egypt.

The Achaemenian Empire fell in its turn, to Alexander the Great, and for almost another 200 years Judea was ruled by Alexander's successors: first by the Ptolemy dynasty of Egypt, who after years of warfare were driven out by the Seleucid dynasty of Syria. Under these Greek regimes the Jews were caught in the swirling currents of Hellenistic culture with its mingling of gods, religions and philosophies from Greece, Mesopotamia, Iran, Syria and Egypt. Some were attracted, some were repelled, and two opposite tendencies developed, one which wanted to Hellenize and modernize Jewish life in tune with the latest intellectual fashions, and one which took its stand on the old ways.

The Hellenizing trend reached its peak under a high priest who took the Greek name of Jason and tried to turn Jerusalem into a Greek city. To the horror of the traditionally minded, young aristocrats and priests promenaded about naked in Jason's new gymnasium and resorted to surgery to make themselves appear uncircumcised. There were riots and the Seleucid ruler Antiochus IV, who called himself Epiphanes, 'the manifest god', came to Jerusalem to restore order. He had supported Jason and he now determined to secure peace and quiet in his dominions by stamping out the Jewish religion. Circumcision, observance of the sabbath and other Jewish customs were prohibited and the Temple was turned into a sanctuary of Zeus, the Greek sky-god. Pigs were sacrificed to Zeus on the great altar of Yahweh and prostitutes were installed in the house of God.

This profanation, 'the abomination of desolation' as it was called, sent a chill of outrage through Jewry. The reaction was swift and fierce. Five brothers of the Hasmonean family, led by Judas, known as Maccabaeus, 'the Hammerer', conducted a successful war against the Syrians. The enemy were driven from Jerusalem and the Temple was purified and rededicated in 165 BC, an event which has been commemorated ever since at Hanukkah, the festival of lights in December. The Jews won the right to keep their own religion and customs, and in 142 BC achieved independence under Simon, the last of the Maccabee brothers, as high priest and ruler. The Hasmonean monarchy survived for another eighty years of unrest, intrigue and bloodshed culminating in civil war, when both sides appealed to Rome for help. Rome sent help, of a sort. The Roman legions under Pompey stormed Jerusalem, killed thousands of its inhabitants and slaughtered the priests at the altar of Yahweh.

Judea was swallowed up by Rome, though for a time governed by puppet-rulers, of whom the most effective was Herod the Great. Notorious

ABOVE View of Jerusalem, dominated by Mount Zion, the hill on which the Temple stood, on the site where David reverently deposited the Ark. Jerusalem has a special place in Jewish, Christian and Muslim affection. In Judaism it is a symbol of God's covenant with his people and his promise of a glorious future. In Christian tradition it is the centre of the world, a symbol of the Church and an image on earth of the city of God in heaven. The Arabic name for it is al-Kuds, 'the Holy One', and the site of the Temple is now occupied by a Muslim mosque, the Dome of the Rock.

LEFT The cover of the Sion Gospels, German, 11th and 12th centuries, overlaid with gold and enriched with precious stones. In the centre is Christ, his right hand raised in blessing. Christians share with Jews and Muslims a reverence for scripture as inspired directly by God.

The Crucifixion, from the Regensburg Lectionary, German, 13th century. Christ is shown crucified by the Virtues because, in Christian theory, it was the death on the cross which released mankind from the power of evil. Pity, Wisdom and Obedience hammer the nails into the hands and feet, and the Church as the Bride pierces Christ's side.

LEFT In this illustration from a 10th-century manuscript Mattathias, leader of the Maccabean uprising against the Syrians, kills a Jew who is about to sacrifice a pig, an unclean animal in Jewish law.

ABOVE Mattathias's son Judas Maccabeus leads his army against the Syrian war elephants, an engraving by Gustave Doré.

LEFT Illustration from a 15th-century Hebrew manuscript, showing the lighting of the candlestick at the Hanukkah festival, which celebrates the purification and rededication of the Temple after the expulsion of the Syrians.

for his political murders and his numerous and sometimes incestuous marriages, he succeeded in keeping the peace, rebuilt the Temple with great magnificence and died of an obscure and singularly repulsive disease which his enemies described as God's punishment for his iniquities.

In the turmoil and suffering of the second and first centuries BC, when foreign powers and foreign beliefs threatened the Jewish way of life with extinction, ideas came to the fore which had developed earlier, during the Exile and the Persian period. These ideas did not at this point form any coherent system and most of the writings in which they were expounded, in tones of high visionary excitement, never found a place in the Bible. They centred around the old concept of the Day of Yahweh (which goes back to before the Exile), the hope that Israel's sufferings would be brought to an end in the future when God would arise in power and wrath, scatter the enemies of Israel and rule the world from Mount Zion, the hill in Jerusalem on which the Temple stood. Some writers expected God to send a Saviour, the Messiah or Anointed One, a king of the house of David, who would lead Israel to victory over her foreign oppressors and tormentors. The foreign nations would be annihilated or subjugated or converted to Yahweh, and the Messiah would establish the kingdom of God with its capital at Jerusalem, a kingdom of righteousness, peace and prosperity. The idealized kingdom of David in the past was here projected into the future and the Messiah, a superhuman figure but not a divine one, was also called the Son of David or the Chosen One. The concept of the final victory of God was transmuted by some writers into a picture of a colossal battle between cosmic powers, the forces of light and the forces of darkness. Some believed that after his triumph God would destroy the old world and create a new one, an ideal world of holiness, beauty, fertility and happiness which would last for ever.

It was also believed in some quarters that not only the faithful who were living at the time but also the faithful dead would see God's kingdom. The older Jewish tradition had been concerned with the destiny and ultimate triumph of the nation as a whole, not with the salvation of individual men and women. The purpose of living was to serve God and multiply his holy nation by having children. No hope was generally held out for the dead, whose usefulness to God and the nation was over. Their bodies decayed in the grave and what little survived, a fleeting shadow of the former self, went down to a dreary underworld of darkness and silence beneath the ground, soon forgotten by God as by men. Now, however, this old tribal concept was challenged by beliefs about a life after death and rewards and punishments based on individual conduct on earth. The good would go to a paradise in the sky and the bad would be punished in hell, in the fires of Gehenna, which took its name from a valley outside Jerusalem where the city's rubbish was burned. At the end of time, God would raise up the dead in their reconstituted physical bodies and all, living and dead, would be judged. The righteous would enter God's kingdom, in heaven or on the perfected earth, and the wicked would be consigned to hell for ever.

These ideas were the products of oppression, persecution and hope for triumph and revenge. They were also a response to the central problem of

The mosaic of the Good Shepherd, Mausoleum of Galla Placidia, Ravenna, 5th century. The symbol of Christ as the shepherd of his flock is connected with Psalm 23, 'The Lord is my shepherd', and is used here in a tomb to depict Christ as the loving guide who shepherds the departed soul safely to heaven. It seems to have been taken over by Christians from contemporary pagan funeral art, in which the symbol of the loving shepherd was used in the same way.

LEFT Hostility between Jews and Christians was an early growth. The wicked King Herod, who tried to murder the infant Jesus, became a stock Jewish villain in Christian eyes, though the real Herod was not in fact a Jew and was detested by many Jews as a foreigner, an evil-liver and a Roman puppet. Herod ordering the Massacre of the Innocents, from the Basilica of S. Stefano, Bologna.

monotheism. How can evil and undeserved suffering exist, as they plainly do, in a world made and ruled by God? On the face of it, the conclusion would seem to be that if God is good, he cannot be all-powerful, or if he is all-powerful, he cannot be entirely good. Though the details varied from one writer to another, the general outline of the Jewish solution was that the sufferings of the faithful would earn their reward, initially in the life after death and ultimately when God intervened in the world to set all things to rights. The details – the future Saviour, the dualistic battle of good and evil, the final victory of good, the bodily resurrection of the dead, the Last Judgement, heaven and hell, the world made perfect – are so similar to the Zoroastrian pattern as to suggest strong Zoroastrian influence during the Persian period.

Although this whole constellation of beliefs was extremely important in later Judaism (and in Christianity), the new interest in individual salvation in the afterlife was not welcomed by the Sadducees, the party which principally represented the priests and wealthy aristocrats and which preserved the older emphasis on Israel's destiny as a nation. The new emphasis came from the opposing party, the Pharisees, many of whom were not priests but teachers in the synagogues. Respected for their piety, learning and humanity, they had considerable popular influence and they may well have found that confidence in another and happier life beyond death sustained ordinary people's faith during times of severe stress. Belief in the Messiah and in personal salvation also sustained small groups which retreated from a world they felt unbearably sinful and corrupt to lead lives of piety and strict observance of Jewish law in secluded communities like the one at Qumran on the shore of the Dead Sea which produced the Dead Sea Scrolls. They believed that the Day of Yahweh was at hand and they awaited the imminent arrival of the Messiah.

Zion Laid Waste

What in fact awaited the Jews was not triumph but disaster. For most of the period after Herod's death Judea was ruled directly by Roman officials. A fiercely militant group, the Zealots, formed under the leadership of Judas of Galilee, determined to win independence from foreign domination once and for all, to rid the Promised Land of the heathen presence which polluted it and restore it to God, the chosen people and the Torah. The militants were opposed by the more realistic, the less fanatical and those who preferred a quiet life, but after years of tension, protests and riots, Menahem, the son of Judas, led the Zealots in a revolt which dragged Palestine into a hopeless war against Rome. Two future Roman emperors, the general Vespasian and his son Titus, moved slowly down through Galilee and in March of the year AD 70 laid siege to Jerusalem, where the Zealot leaders were conducting their own reign of terror against all who questioned their aims and tactics. Gripped by famine, the city held out until September, when the legions broke in, killing, looting and burning. The Temple was burned to the ground and its treasures were carried off to Rome to adorn Titus's triumph. The remaining Zealot strongholds were

LEFT Part of a plaque attached to a barrier outside the inner court of the Temple, warning Gentiles to go no further. St Paul was arrested by the Roman authorities after a riot, in which he was attacked for speaking against the Jewish law and defiling the Temple by taking Gentiles into it.

OVERLEAF LEFT Christ crowned with thorns, by Hieronymus Bosch. The crowning was in cruel mockery of the claim that Jesus was the king of the Jews as the Messiah, the great leader who was expected to free the Jews from the foreign yoke. His disciples had hailed Jesus as the Messiah, but it seems clear that he did not regard himself as a political leader.

OVERLEAF RIGHT Angels waft the Virgin Mary gently up to the throne of Christ in the sky, where her crown as queen of heaven awaits her, from the *Très Riches Heures du Duc du Berry*. The Virgin has a complex role in Christian symbolism as both the bride and the mother of God. The painting superbly conveys the beauty and serenity of the Christian concept of heaven.

Conuerte
nos deus
salutaris
noster.

Et auerte iram tu
a nobis.

Deus in adiuto
rium meum

The Menorah, carved in the ruins of a synagogue at Capernaum, 2nd or 3rd century AD. The seven-branched golden lamp was kept burning perpetually in the Temple before the presence of the God who created light. The seven branches may have stood for the sun, the moon and the five planets known in antiquity, created by God on the fourth day.

reduced, despite brave resistance. At the hill-top fortress of Masada the defenders killed their wives and children and finally themselves rather than surrender.

A distinguished teacher, Jochanan ben Zekkai, had escaped from Jerusalem during the siege by feigning death and having himself carried out of the city in a coffin. With Roman permission he founded a teaching college at the coastal town of Jabneh (or Jamnia). He and his colleagues continued the work which the Pharisees had begun, of interpreting the Torah for practical purposes of everyday living and adapting it to changed conditions, and it was at Jabneh that the canon of the Old Testament was finally settled.

Armed resistance to Rome in Palestine was not yet finished. A fresh revolt broke out when the Emperor Hadrian ordered a temple of Jupiter to be built on the ruins of the Temple in Jerusalem. The rebellion was led by Simeon, who called himself Bar-Kokhba, Son of the Star, and was hailed as the Messiah by Rabbi Akiba, the leading light of the Jabneh centre. Roman troops subdued the country once more. Jerusalem was destroyed, many of the inhabitants were killed or deported as slaves, the site of the city was ploughed up and Jews were forbidden to go anywhere near it. Hoping to

The hill fortress of Masada was the scene of obdurate Zealot resistance to the Romans after the storming of Jerusalem. The defenders, believing in their divine mission to throw off foreign domination, killed their wives and children, and finally themselves, rather than surrender.

rid Rome once and for all of this troublesome and obstinate religion, Hadrian closed the Jabneh school and issued what proved to be a short-lived order banning the study and practice of the Torah. Akiba and many other Jews who publicly defied the order were executed.

Zion, the holy city, which had been the centre of Jewish hopes and emotions for so many centuries, was laid waste. Hadrian rebuilt Jerusalem as a Roman city, Aelia Capitolina, with temples of Roman gods and a shrine of Jupiter on the site of the Holy of Holies. Not for another eighteen centuries was Israel to recover the Promised Land. When Jerusalem again became a sacred centre it was not as a Jewish city, but as a Christian one in the fourth century and a Muslim one in the seventh.

Talmudic Judaism

Jewry was scattered but not obliterated. Jews had been leaving Palestine for centuries. There were Jewish communities in Babylonia, Iran, Syria, Egypt, the Yemen, in Rome itself and in many other cities of the empire, and in time Jews settled in every continent of the world. After the destruction of the Temple the priesthood became virtually extinct and

Interior of a synagogue, built in 1568 in Cochin, India. The Ark containing the Torah scrolls is approached by steps. It is usually on the side of the building towards Jerusalem. On the platform in the foreground is the reading desk from which services are conducted.

LEFT Scroll of the Torah, with a pointer. Hebrew, in the Jewish tradition, is the language of God and the language with which God brought the world into being.

Ceremonial silver crowns used for decorating the handles of the Torah scrolls.

Equally crucial to the survival of Jewish identity was the continued observance of Jewish law and custom. The period from the destruction of Jerusalem to the end of the fifth century saw the compilation in Babylonia and Palestine of the Talmud, which takes second place only to the Bible as the authoritative regulator of Jewish life and faith. The Talmud records the precepts of learned rabbis as to the correct interpretation of scripture and the right living of daily life, and includes ethical rules, religious and civil laws, marriage laws, rules of diet and hygiene, and regulations for services and festivals. The Talmud is also a treasury of sermons, moral tales, legends and popular lore. Although the Bible has remained the ultimate authority in Judaism, it is the Bible as seen through the Talmud, and the existence of this fount of piety and collection of detailed rules for Jewish life was a vital factor in preserving the existence of Jewry, in keeping the Jews Jewish.

Though there have naturally been changes over the centuries, the Talmud remains the foundation of traditional Jewish devotions and rites. Many of them are observed at home, though the extent to which they are kept up nowadays varies enormously from the most strictly orthodox to the more 'liberal' households. The tendency now is to interpret these customs symbolically, but at the popular level in the past they also had a magical function as ways of ensuring God's favour and protection, and keeping evil forces at bay. The first obligation of the devout on waking up is to thank God for the gift of another day, and the next is to wash the hands, both for purification and as a mark of fresh dedication to God. Ritual purity has always been important. The hands must be washed and grace said before all meals and there are complicated rules about what food is 'clean' or 'fit' (*kosher*) and what is not. Prayers are said in the morning, afternoon and evening. Strictly speaking, a fringed garment, the *tzitzith*, should be worn at all times as a symbol of being wholly consecrated to God. During morning prayers a fringed shawl, the *tallith*, is worn, and on weekdays also the *tefillin* or 'phylacteries' on the head and the arm, near the heart. These are small boxes containing texts from the Bible, written in Hebrew on parchment, which instruct the faithful to love God and to give mind, hand and heart to his service. A *mezuzah*, a metal or wooden case enclosing some of the same texts, is fixed to the front door, and sometimes to inner doors as well, as a sign that the house is dedicated to God's law and is worthy of his presence and protection. On going in and out of the house the pious touch the mezuzah with their fingers and then put their fingers to their lips.

Prayers are also said daily, in Hebrew, in the synagogue, where worshippers keep their heads covered as a mark of reverence. Each synagogue recalls the Temple. A lamp burns perpetually, just as the Menorah, the great seven-branched golden lamp, was kept permanently burning in the Temple before the presence of the God who created light. The reading desk in the synagogue recalls the altar of the Temple. The scrolls of the Torah, hand-written and hung with tinkling silver bells, are kept in the Ark at the east end, which the congregation face. During the sabbath service of readings, prayers, psalms and sermon, a scroll is taken from the Ark and carried round in procession while the worshippers stand.

A mezuzah, containing texts from the Bible and fastened to the door of a house, is a sign that the house and its occupants are dedicated to God. This 15th-century example comes from Italy.

The great festivals similarly recall the past and remind the faithful of Israel's historic and continuing mission. Among them are Passover in the spring, which celebrates the rebirth of life after winter and commemorates the exodus from Egypt as the birthday of Israel. At home the family eat unleavened bread and bitter herbs as a reminder of the affliction of slavery and drink wine for joy in the escape to a new life of freedom. Seven weeks later the revelation on Mount Sinai is commemorated at Shavuoth. In the autumn the harvest festival of Sukkoth is celebrated. Rosh Hashanah, the New Year festival in the autumn, is the birthday of the world, the anniversary of its creation. The Shofar, the ram's horn trumpet, is blown in the synagogue to hail God as the king of the world and to call all mankind to him, and prayers are offered for a good year to come. The following ten days are a time for considering one's sins, admitting and repenting them, and asking God's forgiveness. This period of introspection and contrition culminates in the fast on Yom Kippur, the Day of Atonement, when long ago in Palestine the sins of the people were ritually placed on the head of a goat, which was driven out into the desert, carrying the people's sins away with it. Nothing should be eaten or drunk on this day, which is spent in prayer in the synagogue, where a confession of the community's sins is recited. The fast ends with the sounding of the Shofar. To atone means literally to become 'at one' with God through repentance and his forgiveness, and it is on this day that God's presence is most closely sensed by the devout.

ABOVE The sound of the shofar, the ancient ram's horn trumpet, symbolizes God's lordship of the world. When Yahweh descended upon Mount Sinai in flame, the loud blast of a trumpet was heard and all the people trembled.

LEFT Sukkoth in Jerusalem. This autumn harvest festival commemorates the period in the wilderness after the escape from Egypt, when the people lived in booths. During the festival meals are eaten in booths covered with straw or branches, and the four plants – citron, palm, myrtle and willow – are waved in the air and carried in procession to the synagogue. Ceremonies of this kind are not mere reminders of the past but create a sense of unity with previous generations.

Philosophy and Persecution

Christianity's triumph as the dominant religion of the Roman Empire and its successor states boded ill for Jewry. Christians worshipped the same God, but they believed that their religion had superseded Judaism as the true universal faith. They blamed the Jews for killing Christ – somewhat illogically, since without the Crucifixion there would have been no Christianity – and the nonsensical notion of inherited guilt made Jews in every generation supposedly responsible for the crime. Once Christianity had suppressed the pagan religions of the ancient world, the Jew was almost the only outsider left in Christian society (the others being the black magician and the witch, with whom Jews were frequently linked in popular belief). The Jew was the stranger within the gates on whom blame for disasters and misfortunes could always be loaded. Some Christian authorities protected the Jews, however, if only as horrible examples to Christians of what they should not be. The popes were generally tolerant and the Jewish community in Rome came through the Middle Ages comparatively unscathed.

Despite sporadic persecutions and frequent harrassment, Jewish intellectual life flourished in the early Middle Ages, especially in Muslim countries such as Spain and Egypt, Islam being more tolerant of a people who shared its own strict monotheism, respect for the Old Testament and disbelief in Christ. With the compilation of the Talmud, Judaism had become the religion which essentially it has remained ever since, and medieval intellectuals concentrated on interpreting it. Jewish philosophers, much influenced by Greek and Arab thinkers, tried to provide rational proofs of Judaism, though their writings never attained the authority of the Bible and the Talmud. An Egyptian Jew, Saadya ben Joseph, who taught in Babylon, has been called the father of Jewish philosophy. In Spain the poet and philosopher Judah Halevi of Toledo set out to demonstrate the superiority of Judaism to both Christianity and Islam. The most influential of the philosophers, in Christian as well as Jewish circles, was another Spanish Jew, Moses Maimonides of Cordova, author of *The Guide for the Perplexed*, who formulated what he regarded as the thirteen fundamental beliefs of Judaism. They include belief in a single Creator, eternal and omniscient, who alone should be worshipped, in the authority of the Torah and the prophets, in the coming of the Messiah and the resurrection of the dead but, curiously, not the belief in Israel as the chosen people.

By Maimonides's time the complex and obscure system of mystical philosophy known as the Kabbalah (Tradition) was beginning to develop in southern France and Spain. It was based on the traditions of earlier small esoteric groups whose adepts taught ways of achieving visionary experiences, culminating in a vision of the terrifying, overwhelming splendour and majesty of God. The Kabbalists believed that the original perfect harmony of God and his universe had been broken by the sinfulness of man, beginning with Adam's disobedience in Eden, as a result of which evil had entered God's good world. This was seen as a split in the divine nature itself, a cosmic tragedy, and the task of man, and especially of Israel, was to work for the recovery of the original harmony, to restore the wholeness of God. This could be achieved through obedience to God's law and good moral conduct, through kindness and meekness, and through ecstatic experience of loving communion with God. The major work of the Kabbalah, the *Zohar* (Book of Splendour), is a commentary on the Pentateuch intended to reveal the hidden meaning of the scripture, probably written in Spain in the thirteenth century by Moses de Leon. Outside Judaism, the Kabbalah has had an important influence on Christian mysticism and on modern occultism.

In Christian Europe conditions for the Jews changed radically for the worse with the Crusades, when Christian fanaticism against the Muslims spilled over on to the Jews as well. Jewish communities were pillaged and massacred. Persistent stories circulated among Christians of Jews slaughtering children to use their blood in abominable secret rites, blasphemously abusing consecrated hosts to mock and torture Christ, poisoning wells and causing bad harvests by black magic. Jews were forced to live in ghettos, walled-off quarters in towns, and often to wear a yellow badge as a distinguishing mark. The fact that money-lending was largely a Jewish preserve, usury being forbidden to Christians by the Church, created the caricature of the grasping, extortionate Jew. The Jews were expelled from the western European countries. So many German Jews fled from pogroms to Poland and Lithuania that by the early seventeenth century more than half of Jewry was concentrated there, but the respite was only temporary. Many Jews were massacred during the Polish wars against Russia and Sweden, the Russian Cossacks earning an infamous reputation for cruelty. The partitions of Poland in the eighteenth century put a million Jews under Russian rule and the Jewish 'pale' was established, an area stretching from the Baltic to the Black Sea at Odessa, to which the Jews were confined. The only exception was for Jewish prostitutes, who were benevolently permitted to live anywhere in Russia. After a hundred years of intermittent persecution, a series of atrocious pogroms between 1880 and 1910 drove Russian Jews to America in a flood. Jews from other European countries also emigrated, and between 1870 and 1940 the Jewish population of the United States rose from a quarter of a million to four and a half million.

Reform, Orthodoxy and Zionism

In western Europe, however, the nineteenth century saw the release of the Jews from medieval conditions. The eighteenth-century worship of Reason carried with it an impatience for tradition and a demand for freedom, tolerance and equality for all. The French Revolution proclaimed liberty, equality and the brotherhood of man, and Napoleon opened the ghettos all over Europe. The consequences were double-edged. Liberated from isolation in the ghettos, Jews were able to contribute to philosophy, science, the arts and scholarship in the West with remarkable effect – as the names Karl Marx, Sigmund Freud, Gustav Mahler, Marcel Proust and Albert Einstein suggest. But at the same time liberation exposed the Jewish

The plunder of the ghetto in Frankfurt, following riots in 1614. Jews were for centuries objects of intense suspicion and hostility in Christian Europe. The Jew was the outsider, the stranger within the gates, on whom could be fastened blame for poor harvests, epidemics, unexplained deaths and other disasters.

communities to the non-Jewish world, to the same western influences which transformed traditional ways of life in India, China and Japan. It also exposed them to a fresh wave of virulent anti-semitism. In their old seclusion, fraught with danger and humiliation as it was, the Jews had stayed Jewish. The escape raised the question whether they could, or even should, remain Jewish.

The principal Jewish schools of thought today all stem from this situation. The founding influence on the Reform movement was the philosopher and educator Moses Mendelssohn, who spent most of his life in Berlin, hailed as the German Plato. Mendelssohn reduced the fundamentals of Judaism to three: belief in God, in God's providence or plan for the world, and in the immortality of the soul. He also suggested that truth might be plural and not singular, that no religion might have a monopoly on truth, that different people might need different religions and that the test of a religion should not be its doctrines but its effect on behaviour. His translation of the Pentateuch into German encouraged German Jews to speak German instead of Yiddish, the German Jewish vernacular, and to think of themselves as Germans as well as Jews. Most of his own family ceased to be Jewish by religion. His grandson, the composer Felix Mendelssohn, for instance, was baptized as a Lutheran Christian.

The first Reform temple was opened in Germany in 1810, the name temple instead of synagogue implying the abandonment of the old hope for the restoration of the Temple in Jerusalem. The Reform movement, which has flourished particularly in the United States, set out to modernize the faith and simplify the ritual for the Jew who had emerged from the ghetto and wanted to live on equal terms with his non-Jewish neighbours as a full and loyal citizen of a Gentile state. It played down the idea of the chosen people, claimed that Judaism ought to be a purely religious and not a nationalist phenomenon, and converted the personal Messiah into a Messianic age in which all mankind would share. The Reform leaders regarded many of the traditional rules and observances of Jewish life, including the dietary laws, as unnecessary and non-binding, creations of man not of God. They welcomed the new critical attitude to the Bible, which undermined belief in the divine authorship of scripture and weakened respect for tradition.

Reform was bitterly opposed by the conservatives, or Orthodox, who criticized it for abandoning Jewishness, reducing the religion to a vague ethical monotheism and encouraging apostasy. The Orthodox maintained that the Torah came directly from God and was binding on the faithful, and continued to believe in the personal Messiah. Numerous compromises are possible between the two extreme positions. On the whole, European Jewry is more or less Orthodox. In the United States the three main divisions, each with its own synagogues and schools, are Reform, Orthodox and Conservative. The Conservative movement was led in its early days by the distinguished scholar Solomon Schechter. It stands halfway between the other two. Accepting the traditional law, but with allowances for modern conditions, it leaves room for a wide variety of belief and practice. Conservatives do not keep the sexes apart in the synagogue, as the Orthodox do, and the services include prayers in English as well as in Hebrew.

In the nineteenth century, influenced by the desire to live at one with their neighbours and by the scepticism and materialism of the times, many western Jews either turned Christian or ceased to have a religion at all. The reaction was a revival of militant Jewish nationalism, with demands for the creation of a Jewish national state. The effective founder of the Zionist movement was Theodor Herzl, a Hungarian Jewish journalist, who called for the establishment of a home for the Jewish people in Palestine, secured by international law. The first Zionist Congress was held in Switzerland and the movement attracted strong support from oppressed Jewry in eastern Europe. In the West, where Reform leaders were usually hostile but many of the Orthodox approved, Zionism proved to have an unexpected appeal to Jews who had lost interest in their religion altogether. After 1917, when the British government pledged support, Jews began to emigrate to

This section of Herod's wall is all that is left of the Temple in Jerusalem and is venerated as a holy place. Known as the West Wall in Hebrew, it was called the Wailing Wall by Gentiles, who saw Jews there lamenting the destruction of the Temple, the departure of the divine Presence and the dispersion of Israel.

Palestine in thousands, to the dismay of Arabs who had been settled there for centuries.

Tragically, what brought Zionism success was the previously unparalleled Nazi massacre of Jews in Germany and German-occupied countries during the Second World War, in which one-third of the entire Jewish population of the world was exterminated. Previous opponents of Zionism changed their minds, the previously lukewarm became committed, and the new state of Israel was proclaimed in 1948. At last, after 2000 years of exile and dispersion, Zion was regained, the Promised Land was once more Jewish land. In the first ten years a million impoverished exiles from sixty different countries were absorbed into the new state and a country which had been largely desert began to blossom. Zionism was in principle a political not a religious movement, but it inevitably appealed to religious sentiment and to echoes of the towering promises of the prophets in the Bible. There were Zionists who saw, and still see, the creation of the Jewish state in Messianic terms as the beginning of the fulfillment of Israel's divine mission, a giant step towards the coming of the kingdom of God on earth. Outside Palestine itself, the state of Israel and Israeli achievements have given Jewish communities a fresh sense of pride, a greater feeling of solidarity and a revived confidence in their national and religious tradition.

7. Christianity

Christianity began as a splinter movement within Judaism. The founder and all the early leaders were Jews, but respectable Jewish opinion condemned the new sect as disreputable. When it spread to the Roman world outside Palestine, Christianity was at first dismissed with contempt by sophisticated people as a novel superstition which appealed to slaves, women and other irrational and excitable persons. Fiercely intolerant, the Christians refused to recognize any god other than their own. Their meetings involved anarchic and undignified shouting and raving. They worshipped a Jewish healer who had been executed as a rebel against Rome and absurdly claimed that their dubious holy man had come back to life again, had risen into the sky and would return at any moment trailing celestial clouds of glory to found a heavenly kingdom on earth. The oldest picture of the Crucifixion that has survived is a scrawl on the wall of a house in Rome showing a Christian worshipping a crucified donkey.

This despised faith now has the largest following of any religion in the world, estimated at close to 1,000 million, of whom about fifty-eight per cent are Roman Catholics and thirty-five per cent are Protestants. The devout see in Christianity's progress the working out of the purposes of God, and at the least it is clear that a religion which commands the allegiance, in all shades from real to nominal, of one human being in every four has a remarkable appeal. One of the reasons for the success of Christianity is the goodness and strength which shine through the New Testament picture of Jesus, allied to the manner and, in the Christian view, the meaning of his death. Gods who live on earth in human form are known in other religions, but a god who is the Saviour of the world yet whose human life ends in rejection, torture and execution is not. The broken body on the cross is an extraordinary and mysterious symbol of godhead and salvation which has struck a deep chord in millions of hearts. At the same time, Christianity's Jewish moral code is straightforward and satisfying, while it is not so inextricably mingled with the whole traditional way of life of any one people as to create a barrier to widespread acceptance.

Christianity takes its name from Christ, the Greek translation of the Hebrew word Messiah and the title given by Christians to the founder of their religion, believed to be both God and man. He is the Son of God, who lived, taught and died on earth as Jesus of Nazareth. He did this out of compassionate love of mankind. By living a humble human life and suffering rejection and death, the common fate of humanity, he bridged the gulf between godhead and manhood, not only in himself but potentially for everyone else. To those who believe in him and do their best to follow his teaching, he offers loving understanding, forgiveness of sins, survival of death and a happy immortality in heaven. If this brief outline of Christian doctrine seems simple, the impression is misleading. Its implications and ramifications are such that Christianity is enriched or burdened, according to the point of view, with a theology of a weight and complexity unrivalled by any other religion.

Christianity inherited from Judaism the principle of monotheism, the concept of God as the divine Father who loves, protects and disciplines his human children, the sense of being entrusted with a divine mission and the view of history as the working out of God's plan, and some of the most inspiring and beautiful religious literature ever written. Christians accepted the Hebrew Bible, or Old Testament, and in time added books of their own to form the New Testament. This consists principally of the letters of Paul, which are the earliest surviving Christian documents; the gospels or 'good news' attributed to four of Jesus's disciples, of which Mark is thought to be the oldest; the Acts of the Apostles, which recounts events during the first thirty years or so after Jesus's death; and the book of Revelation, which is a vision of the future and the end of the world.

Jesus of Nazareth

That Jesus was at the least a great moral teacher is rarely denied, but attempts to write a convincing biography of him have failed, partly for lack of adequate information and partly because he was, to those who knew him, an enigma. He taught by word of mouth and nothing written by him has survived. There is very little evidence about him outside the gospels, which concentrate on his brief public career and were put together between about forty and seventy years after his death. Though based on earlier traditions and the memories of people who knew him, they were not written as impartial biographies but for missionary purposes, to convey the Christian view of his character and teaching. Very different interpretations of Jesus can be drawn from or read into the New Testament.

Jesus is the Greek form of the common Hebrew name Yeshua or Joshua, which means 'Yahweh helps'. He grew up in a Jewish family at Nazareth in northern Palestine, with several brothers and sisters. His mother's name was Miriam (Mary) and his reputed father was Joseph. According to the gospels, his real father was God, but later Jewish opponents of Christianity said that he was the bastard son of a Roman soldier. Joseph was a carpenter and Jesus followed the same trade.

Jesus was presumably given the normal religious training of a Jewish

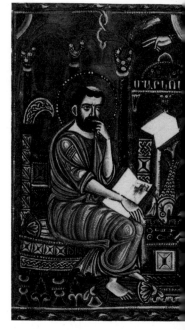

ABOVE St Mark, from an Armenian edition of the gospels, 14th century. The guiding hand of God, in the top right corner, has two fingers extended, presumably because Mark is the second gospel. The fish was employed as a symbol of Christ from very early on because the letters of *ichthus*, 'fish' in Greek, can be used as the initial letters of the Greek phrase 'Jesus Christ, Son of God, Saviour'.

RIGHT The Adoration of the Magi, by Hieronymous Bosch, in the Église Collegiale, Anderlecht. The visit of the three magi, or kings, was interpreted as the three parts of the known world doing homage to the infant Jesus. One of the conventional divisions of the world was Africa, hence the convention that one of the kings was black.

AMBVLANS IHC IVXTA MARE GALILEAE·
VIDIT DVOS FRS· PETRVM ET ANDREAM ET
VOCAVIT EOS· AT ILLI RELICTIS RETIBVS SECV
TI SVNT EVM·

ET PCEDENS INDE· VIDIT ALIOS
DVOS FRS· IACOBVM ET IOHANNE
CVM ZEBEDEO PATRE· ET VOCAVIT
EOS· ET RELICTIS RETIBVS ET PATRE
SECVTI SVNT EVM

LEFT Jesus gathering his first disciples among the fishermen on the Sea of Galilee, from a German Bible, 11th century. Jesus, whose halo contains the cross, is seen twice. As described in the gospel of Matthew, he first calls Peter and Andrew, and then James and John, who are in the boat with their father, Zebedee.

boy at home and in the synagogue. When he was in his thirties he emerged from obscurity in Nazareth into a public career as a teacher and healer, and between one and three years later he was dead. For most of this time he moved about in the area near the Sea of Galilee, speaking in the synagogues and also in the open air in the countryside. He gathered a group of disciples and a motley crowd of admirers; one of the things that surprised people about him was his indifference to class distinctions and his sympathy for social outcasts. The gospels stress the effects in drawing people to him of his authoritative and mysterious personality, his deceptively simple but profound parables and his apparently supernatural powers of healing.

Finally Jesus went to Jerusalem for the Passover and entered the city with his followers hailing him as the Messiah. Infuriated by finding traders chaffering in the Temple precincts, which was a source of income to the Temple, he assaulted them. He was soon arrested as a troublemaker by the Jewish authorities and handed over to the Roman governor, Pontius Pilate, as a rebel against Roman authority, a would-be king of the Jews. Pilate found him guilty and had him crucified outside the walls of the city.

The next episode of the story, the Resurrection, is the cornerstone on which the whole of Christianity rests. On the third day after his death in agony on the cross, Jesus came back to life. He was seen by various of his followers, though by no one who was not a follower, and he was last seen ascending into the sky.

It is unlikely that the disciples made this story up and then stuck to it through humiliation, persecution and sometimes a painful death. They evidently had experiences in which they saw Jesus still alive. Whatever may be thought of the validity of these experiences, they convinced those who

ABOVE Jesus enters Jerusalem, from a 13th-century French manuscript. According to the gospels, Jesus rode into the city on an ass, in fulfillment of an Old Testament prophecy that the Messiah would appear mounted on an ass.

The Resurrection is the cornerstone on which the whole of Christianity rests. This ivory panel, about 400, shows an angel telling the astonished women that Jesus has risen from the tomb. Above, Jesus is shown being pulled up into heaven by God, while one disciple hides his face and the other is astounded.

had them that Jesus had risen from death. Jesus's followers had already identified him as the expected Messiah, before his execution, and they now concluded that he had indeed been the Messiah, tragically unrecognized by his own people, but bringing a true message of the approaching kingdom of God.

Jesus himself was not a philosopher or a theologian and he was not given to precision of utterance. His sayings are frequently mysterious and sometimes mutually contradictory. His followers found him both fascinating and puzzling, and what he thought about himself is a mystery. Nowhere is he quoted making a plain and unambiguous statement that he was divine. The sayings which seem most clearly to imply it – 'I and the Father are one', for instance, and 'I am the way, the truth and the life' – come from the latest of the gospels, John, and may represent later Christian belief rather than Jesus's own belief.

Jesus may have thought that he was the Messiah, though a different kind of Messiah from the all-conquering king of popular expectation, and identification of him as the Messiah did not in current Jewish terms mean that he was divine. He sometimes called himself 'the Son of Man', a title which earlier writers had given the Messiah, but he also spoke as if the Son of Man were someone else. When the impetuous disciple Peter burst out with the words, 'You are the Messiah', Jesus in characteristically enigmatic fashion neither accepted nor rejected the title, but told the disciples not to use it in anyone else's hearing (Mark, chapter 8). He may perhaps have been less certain of his own role than his followers have been. At the end he foresaw his own death and believed that in some way his blood would be 'poured out for many' (Mark, chapter 14).

The message which Jesus did proclaim, repeatedly, was that the kingdom of God was near and that people should prepare themselves to belong to it by repentance and single-minded devotion to God. Again, however, what exactly Jesus meant by the kingdom is not at all clear. The hope that God would soon free his people from foreign domination, humble their enemies and inaugurate a glorious reign on earth was common currency in Palestine at the time, but it took several different forms. Some hoped for the arrival of the Messiah as their leader and king. The Zealots wanted a rising which would oust the Romans, but although at least one of the disciples was a Zealot, Jesus took an entirely different line. He does not seem to have conceived of the kingdom in political terms at all, but more as the reign of God in human hearts, and it was this kind of kingdom, perhaps, which he saw himself ushering in as the Messiah.

Saint Paul

After the Resurrection, the centre of the new sect was at Jerusalem. Led by Peter and the other disciples, the Nazarenes, as they were disapprovingly called, did not think of themselves as pioneers of a religion distinct from Judaism but as devout Jews. They worshipped in the Temple and observed Jewish law. They preserved their solidarity as a group by meeting in private homes to eat together. This was the origin of the early Christian *agape*, or 'love-feast', a meal that commemorated the last supper which Jesus had eaten with his disciples before his arrest, when he had told them to break bread and drink wine together in his memory.

There is unfortunately extremely little reliable evidence about the beliefs of the Jerusalem Christians, but they seem to have been confident that Jesus was the Messiah, that God would shortly establish his kingdom, which would vindicate Jesus, and that God had meantime infused them with his Spirit, to guide them. They had some notable successes in healing in the name of Jesus and they made converts, but they also aroused fierce hostility. The leaders were imprisoned more than once and one, Stephen, was stoned to death by an angry mob.

The situation was transformed by the arrival on the scene of Paul of Tarsus, the most remarkable figure after Jesus himself in the history of Christianity and the architect of the religion as it is known today. Described as short, bald and bow-legged, Paul was a man of volcanic energy, hot-blooded enthusiasm and indefatigable persistence. Brought up in a prosperous Jewish family outside Palestine, in the Greek city of Tarsus in Asia Minor, he was a zealous Jew thoroughly trained in the Torah, but he spoke Greek and he was better educated and altogether more formidably equipped intellectually than the disciples in Jerusalem. He had never met Jesus and he detested the Nazarenes and energetically persecuted them until, on his way from Jerusalem to Damascus, he had a vision of Jesus which left him blind for three days and changed his life.

This experience convinced Paul that Jesus had risen from death, and in time it persuaded him of a good deal more. He felt that he was as much an apostle or 'messenger' of Jesus as those in Jerusalem; that Jesus had been revealed to him as the divine Saviour of the whole world; and that it was his special mission to carry the message to the Gentiles, the non-Jews. For the rest of his life he carried out his mission in defiance of opposition, dangers and hardships, travelling to Syria, Cyprus, Asia Minor and Greece, founding Gentile Christian communities in the cities, revisiting them, advising them in letters and maintaining his personal authority over them. All this zealous activity by a former enemy was not entirely to the liking of the leaders in Jerusalem. They doubted whether Gentiles should be admitted to the flock at all and, when they conceded that, there was a serious dispute over the Jewish law. The Jerusalem leaders, who regarded their movement as true Judaism, thought that Gentile converts must be circumcised and should observe the dietary rules and all the other prescriptions of the law. Paul vigorously opposed this requirement, which would drastically have reduced the number of converts. He had his way and the effect was to detach the Christian movement from Judaism and turn it into a separate religion.

Paul seems to have been the first to formulate the central distinctive doctrine of Christianity by proclaiming Jesus not as the Messiah of the Jews but as God, who came to earth in the person of his Son to die for the salvation of the world. This is disputed, however, by those who believe that the Jerusalem Christians were already teaching the same thing. The difficulty is created by the discrepancy between the Paul we see in his letters

St Paul, from a 12th-century mural in the Lagoudera monastery, Cyprus. An early apocryphal book, the *Acts of Paul*, describes the apostle to the Gentiles as a short man with bow legs, thinning hair, a hooked nose and joining eyebrows. The description may be based on an actual memory of Paul, the most influential figure after Jesus himself in the entire history of Christianity.

and the Paul of the Acts of the Apostles, who might almost be two different people. The Acts of the Apostles was written later and apparently attempted to cover up sharp disagreements between Paul and his opponents in the movement.

The type of Christianity which Paul preached could not be accepted by any Jew who remained within Judaism. Not only did he make disparaging remarks about the Jewish law, but to proclaim the Messiah as a second God was, from the Jewish point of view, a gross breach of monotheism. Paul did not go quite so far, but he went far enough for Jews to condemn him bitterly as an apostate, and Jewish feeling against him is not dead to this day. Paul said that Christ was the Son of God, not as a literal fact of family relationship but as a metaphor. Christ was the Son possessed of all the power and majesty of the Father, the ruler of all creation, at whose name every knee should bow. Paul never cleared up the ambiguities involved and spoke sometimes as if the Father and the Son were identical and sometimes as if they were separate.

The apostle to the Gentiles was not primarily interested in the human Jesus of Nazareth he had never known, but in the divine figure who had commissioned him. He thought that the old covenant, the agreement and special relationship between God and Jewry, had been cancelled when the Jews rejected Christ. There was now a new dispensation or a 'new testament'. The Christians were now the true Israel and Jewishness was no longer required. In his death and resurrection, in an astonishing act of divine favour and grace, Christ had rescued mankind from evil and death, reconciled man with God and brought all human beings the possibility of living for ever. If he identified himself with Christ, the Christian would triumph over evil and death as Christ himself had done.

Belief that immortality could be achieved through identification with a god was already flourishing in the Roman world, in Mithraism and other esoteric cults with a limited membership and complicated initiation rituals. The main reasons for the rapid spread of Christianity were probably its conviction of the supreme love and self-sacrifice of God and its offer of immortality to everyone, rich and poor, educated and ignorant, male and female, master and slave, through belief in a Saviour who was not a figure of remote antiquity but who had recently lived and died among men.

Identification with Christ meant faith in him and personal commitment to him, which Paul regarded as more important than 'good works'. Good moral behaviour was required of the Christian, certainly, but Paul was convinced that sinfulness was endemic in human beings and that no human effort by itself could rescue men and women from human nature. Identification with Christ also meant being part of the Christian community, which was the 'body' of Christ on earth, so that to belong to it was to be 'in Christ'. Initiation was by baptism, which symbolically assimilated the novice Christian to the Lord's death and resurrection. Submerged naked in the water, the novice 'died' and then 'rose again', spiritually clean and transformed.

Paul was also convinced that the Lord would come back to the earth, not this time in a humble home in Nazareth but in glory, to destroy every other

Allegory of baptism and the Mass, from a German Bible, about 1000. In the centre the Christian is assimilated to Christ's death and resurrection through immersion in and raising from the water of baptism. At the top, the Christian is again identified with Christ through drinking the Communion wine, which is the blood of the crucified Saviour.

power and authority. The Second Coming, which was again a totally un-Jewish concept, was expected at any moment. Meanwhile, Christians should stay as they were and not waste effort trying to improve their social condition. Nor was there any need to produce children when the world was about to come to an end. Paul himself had no sexual relationships and would have preferred everyone else to be like him, but he did reluctantly concede that it was better for the faithful to marry than to burn with unsatisfied desire.

When Christians gathered to worship, their meetings tended to be lively, noisy and disorganized because they believed themselves to be infused with God's Spirit. People would break into spontaneous prayer or 'prophesying', which meant delivering a message inspired by the Spirit, or they would speak or sing in unintelligible languages, known as 'speaking in tongues', which others would be inspired to interpret. There would often be several worshippers talking and singing at once. Although Paul was no stranger to ecstatic experience himself, he disapproved of the confusion and said that outsiders would think the Christians were mad. Some outsiders did think so, but ecstatic behaviour is contagious and it probably helped to make converts.

The most important Christian ritual, apparently, was the Lord's Supper, which through breaking of bread and drinking of wine commemorated Jesus's last supper with his disciples. This was part of the love-feast, or common meal, but gradually became distinct from it. The meaning and effect of the Lord's Supper has remained a matter of profound disagreement between Christians, but in Paul's time it was more than a simple act of remembrance. It enshrined a mystery and before long, if not already, only baptized Christians in good standing were allowed to take part, which prompted accusations of cannibalism among pagans who heard that the Christians secretly feasted on someone's body and blood. Paul regarded the ceremony as a method of identification with the Lord in his death and resurrection, a participation or communion in the body and blood of Christ.

In about the year AD 58 Paul returned to Jerusalem, where he was arrested as a troublemaker by the Roman authorities and, being a Roman citizen, appealed to Caesar. He was sent to Rome, where there was a thriving Christian community, though no one knows how it started. He lived there under house arrest for two years and whether he ever left Rome again is uncertain. He was perhaps in his sixties at this time. According to an old and probably reliable tradition, Peter was also in Rome and the two apostles were martyred during a fierce persecution initiated by the Emperor Nero, when some Christians were torn to pieces by dogs, some were crucified and some were tied to crosses and burned as living torches to illuminate an entertainment in Nero's gardens. Peter is believed to be buried beneath the high altar of St Peter's, Rome, and Paul on the site of St Paul Outside the Walls.

The Jerusalem Christian leaders had retained great prestige and influence in the movement, but within a few years the Jerusalem community was obliterated during the Zealot revolt and the Roman siege and sack of the city. Jewish Christianity lost its headquarters and its source of authority. It was Paul's Christianity which survived. The four gospels, which were produced in the Gentile communities and whose message would eventually be carried to millions, fused Paul's belief in the divine Saviour with traditions of the Jesus the disciples had known. Paul has been attacked for submerging the simple precepts of Jesus under torrents of a difficult theology which sometimes offends modern liberal humanitarianism. But the supposed simplicity of Jesus is more apparent than real and, without Paul, it is difficult to see how Christianity could have made any mark on the world. Without Paul, we would scarcely have heard of Jesus at all.

The Growth of the Church

When Paul died, Christianity was an obscure, eccentric sect, disliked or more often ignored by its contemporaries. By the year 200 there were Christians in every province of the Roman Empire and the faith had begun to spread outside the empire. By 300 there were more Christians than Jews, and by 400 Christianity was the official religion of the Roman state. The principal early centres were in Rome, in the eastern Mediterranean area at Alexandria and Antioch and in Asia Minor, and at Carthage in North Africa.

A cross from Corinth, 3rd century. The cross was a symbol of the Christian faith from very early in the history of the Church because the heart of the Christian message was that God had sacrificed himself on the cross for all mankind. The peacocks stand for immortality, because of the old belief that the bird's flesh did not decay.

The time was ripe for the rise of a new popular religion. Rome had swallowed up independent states and urbanization concentrated people in cities, making the individual feel small, lost and helpless. Cosmopolitanism and increased social and physical mobility caused restlessness and anxiety. Old institutions, old gods, old rituals seemed outworn and there was a demand for a more direct, personal and certain relationship with the divine than the established cults could supply. This demand Christianity met, especially in the cities, where it was most acute. The new religion was so much an urban phenomenon in its early days that *paganus*, the Latin word for a countryman, came to mean an unbeliever.

Not that the Christian path to power was strewn with roses. Down into the early fourth century there were outbreaks of intensive persecution, because Christians refused to sully themselves with the Roman state religion, the cult of the emperor as divine, which the authorities considered vital to the cohesion of the empire. In the face of persecution some Christians gave way and some died bravely for their beliefs, but not only was there external opposition, there were also enemies within. The faithful disagreed violently with each other over their doctrines, because the concept of Christ as the Son of God in human form raised formidable intellectual difficulties. Believing that they were informed by the Holy Spirit, Christians inherited the Old Testament prophets' conviction of possessing the truth direct from God. It was in this conviction, after all, that they made converts from the pagan cults and their certainty of their own rightness made them highly intolerant.

Almost every disputing faction could find a warrant for its opinions somewhere in St Paul, including people of gnostic inclination, and varieties of gnostic Christianity developed. Gnosticism (from Greek *gnosis*, 'knowledge') was a current of ideas centred round the belief that the human body and the material world are evil, the prison of the immortal soul. Gnostic Christians denounced the god of the Old Testament as the evil creator of the prison. They could not accept that he had sent the Saviour or that the Saviour had been human. Christ's body and his suffering on the cross must have been illusory. These beliefs subverted the central Christian doctrine that the Father had sent the Son to redeem humanity by becoming human. Mainstream Christians were outraged and the ominous word heresy was first used against the gnostic sects.

These early wranglings implanted in the Christian movement a lasting conviction of the dangers of unrestrained individualism. The expected Second Coming of Christ did not materialize and Christians, it began to seem, might have to live in the world for many generations. Harassed from outside and threatened with chaos within, the movement needed order and discipline. Order required authority, and authority required conformity. The distinctive ideas and institutions of Christianity took shape in response to the need for order, prominent among them the Church. The word comes from Greek *kyriakon*, meaning 'belonging to the Lord'. It was used for the buildings in which Christians worshipped, but it also meant the whole community of orthodox Christians forming the 'body' of Christ on earth. The term Catholic Church, meaning both universal and orthodox, was in use by the second century. Since numerous different groups of Christians have classified themselves as orthodox, there has been more than one Church, but there has also been a persistent feeling that there ought not to be more than one, and most Christians have always thought it essential to belong to a Church as a source of authority.

Anyone who is outside the Church is in spiritual danger, and in the past might well be in physical danger as well. This was especially the case if he was not an unbeliever, a pagan living in lamentable error, but a Christian of a different persuasion. This Christian was a heretic, a wilful perverter of the truth. For his own sake and that of others whom he might infect he must either be won back to orthodoxy or stamped out. Linked to the old Jewish principle of the holy war, the concept of heresy has been responsible for much cruelty and suffering.

The early campaigns against deviationism raised the whole question of where authority was to be found, to which the natural answer was in the teachings of the apostles, the earliest messengers of the faith, commissioned by Christ himself. To controvert the gnostics a statement of fundamental beliefs was worked out, which was called the Apostles' Creed. Numerous books were in circulation claiming to have been written by one apostle or another, but often tainted with gnosticism. A canon of orthodox scripture was needed and by about AD 250 the New Testament in its present form was widely accepted. Christians share with Jews and Muslims a reverence for scripture and, until recently at least, they also shared the belief that those who wrote the scriptures were inspired by God.

At the same time, in response to the need for authority, the Church began to develop a hierarchical structure unparalleled in other religions.

The bishop (in Greek *episkopos*, 'superintendent') was the leader and spiritual ruler of a group of local congregations. The theory grew up that the apostles had appointed bishops as their successors, who had been succeeded by other bishops in an unbroken chain of apostolic authority. Below the bishop someone was needed to conduct the services and supervise each local congregation, and he required a source for his authority. It came to him from the apostles, and so ultimately from Christ, by way of the bishop who ordained him. By 200 there was a clear distinction between the priest (from Greek *presbyteros*, 'elder') and the layman, one by-product of which was to give priests a certain magical mystique among the laity.

The monastery of St George at Wadi Kelt. Monks lived under a rule which prescribed regular services and set periods for prayer, work, meals and sleep. Ideally, the monastic life was calm, God-centred and largely free of personal responsibility for survival. It was only in an organized and disciplined community that the ideal had any hope of realization.

The temptation of St Antony, by Martin Schongauer. The saint, a desert hermit of the 4th century, was famous for the attacks made on him by demons in grotesque and monstrous forms. Christianity grew up in a hostile world and Christians believed that the resistance and persecution they encountered were inspired by evil supernatural forces, the legions of the Devil.

OVERLEAF The Trinity with saints, by Pesellino, 15th century. The Father stands behind the cross on which the Son hangs, and the dove of the Holy Spirit perches above the Son's head. The concept of three 'persons' in one God raised formidable intellectual difficulties, especially in defining the relationship between the Father and the Son. Some Christians broke away and formed separate Churches because they could not accept the majority position.

The bishops began to meet, in synods or councils, to regulate the affairs of the Church and to decide what was or was not orthodox. After the destruction of Jerusalem, Rome as the capital of the empire was the chief centre of Christianity, and in time the bishop of Rome claimed to be the head of the Church as the successor of Peter.

With the need for authority and conformity, the ecstatic praying and prophesying and speaking in tongues of the early congregations grew increasingly suspect, and by the Middle Ages behaviour of this kind was no longer believed to be inspired by the Spirit but was put down to the sinister influence of the Devil. Christian services became orderly and followed set patterns of Bible readings, prayers, psalms, hymns and a sermon, which owed much to the pattern of worship in the Jewish synagogues. The sabbath for Christians was not Saturday, as for Jews, but Sunday, the day of the Resurrection. The two major festivals of the year were Easter, celebrating the Crucifixion and Resurrection, which replaced the Jewish Passover, and Christmas, celebrating the birth of Christ.

Partly in reaction against the growing authority of the Church, from late in the third century Christian ascetics retreated into the Egyptian and Syrian deserts, where remote from the bustle of the world they could live close to God in prayer and meditation, poverty and chastity. St Antony of Egypt became famous for the attacks made on him by hordes of evil spirits in monstrous forms, which supplied a favourite theme for painters. St Simeon Stylites lived austerely for forty years on top of a column sixty feet high in the mountains outside Antioch, but most of the ascetics clustered together in small groups. Communities grew up which followed a common pattern of life, or 'rule', with regular services and periods for prayer, and compulsory manual labour for the community's support. The traditions of Indian asceticism and the Buddhist monks may have influenced these communities, which were the first Christian monasteries. Basil the Great, bishop of Caesarea in Asia Minor, drew up the rule which is still the basis of the monastic life in the Eastern Orthodox Church. During the fourth century the monastic movement spread to the whole Roman world from the eastern deserts to Britain. A life of poverty and self-denial in concentration on God and seclusion from the world became an admired pattern of Christian holiness.

The Triumph of Christianity

Christianity found its first imperial patron in Constantine the Great. His mother Helena was a Christian and was believed to have been divinely guided to find the true cross, on which Christ died, at Jerusalem. Constantine himself seems to have blended Christian and pagan beliefs in a way which was probably common at the time, but he insisted on official toleration of Christianity and built churches in his new eastern capital of Byzantium or Constantinople (modern Istanbul). It was he who summoned a council of bishops at Nicaea in Asia Minor to resolve the Arian controversy.

To outsiders, the Christians appeared to have three gods, the Father, the Son and the Holy Spirit. Christians, however, regarded themselves as monotheists, worshipping the Trinity of three 'persons' in one God. This is not an easy concept to grasp, and it raised awkward questions. An Alexandrian priest named Arius argued that the Father must have existed before the Son and that the Son could not therefore be eternal and the Father's equal. His opponents, led by the formidable bishop of Alexandria, Athanasius, said that this would not do because if Christ was not fully God the salvation of believers who identified themselves with Christ was not assured. The bishops at Nicaea decided that Arius was a heretic and that the Son was 'true God' and 'of the same substance with the Father'. Constantine sent Arius into exile and ordered the burning of his books. The Church was now able to have heresy punished by the state.

The Arian heresy was by no means dead, but towards the end of the century the Emperor Theodosius the Great, a redoubtable soldier and a convinced Christian, made Catholic, non-Arian Christianity the official religion of the empire. He penalized the Arians and banned all the pagan cults. With his encouragement, bands of zealous Christians demolished and defaced pagan temples, sanctuaries and images.

Only a minority of Theodosius's subjects were Christians, but the support of the state was decisive and during the next hundred years the bulk of the empire's population became at least nominally Christian. The Germanic peoples of the north, who infiltrated the empire, adopted Christianity and so did the Celts in Britain and Ireland. From the sixth century missionaries began the conversion of the Slavs, and eventually all Europe would consist of Christian kingdoms.

Christianity had now formed the alliance with the state that has both sustained it and dogged it ever since. The state was influenced by Christian principles and society improved by Christian ethics, but at the same time the Church inevitably grew more worldly and more pagan. Greatly though the faith was strengthened in numbers, the mass of pagan converts brought their own mental furniture with them. The Church's sensible response was to absorb and Christianize pagan beliefs and practices, but the process worked both ways. Festivals and customs intended to promote fertility and prosperity became part of the Christian year, but retained much of their pagan and magical feeling. The worship of pagan gods was forbidden, but polytheism crept in by the back door. Christianity's lack of a bountiful and protective mother-goddess was repaired at the popular level by the cult of the Virgin Mary. Christian saints and martyrs were prayed to for help in everyday life, virtually as godlings, though theologians always distinguished the veneration properly due to the Virgin and the saints from the worship due to the Trinity. Relics of Christ, the Virgin and the saints were regarded by many ordinary Christians as objects containing supernatural magical power and there was a brisk trade in bits and pieces of martyrs' bodies, the Virgin's chemises and fragments of the true cross. Pictures of Jesus, the Virgin or a favourite saint have an honoured place in many Roman Catholic households to this day, in something of the same way as images of deities are kept in oriental homes.

LEFT The Assumption of the Virgin, by Matteo di Giovanni, 15th century. In the foreground is St Thomas. According to legend, Doubting Thomas opened Mary's grave. He found it empty and saw a vision of her rising into the sky.

LEFT St Helena carrying the true cross, from Luttrell's Psalter, 1340. The Empress Helena was believed to have found the cross on which Christ died.

ABOVE Clergy exhibiting relics of the Crucifixion to the emperor at Constantinople, Flemish manuscript, early 15th century. Relics of Christ, the Virgin and the saints were naturally treated with reverence by Christians, and at popular levels they were credited with magical powers.

From Augustine to the Crusades

Meanwhile, gnosticism had raised its head again in the form of Manichaeism, a religion founded in the third century by a Persian, Mani, who believed that God had commissioned him as a prophet. He thought that the same truths were to be found in the teachings of Jesus, Zoroaster and the Buddha, but had been misunderstood. His system combined the gnostic conviction of the evilness of matter and the human body with the Zoroastrian dualism of two great forces of light and darkness, good and evil, at work in the world. To escape from the grip of evil and matter, rigorous asceticism, vegetarianism and abstention from sex were required of the elite of his followers, though the demands on ordinary believers were much less severe. In time there were small groups of Manichees from Spain and France across North Africa and the Middle East to Central Asia and China. The religion did not survive, but Manichaean ideas influenced various medieval heresies.

Christianity is not a dualistic religion, in theory at least, and Manichaeism contradicted the Christian principle of the goodness of the world which was created by God. On the other hand, there is a world-rejecting, body-hating and sex-fearing strain in Christianity, and a powerful intellectual impulse was given to it by Augustine, bishop of Hippo in North Africa, author of the *Confessions* and the *City of God*, and the most influential theologian of the western Church. As a young man he was for several years a Manichee. He returned to Christianity, in which he had been brought up, when a child's voice directed him, as he believed, to a passage in St Paul: 'But put on the Lord Jesus Christ, and make no provision for the flesh, to satisfy its desires' (Romans, chapter 13).

The text is significant, because Augustine was troubled by the flesh and its desires. Introspection persuaded him that human nature is shot through with depravity and he was the effective founder of the doctrine of 'original sin', that all human beings are tainted with sinfulness from birth. He saw a yawning gulf between tarnished humanity and God, which could not be crossed by any human effort but only by the grace of God, freely given, a grace which God does not confer on everyone. If goodness could be achieved by human effort, there would be no need for Christ and no need for the Church. The effect was to strengthen the belief that only through the Church could man find salvation and that all those outside the Church were lost souls, condemned to hell. Augustine also had a lasting influence on Christian attitudes to sex. He considered the procreation of children to be the only proper purpose of sex and he disapproved of the excitement of animal passion in which human beings lose control of themselves. He provided a warrant for the exaltation of virginity as a virtue, for the rule that priests must be celibate and for Roman Catholic teaching on sex and contraception in marriage.

In the east, disputes about the divine and human nature of Christ caused serious splits in the unity of the Church. The Monophysites claimed that Christ was far more divine than he was human. Condemned as heretics, though otherwise orthodox in their teachings, they survive today in the Coptic Churches of Egypt and Ethiopia, the Jacobite Church of Syria and the Armenian Church. Among the theologians who opposed them was Nestorius, briefly bishop of Constantinople in the fifth century, who believed there were two different persons in Christ, one divine and one human. This view was also condemned as heretical, the majority view being that Christ was truly God and truly man, in one person. The Nestorians broke away in their turn and Nestorian Christianity in time gathered a considerable following in Syria, Mesopotamia, Iran, India and China, and survives today in Iran.

When imperial power collapsed in the west and the empire was splintered into Germanic kingdoms, the Church was the only unifying institution left, through which order and efficient administration could be maintained. Bishops and clergy took an important part in the running of the new kingdoms, acquiring much of the secular power of the previous Roman officials, and the western Church with its headquarters at Rome inherited the tradition and something of the mystique of ancient Rome. The bishop of Rome, the pope or 'father', as heir of the emperors, claimed to be the supreme spiritual authority in Christendom.

The churches of the eastern empire with their political and religious centre at Constantinople, where an emperor still ruled, were ready to honour Rome as the see of Peter, but not to grant more than that. The effective head of the eastern Church was the emperor and the patriarch of Constantinople was the senior bishop, but no eastern bishop claimed supreme authority over his colleagues. With political unity broken, the Greek-speaking east and the Latin-speaking west went their separate ways. Relations between the two Churches steadily worsened, though the final split did not occur until the eleventh century, when the pope excommunicated the patriarch of Constantinople.

The seventh century brought the thunderclap of the rise of Islam. About half the territory of Christendom was overrun as Arab armies conquered North Africa, Spain and much of the Byzantine east. Christian communities survived under Muslim rule, but they lost the support of the state and with it much of their vitality. In 718 Constantinople itself was besieged, but the Byzantine Empire held fast for another seven centuries. In the west the threat that western Europe might fall to Islam receded after the Frankish leader Charles Martel defeated the Arabs at Poitiers in 732, though it was to take hundreds of years to win Spain back from the Muslims.

Charlemagne, Charles Martel's grandson, was crowned emperor in Rome by Pope Leo III, but the western Roman empire was dead and, after many vicissitudes, the attempt to resuscitate it as the Holy Roman Empire was a failure. Europe became a patchwork of small states. The Church, however, was international and the nearest thing to a western emperor for the next five hundred years was the pope. The authoritarian tendency in the Church grew even stronger and papal claims rose to new heights. In the ninth century the papacy declared itself to be *caput totius orbis*, 'head of the whole world'. Pope Gregory VII, one of the most formidable of the many formidable men who have occupied the chair of Peter, pronounced that kings were as much representatives of the Church as bishops and should be equally subject to papal authority.

The mouth of hell, from the Winchester Psalter. Hell is the polar opposite of heaven, dark, flame-streaked, pain-wracked, cacophonous, desolate, the kingdom of the Evil One. Here its entrance is the gaping jaw of Leviathan, the titanic sea monster which battled with God in the Old Testament.

RIGHT Interior of the Benedictine abbey church of La Madeleine, Vézelay, France. The Last Judgement is carved in the arch as both a promise and a warning to the faithful. The figure of Christ as Judge towers over the scene. To his left an angel sounds the last trumpet, to his right St Peter holds the keys of heaven and hell.

The effort to establish a theocracy, the rule of God administered by priests, necessarily entangled popes and bishops in the labyrinth of contemporary politics, but at the same time the quiet, contemplative life was flourishing in the great Benedictine monasteries. The Benedictines, called 'black monks' after their black robes, followed the rule drawn up by St Benedict, who had founded the famous monastery at Monte Cassino, between Rome and Naples, in the sixth century. A monk normally remained a monk for life. The round of poverty, chastity and obedience to his superiors which he shared with his brethren was austere but not ferociously ascetic. Each day was parcelled out between services in the church, private prayer and meditation, work in the house or the fields, meals and sleep. Ideally, life was calm, God-centred and largely free of personal responsibility for survival. It was only in an organized community with reasonably strict discipline that such an ideal had any hope of realization.

The monasteries had much to do with spreading Christian principles among the people at large. Many of them were in or close to centres of population and they cared for the sick, helped the poor, taught children, provided lodging for travellers and gave an example of Christian goodness in action. They were also centres of learning, the arts and efficient agriculture. Through gifts from appreciative laymen they acquired estates, tied labourers and commercial interests; successive reform movements were required to keep these valuable properties true to spiritual aims and out of the hands of predatory landowners, lay and ecclesiastical. During one of these waves of reform, in the late eleventh century, the Cistercian order was founded in France. The Cistercians or 'white monks' put a greater stress on poverty, simplicity and austerity than the Benedictines. Their monasteries were in remote places and they were successful land-reclaimers and farmers.

The northern European peoples, the Norse and the English, were converted to Christianity by the Roman Church. The Eastern or Orthodox Church carried the faith to the peoples of the Balkans and Russia, where a bridgehead was won with the conversion of Prince Vladimir of Kiev and his marriage to a Byzantine princess. On its eastern front, however, the Byzantine Empire was menaced by the Seljuq Turks, who overran most of Asia Minor. They had already taken Palestine and Syria and they made life difficult for pilgrims visiting the Christian holy places in Jerusalem. In 1095, in response to an appeal from the Byzantine emperor, Pope Urban II proclaimed a holy war against Islam, a great campaign under the emblem of the white cross to recover the Holy Land from the infidel.

The pope's appeal found an emotional and enthusiastic response from European fighting-men, who could now put their skill in war and their appetite for it at the service of God, with the Church's promise that anyone who was killed had a passport to heaven. Muslim warriors were encouraged by the same promise on their side. The first crusade fought its way bravely across Syria and Palestine to storm Jerusalem in 1099. The crusading leaders carved out small principalities for themselves, including a kingdom of Jerusalem, but their position was precarious. Numerous other crusades set off to their aid during the next two centuries. Valuable commercial interests were involved and the fourth crusade, in 1204, so far forgot itself as to go nowhere near the Holy Land but capture and plunder Constantinople instead and set a western adventurer, Count Baldwin of Flanders, on the Byzantine imperial throne. In 1212 thousands of children in France flocked to follow a shepherd boy on crusade. They were kindly transported to Alexandria by traders, who then sold them all into slavery. A similar episode in Germany, when children followed a leader on crusade, left behind it nothing but the legend of the Pied Piper.

In the end the Muslims recaptured Jerusalem and the Greeks recovered

The crusaders storm and capture Jerusalem, from William of Tyre's *History*, late 13th century. Scenes from Christ's passion are enacted in the church. At the top left is the Ascension, with Christ vanishing into a cloud, and at the bottom left is the death of the Virgin Mary.

RIGHT St Basil's Cathedral, Moscow. The earliest Christian churches were purely functional buildings in which congregations met to worship. In time they became far more elaborate and symbolic, the domes of eastern churches conveying the idea of the divine descending upon the world and transforming it.

their empire. The crusades petered out. The papacy had hoped for a reunion of the western and eastern Churches, but mutual suspicion and incomprehension went too deep.

The Friars, the Inquisition and the Mass

The western and eastern Churches were separated from each other by various points of doctrine and practice besides the question of the supremacy of Rome. The east, for instance, did not believe in purgatory, did not require all priests to be celibate and baptized by complete immersion in water instead of by pouring. More fundamental were differences of attitude. Very broadly speaking, the west tended to emphasize man's sinfulness and the east man's potential goodness. The west saw Christ as the tortured victim sacrificed for man's sin, and the crucifix was its favourite symbol. The east saw Christ as the victor triumphing over evil and death, and preferred the empty cross. The west talked more of man's redemption through Christ, the east of man's deification through Christ. In the west orthodoxy meant right thinking, in the east it meant the right way of worshipping. The ceremonies of the Eastern Orthodox Church are long, elaborate and quite extraordinarily magnificent and colourful, as a revelation of the divine presence among men. The towers and spires of western churches expressed the idea of rising up from the dark earth and mortal clay to find safe harbour with God. The domes of eastern churches conveyed the idea of the divine descending upon and transforming the earth.

In the west, the papacy reached the summit of its temporal power under Pope Innocent III, who styled himself Vicar of Christ, God's deputy on earth. The bishops were kept under close control, recalcitrant kings were rapped sharply on the knuckles and England, Portugal and Sicily were for a time papal dependencies, technically at least. In reality, there was no theocracy, but Church and state were mutually dependent. The bishops were important state officials and the hierarchy was a ladder to secular as well as spiritual power, especially for those equipped for success by brains and determination but not by birth. The Church was bound up with the established order of society, which it regarded as the order established by God, and was as committed as any Confucian or orthodox Hindu to the principle that each person should keep to the station in life to which it had pleased God to call him. Any threat to the established order was seen as a threat to the Church, which had acquired great wealth and vast estates. It all seemed a far cry from the apostles and there were complaints that the Church had been corrupted by power and riches, and that it had failed to win many of its flock to a Christianity that went more than skin-deep.

One response was the emergence of a new kind of monastic order, the friars. They followed the pattern of communal monastic life with its ideals of poverty, chastity and service to God, but they went out to preach to all and sundry, especially in the cities. Living by begging, they were missionaries to the nominal Christians of western Europe. The two principal orders of friars were founded by St Francis of Assisi and

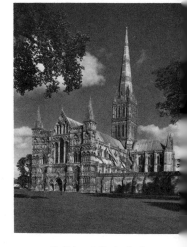

ABOVE Salisbury Cathedral, England, from the south-west. Most western churches are signs of the cross in stone, built to a cruciform ground plan, and their soaring arches, towers and spires express the idea of rising to heaven to find salvation and happiness with God.

RIGHT St Francis preaching to the birds, by Giotto. Francis of Assisi is the patron saint of animals, and his love of nature makes him an admired and attractive figure.

St Dominic. St Francis, whose gentleness and delight in nature make him an immensely attractive figure, was driven to a missionary life by hearing the voice of Christ commissioning him as he had commissioned the first disciples to preach repentance and the kingdom of God. St Dominic, a Spaniard, was sent on a mission to the Albigensian heretics in the south of France and decided that they were unlikely to be won back to the Church by mitred bishops and bejewelled clergy, and that a new preaching order was needed.

The Albigensians were strongly influenced by Manichaean ideas and regarded the Church as an engine of the Devil. When missions failed to persuade them of their errors, the sword of holy war was drawn against them in a ruthless 'crusade' launched by the papacy. They were slaughtered and subdued but their ideas were not extinguished and there were still hotbeds of heresy elsewhere in Europe. The Holy Office of the Inquisition was established to deal with the problem by Pope Gregory IX in 1233. Twenty years later, the Inquisition was permitted to use torture. Penalties ranged up to confiscation of property, imprisonment for life, and execution, usually by burning to death. The Church did not execute heretics itself, but handed them over to the laity for dispatch. Often, though not always, the condemned were mercifully strangled before their bodies were burned. Various nests of heresy were smoked out, but the more suspects the Inquisition tortured into confessing their guilt and naming their accomplices, the more heretics there seemed mysteriously to be. The Spanish Inquisition, which was peculiarly notorious, was not established until the fifteenth century, to deal with Jews and Muslims who had been forcibly converted to Christianity and whose sincerity was in doubt.

Dominican and Franciscan friars, valued for their learning and their skill in argument, played a prominent part in the Inquisition. Others put the same gifts at the service of Christian philosophy. As in Judaism, philosophers set out to demonstrate that the religion was right not only as a matter of faith but as a matter of reason. The greatest of them was an Italian Dominican, Thomas Aquinas, whose systematic Christian philosophy is the basis of Roman Catholic theology. A German Dominican, Meister Eckhart, explored the path to God through mystical experience, through turning inward to find the divine presence in oneself. Mysticism attracted other men and women in the later Middle Ages, but has never been a major factor in Christianity. The overwhelming majority of Christians have sought salvation through a Church, not through the solitary communings of the mystic.

If it seems astonishing that the Church which produced a Francis of Assisi, an Aquinas, an Eckhart, also created the Inquisition, it is essential to remember the conviction of churchmen that a heretic would burn in agony for ever in hellfire if he could not be recovered for the true faith. The medieval Christian afterworld had three main departments, which in theology were spiritual states or conditions, but which were popularly imagined as places. Christians of exceptional goodness would go to heaven. Unbelievers, heretics and Christians of exceptional wickedness would go to hell. The great majority of sinful but redeemable Christians would go to

TOP Christ gives the wine which is his blood to the eleven disciples, Judas having hurried away to betray him. 15th-century mural from a church in Cyprus.

ABOVE Pilgrims, from John Lydgate's *Troy Book*, 15th century. Pilgrimage to the tombs of famous saints and other sacred sites was a common medieval custom.

purgatory, where they would be painfully cleansed of their sinfulness to fit them for heaven. Prayers offered by the faithful on earth could help the dead through the punishments in purgatory. At the end of time Christ would come in majesty as both Judge and Saviour, the dead would be resurrected and all would be judged and sent finally to heaven or to hell.

Vivid pictures of the Last Judgement and hell were painted in churches as warnings and reminders. Presiding over hell was the grim and monstrous figure of the Devil. Christianity inherited Satan from Judaism, but he never played as important a role in Jewish belief as among Christians. Jewish thinkers were prepared to recognize, as monotheists, that the ultimate root of evil must lie in God, that good and evil were part of the divine ordering of the world. Christians tended to see the world in more dualistic terms, as the battlefield of contending forces of good and evil. They believed not only in God the Father but also in God the Son, who saved man from evil. If the Saviour was necessary, then the power of evil must clearly be formidable. Satan was not the equal of God, for God had no equal. He was the rebel against God, the arch-enemy of man, the inspiration of all evil and wrong. And since, as always, evil and wrong were everywhere apparent, the enemy's resources must be massive and his malice insatiable.

For many generations of Christians the Devil and the armies of demons under his command were an alarming reality. At the popular level, one of the most important functions of the Church was to provide magical protection against evil. Christians made the sign of the cross over themselves and their children, houses, cattle and crops to ward off disease, blight, unfavourable weather and every kind of misfortune, and for protection in moments of danger. They wore amulets inscribed with the cross or with gospel verses. Holy water, blessed by a priest, was taken home from church and sprinkled on the beds at night against the evil spirits that clustered in the dark.

Christians lived in districts called parishes, each with its priest and its church, where services were held, children were baptized, couples were married and the dead were buried. The parish church was often a general community centre, used for meetings, dancing, games and markets, so that the life of the congregation, individually and collectively, was closely linked with the church. The most important service remained the Lord's Supper or Mass. After 1215 it was official doctrine that the words and gestures of the priest 'transubstantiated' or transformed the bread and wine into Christ's body and blood, though they retained the outward appearance of bread and wine. Through consuming the Saviour's body the worshipper was identified and united with Christ. Mass was said in Latin, which most of the congregation and sometimes the priest himself could not understand, but the correct Latin words were considered essential to the efficacy of the rite.

Since Christ was present in the consecrated host, the Mass-bread, the custom grew up of keeping it on the altar in a transparent vessel for the adoration of the faithful. It could also be taken out of the church and round the district in procession, just as gods are carried in procession in oriental countries. Figures of Christ, the Virgin Mary and the saints were also carried in procession at festivals to bless the district with their presence. People made pilgrimages to sacred sites, to the shrines of St James at Compostela in Spain or Thomas Becket at Canterbury, to Rome, to the scenes of Jesus's life and death in the Holy Land, so that the inherent holiness and supernatural power in such places might, as it were, rub off on them.

The Protestant Reformation

Medieval Christianity had much to its credit as a powerful moral and civilizing force, a nourisher of art and learning, a fount of education, a comforter of the suffering, an ameliorator of misery in a harsh world, a source of spiritual security in this life and of a surer hope for a life after death. In the later Middle Ages, however, the ship of the Church sailed into heavy seas. The papacy's power and prestige dwindled with the emergence of France, England and Spain as nation-states, whose rulers were determined to control the ecclesiastical establishment in their own territories. The French went further and for almost seventy years in the fourteenth century held the papacy prisoner at Avignon. All the popes of this new 'Babylonian captivity' were French. When the last of them, Gregory XI, escaped from the gilded cage back to Rome there was a prolonged schism, with one succession of popes in Rome and another in Avignon, busily hurling anathemas at each other. At one point there were three different Vicars of Christ claiming the faithful's allegiance.

The Church was part of the established order of society, but the established order was breaking up and the Church was splintered with it. The old feudal system was crumbling, capitalism was on the march, familiar institutions were changing. The bounds of known geography were suddenly pressed back with the opening of the sea route to the East and the discovery of America, and the renaissance of interest in pagan classical literature, art and philosophy widened intellectual horizons. The consequence was widespread anxiety and unrest, sharpened by wars, famines and epidemics, including the terrifying pestilence called the Black Death. Insecurity, restlessness and dissatisfaction focused on both the social order and the Church. There were fierce peasant revolts. The wealth of the Church and its financial exactions were bitterly criticized. The hierarchy was accused of corruption and nepotism, the monasteries of luxury, sloth and vice, the clergy of immorality and spiritual inadequacy. There was growing scepticism about both the authority and the teaching of the Church.

Already in the fourteenth century John Wycliffe in England and John Huss in Bohemia (modern Czechoslovakia) maintained that anyone could understand the Bible by reading it for himself, with the guidance of the Holy Spirit, without needing the Church to interpret it for him. Wycliffe died peacefully in his bed, but Huss was tried by a Church council at Constance in Switzerland and burned alive as a heretic, and his followers were excommunicated. The invention of printing in the fifteenth century brought the Bible in the vernacular languages a far larger readership than

Badges were worn to show where a pilgrim had been, and like modern tourist resorts each place had its own badges and symbols. This badge of the Virgin and the angel Gabriel would have been worn by a pilgrim to Walsingham in Norfolk, where the Virgin was said to have appeared in the 11th century and commanded the building of a shrine.

Des Chur Fürsten zu Sachsen Friedrichs des Weisen Traum zu Schweinitz den 31 Octb 1517.

In 1517 Martin Luther nailed his Ninety-Five Theses on the door of the castle church at Wittenberg in Saxony. This painting by an unknown artist shows him writing on the door with an enormous pen after, in the background, receiving a ray of illumination directly from God on high. At the right he is being sheltered by the Elector Frederick of Saxony.

before and undermined the position of the Church as more and more Christians began to look to the Bible as the source of spiritual authority and doctrine. Printing also enabled the attackers and the defenders of the Church to disseminate their convictions widely in pamphlets and books, creating a ferment of conflicting opinions.

In the east, the Ottoman Turks were on the move. Constantinople was surrounded and the Ottoman armies pressed on into the Balkans. In 1453 Constantinople was attacked by an enormous army under Sultan Muhammad II. After a siege of seven weeks and a heroic resistance the historic city fell. The last of the Byzantine emperors, Constantine XI Palaeologus, died fighting. The great church of the Holy Wisdom, Santa Sophia, was turned into a mosque. The leadership of the eastern Church passed to Moscow, 'the third Rome'. By the early sixteenth century the Ottoman Empire had swallowed up Greece, the Balkans and Hungary. The sultans used the Church to control their Christian subjects, setting up patriarchs of Constantinople and knocking them down again like ninepins. To be a Christian was to be a second-class citizen and the Church suffered in numbers and morale.

In Europe, Martin Luther set the match to the powder train of the Protestant rebellion against Rome when he nailed his Ninety-Five Theses to the door of the castle church at Wittenberg in Saxony in 1517. Of peasant stock, trenchant, forthright and caustic, Luther was now in his thirties, a monk and a teacher at the university of Wittenberg. He had passed through a severe spiritual crisis. Like Augustine before him, he was tormented by a sense of his own worthlessness and convinced of the ingrained sinfulness of human nature and the littleness of man before God. Like Augustine, he despaired of any remedy for human guilt in human effort, and found it in the merciful grace of God, acting in Christ. Necessary though good moral behaviour is, it is not through 'good works' but through heartfelt faith that man is redeemed or 'justified', freed of the penalty of sin. Unlike Augustine, however, Luther came to believe that God's grace does not come to man through the Church, but direct to each believer.

The occasion for the break with Rome happened to be the question of

indulgences. As a way of raising money for the Church, professional 'pardoners' sold indulgences which cancelled all or part of the punishment due to be exacted in purgatory for a person's sins. The theory was that Christ and the saints had a treasury of surplus spiritual merit on which the Church could draw. In 1514 Pope Leo x offered indulgences in return for contributions to the rebuilding of St Peter's, Rome. Luther, who did not believe that good works could buy forgiveness of sins, still less the payment of money, was infuriated and posted his arguments on the church door.

To the surprise of both Luther and the pope, what seemed to be a minor storm turned out to be a hurricane. Luther's stand created intense excitement among churchmen and laymen already restive with Rome, and the dispute quickly moved beyond indulgences to the fundamental question of authority. The Catholic party argued that to defy the Church was heresy. Luther argued that it was possible for the Church to be wrong. Challenged to name his authority for his own opinions, he replied that he took his stand on the Bible and plain reason.

If the Church was not the final authority, then the doctrine that salvation could be gained only through the Church could no longer stand. Luther was condemned for heresy, but was protected by the Elector of Saxony. Other German lords rallied to his support, partly out of religious conviction and partly because they wanted to control the Church within their own borders. Luther circulated tracts in which he denounced the papacy and the mystique of the priesthood, standing between the believer and Christ, and attacked the doctrine of transubstantiation and the Catholic belief that in the Mass the sacrifice of Christ on the cross is repeated. He was a powerful speaker and writer, and he gained increasing popular approval, but what really mattered was the attitude of the rulers of the mosaic of small states in Germany. Some supported Luther, others Rome, and neither party proved strong enough to enforce its will on the other. In this impasse it was eventually agreed that each state would make its own religious arrangements. The result was that Germany was divided up between Protestant and Catholic territories. On the whole, the northern states were Protestant and the southern remained with Rome.

The Protestants regarded themselves as reformers, not innovators. They took over the Catholic churches and retained most features of Catholic ritual, but the services were now in German and the Mass was purged of all references which suggested a sacrifice. Priests turned into or were replaced by ministers, appointed and paid by the state. The monasteries were closed and the clergy were allowed to marry.

The Lutheran movement spread to Denmark, Norway, Sweden, Finland and Iceland, where it became the official state religion. It also had considerable influence in England, especially after Henry VIII broke with the papacy in the 1530s for political reasons and declared himself head of the English Church. Ironically, he had earlier been given the title of Defender of the Faith by the papacy for writing a pamphlet against Luther.

In Switzerland, meanwhile, far more radical changes had been pushed through at Zürich, under the leadership of Ulrich Zwingli, who was determined to restore the early Christianity of the apostles. The city council

The nave of St Peter's, Rome. This huge and magnificent cathedral, dating in its present form principally from the 16th and 17th centuries, stands above the site where, according to a tradition which is probably accurate, the apostle Peter was buried. It was Pope Leo x's offer of indulgences in return for contributions to the rebuilding of St Peter's which provoked Luther's protest.

of Zürich took all images out of the churches, covered the pictures on the walls with whitewash, abolished religious processions and replaced the Mass with a simple commemoration of the last supper. Three other Swiss cities, Basle, Bern and Geneva, became prominent Protestant centres. The Swiss Protestants and Catholics came to blows and Zwingli was killed in the fighting. The Catholic victors had his body publicly quartered and burned with dung.

Protestant ideas were also making an impression in France. John Calvin was born at Noyon in northern France and was intended for the priesthood. By an odd coincidence he studied at the university of Paris at the same time as two of the greatest Catholic figures of the age, Ignatius Loyola and Francis Xavier, but whether he ever met them is not known. When he was in his middle twenties he abandoned the Roman Church and, fearing persecution, went to Basle in Switzerland, where he wrote *The Institutes of the Christian Religion*, an exposition of his doctrines. Before long he moved to Geneva, where he spent most of the rest of his life, and organized the city into a theocracy which gave effect to his principles.

Like Luther and Zwingli, and Augustine earlier, Calvin believed that man is saved only by God's mercy and that the Almighty, for his own inscrutable reasons, does not confer his saving grace on everyone. This can be observed simply by looking about one, at the number of people who are manifestly not imbued with God's grace. There are sheep and there are goats. Some people, the godly 'elect' chosen by the Almighty, are predestined to be saved, and everyone else is predestined to be damned. There is nothing unjust about this on Calvinist principles. All human beings are corrupted by original sin, all deserve God's wrath and damnation, but God in his mercy has chosen some to be saved through his Son.

Predestination does not mean that the elect, sure of salvation, can behave as badly as they like. On the contrary, the elect are known by an upright life, correct belief and attendance at the Lord's Supper, which for Calvin was not only a commemoration of the last supper, but a spiritual contact with Christ. 'Good works' are definitely required of the Calvinist. The duty of the elect is to labour for the establishment of God's kingdom of righteousness on earth. It is also their duty to work diligently in their everyday occupations. Hard work and thrift are Calvinist virtues and one of the great benefits of Calvinism is the vigorous self-confidence which a sense of belonging to the elect inspires. Calvinism has always tended to regard prosperity gained through self-discipline and hard work as a mark of the elect, and honest profit-making as evidence of righteousness. It has consequently appealed to men of business and the 'Protestant ethic' seems to be closely connected with the flowering of capitalism in the West, though not all capitalists have been Calvinists by any means.

The community in Geneva elected its pastors and elders, who supervised the conduct of the congregation and punished backsliding. All citizens were required to belong, and Catholics left the city in large numbers. Attendance at church was compulsory, much Catholic ritual was swept away and the demand for righteousness entailed a moral code which outlawed most forms of amusement. Not surprisingly, there was resistance

Portrait of John Calvin. Far more radical than Luther, Calvin believed that the only practices and institutions which Christians should tolerate were those which could be shown to have been adopted by the early Church. He and his followers swept away much Roman Catholic ceremonial, including crucifixes, incense, images, candles, vestments, pilgrimages and processions.

to the tyranny of Calvin and the elders, which was rigorously put down. By 1546 more than fifty people had been sentenced to death. A doctor named Michael Servetus, denounced to the Inquisition in France for denying the doctrine of the Trinity, fled for his life to Geneva. There he was required to recant his abominable notions and when he refused he was burned at the stake in the name of the Father, the Son and the Holy Spirit.

Calvin was a more systematic thinker than Luther, more austere and less passionate. Sparing of food and sleep, always simply dressed, he is said to have been cheerful and even facetious with his few friends, but he seems to have been essentially a grave and serious man. Calvinism spread from Geneva to France, Germany, Poland, Holland, England and Scotland. In Holland and Scotland it became the official religion.

The Protestant groups disagreed with each other over numerous points but they shared certain attitudes broadly in common. They refused to accept the authority of the Roman Church and substituted for it the authority of scripture. If asked how they knew that their interpretation of scripture was right, they answered that they were guided by the Holy Spirit. With varying degrees of radicalism, they wanted to return to the early Church of the apostles. They had a high regard for the Old Testament, its God and its prophets, whose attitudes they shared and echoed. 'God-fearing' is a word irresistibly associated with them, and they brought the Old Testament back into the forefront of Christianity. They rejected monasticism, the mystique of the priesthood and clerical celibacy. They firmly believed in the Devil, hell and the Last Judgement. They repudiated purgatory and the veneration of the virgin Mary and the saints.

The Calvinists and the Zwinglians were far more severe than the Lutherans and the Church of England in their attitude to ritual and symbolism. They detested the element of magic which they discerned in Roman Christianity. Some of them denounced the Mass as a magical ceremony. They swept away crucifixes, holy water, making the sign of the cross, incense, images, altars, candles, vestments, relics, pilgrimages, processions and the observation of saints' days as popish mumbo-jumbo. They also had no use for the Catholic hierarchy of bishops, archbishops and cardinals. They wanted to achieve a simple, direct relationship between the congregation and God, unimpeded by ceremonial and hierarchy. Believing in the fundamental wickedness of mankind, they had a sharp nose for sin, especially for sexual sin. They sternly disapproved of cosmetics and feminine adornments, and of holidays, games, dancing and theatre-going as frivolities which led to sin and distracted attention from work and God.

Protestants were just as convinced of their own rightness as Catholics and just as intolerant. Each side believed that the other was inspired by the Devil and doomed to eternal damnation if not won over. They fought holy wars against each other and burned each other as heretics. Although Protestants upheld the right of individual judgement, it was the right to reach the same judgement as their own. Protestants no more than Catholics believed that one man's interpretation of scripture was as good as another's, for that way lay anarchy, and both were equally convinced of the need to find authority in a group, a Church.

The Catholic Reformation

The Roman Catholic reaction to the Protestant threat was a mixture of internal reform and vigorous counter-attack, known to Protestants as the Counter-Reformation. Many Catholics disapproved of moral and financial corruption in the Church and a council which met at Trent (Trento in Italy) remedied numerous abuses. On the doctrinal front, however, the council yielded no ground to Protestantism. It declared that the right to interpret scripture lay with the Church and reasserted the doctrines with which Protestants quarrelled. In 1557, to prevent Catholics being infected by Protestant ideas, Pope Paul IV issued an Index of authors and books prohibited to the faithful as 'heretical, suspect or perverse'. The Index has been kept up to date ever since.

A number of new orders emerged, dedicated to practical reform and the battle against heresy. The Theatines were organized to improve the standards of the clergy. The Capuchins, an offshoot of the Franciscans, dedicated themselves to work among the poor. The Ursulines, an order of women, specialized in the education of girls. The Society of Jesus was founded by Ignatius Loyola, a Spanish knight whose military career was cut short by a serious injury to his leg in battle. While he was convalescing, his mind turned to spiritual matters and he saw a vision of the Virgin Mary and Jesus. He went to live in a cave in Catalonia, where he prayed, fasted and scourged himself. As a result of his experiences he worked out a course of meditations, which he later published as his *Spiritual Exercises*. Going to study at the university of Paris, he gathered a small group of kindred spirits, including another Spaniard, Francis Xavier, who vowed themselves to poverty, chastity and missionary work. Pope Paul III approved the new order in 1540. It was organized on military lines, with Loyola as its first General, answerable only to the pope, and set itself to winning both Protestants and the heathen for the Church. The Society's numbers grew rapidly and after a hundred years there were more than 13,000 in its ranks.

Dedicated, disciplined, highly trained, courageous and astute, the Jesuits were feared and hated by Protestants, and many were martyred, but their major successes were outside Europe altogether, in the New World and to a lesser extent in the East. Far from being driven on to the defensive, the ground which Rome lost in Europe was regained in a surge of missionary energy overseas, carried through principally by Jesuits, Franciscans and Dominicans. Francis Xavier was packed off at a day's notice to India, and later went on to Japan. Another Jesuit, Matteo Ricci, went to China. The spectacular gains, however, were made in America. Two years after Luther nailed his arguments to the church door in Wittenberg, Hernan Cortes launched the swift Spanish conquest of the Aztec Empire in Mexico. In the 1530s Francisco Pizarro took Peru. The conquistadors pressed on, missionaries followed and millions of Indians were converted. Almost the whole of Central America and South America were captured for Rome.

In North America the position was more complicated. Mexico was Catholic. Romanism was carried to California and the American south-

RIGHT Matteo Ricci (left), the first Christian missionary to penetrate China, with a Chinese convert. Vast new areas of the world were opened up to European enterprise in the 16th century and part of the Roman Catholic reaction to the Protestant schism was a vigorous missionary campaign outside Europe, spearheaded by Jesuits, Franciscans and Dominicans. Ricci was a Jesuit.

The Council of Trent, by an unknown artist. Summoned by the pope at the instigation of the Emperor Charles V, the Council met in 1545 and sat intermittently until 1563. Its main objects were to mend the split in western Christendom and reform abuses in the Church. Numerous abuses were remedied, but little or no doctrinal ground was yielded to the Protestants and the split was not healed.

west by the Spaniards from Mexico, and to Canada and the Louisiana Territory by the French, but the British won the struggle for the north and Protestantism became the dominant religion of the United States and Canada.

Congregations of Saints

In Europe, the northern countries were Protestant and the southern Catholic. Germany, France, the Netherlands and Ireland were split. The French Protestants, known as Huguenots, were granted freedom of worship by the Edict of Nantes in 1598, but the edict was revoked in 1685. Thousands of Huguenot families fled abroad and France remained a Catholic country until the French Revolution.

England was the leading Protestant power from the seventeenth century on. It was pre-eminently from England that the banner of Protestantism was planted in North America, and later in India, Africa, Australia and New Zealand. The Book of Common Prayer, of 1549, and the Authorized or King James version of the Bible, issued in 1611, have exerted a powerful religious and cultural influence on the whole English-speaking world. The Anglican Church had retained its bishops and too much Catholic ceremonial for the liking of a welter of Calvinist sects, known as Puritans. The royal government and the bishops tried to enforce conformity and persecuted both Roman Catholics and Puritans. After a civil war, the beheading of Charles I, a few years of Puritan rule and the restoration of the monarchy, the Church of England settled down in a compromise position between the Roman Catholic and Protestant extremes. Roman Catholics and dissenting Protestants were discriminated against, but no attempt was made to suppress them.

Although the principal Protestant groups were determinedly authoritarian, the Protestant movement opened the door to a more democratic, more tolerant and more variegated Christianity by taking its stand on scripture. The plain fact was that the Bible could be interpreted in more than one way, and the claim to be guided by the Holy Spirit rested on personal conviction. Already in the seventeenth century some of the radical Protestants were saying that people should be left alone to worship as conscience dictated. If the ideal of religious uniformity was dropped, the state would no longer control the religion of its citizens and, especially in North America, radical Protestantism was a force for political democracy.

One bone of contention among Protestants, linked with the question of democracy, was how the Church should be run: on the Episcopalian system by bishops, as in England; or on the Presbyterian system by 'presbyteries' or committees of ministers and leading elders as in Calvinist Scotland; or on the Congregationalist system, in which each congregation was self-governing. All three systems were exported to the New World. The Anglican Church first established itself at Jamestown, Virginia, where the earliest permanent English settlement in America was founded in 1607. (The American Anglicans declared themselves independent of the Church of England in 1789, as the Protestant Episcopal Church.)

LEFT Christ Church, Shrewsbury, New Jersey, an Episcopalian parish church, built in the 18th century. All the principal Christian denominations established themselves in the New World, but Protestantism became the dominant religion of the United States and Canada. After the thirteen colonies had freed themselves from Britain, the Anglicans in the United States declared themselves independent of the Church of England as the Protestant Episcopal Church.

ABOVE John Bunyan, title page of an 18th-century edition of *Pilgrim's Progress*. In the background is the central character, Christian, treading the path of his pilgrimage.

A Quaker meeting in Amsterdam. The Quakers, who dispensed with church services and ceremonial altogether, were among the radical Protestants who called for people to be left free to worship in their own way, as conscience dictated. This demand in time led to a more variegated and more democratic Christianity. Once the ideal of religious uniformity was dropped, the state no longer attempted to control the religion of its citizens.

It was the Congregationalist system which prevailed. The Pilgrim Fathers, who sailed to America in the *Mayflower* and founded Plymouth Colony, were Congregationalists. They went to the New World to escape from harassment in England and find a place where they could establish the ideal God-fearing society. They believed that each congregation of 'saints', meaning those who lived a godly life, should be independent of outside control, so as to be free to obey the will of God as transmitted to conscience by the Spirit.

The earliest Presbyterian immigrants were French Huguenots, who founded colonies in South Carolina and Florida in the sixteenth century. Many of the British Puritans who settled New England in the following century were Presbyterians, but they veered over to the Congregationalist system of Plymouth Colony. The Baptist congregations were also self-governing. The first Baptist church in America was founded in 1639 at Providence, Rhode Island. The movement had begun among English Calvinist refugees in Holland, a group of whom returned from Amsterdam to London in 1612 and established the earliest Baptist church in England. The distinctive principle of the movement is that only believers should be baptized, which means that small children should not be. Baptism is usually by immersion, not by pouring or sprinkling. John Bunyan, the author of *Pilgrim's Progress*, was a Baptist.

Another radical sect was the Society of Friends, popularly known as Quakers because they trembled and shook with the power of God's Spirit. Their founder, George Fox, went about in the Midland counties of England calling on everyone to repent, and once marched through the town of Lichfield crying 'Woe to the bloody city of Lichfield', to the astonishment and disapproval of the inhabitants. Fox believed that each human being can find truth within himself, through the 'inner light' which is part of God's light. He dispensed with church services, ministers and creeds. There was no fixed programme for Quaker meetings, at which anyone might feel moved to pray aloud, teach or read from the Bible and, when they did not, there would be long periods of silence. The Quakers gave women equality with men in their organization and they practised passive resistance to the persecution they encountered with steadfastness and success. The leaders travelled to America and the Quaker colony of Pennsylvania was founded in 1682 by William Penn. The Friends' insistence on honesty and simplicity of behaviour, their disdain for class distinctions, their pacifism, their charitableness, and later the success which many of them achieved in business, have given them an influence out of all proportion to their small numbers.

Christianity in the Modern World

The fierceness of the religious conflicts of the sixteenth and seventeenth centuries, and the fact that no one group was strong enough to overcome the others, generated a reaction against fanaticism and a policy of live and let live. At the same time a new tide was rising which would become a far more serious threat to all the Christian denominations than they posed to each other. The work of men like Copernicus, Galileo and Newton created a new picture of the world, into which religion was difficult to fit. It was not that the pioneers of science were anti-Christian, usually far from it, but the universe which they revealed was a machine which ran by itself without interference from God. An honorific place was reserved for God as the Supreme Being, the Great Artificer who constructed the machine in the first place and the Prime Mover who set it running, but the Almighty no longer intervened in the world to help or to harm. God became impersonal, remote and, for practical purposes of daily life, powerless.

Inevitably, it began to be asked whether there was a God at all, and the lack of scientific evidence for God's existence created scepticism. As God receded into improbability, so did Christ, so did the Devil, so did heaven and hell. With them went Christianity's central promise of salvation and a happy afterlife, and the Church's role as a shield against evil and misfortune. If there was no afterlife, then this life was no longer a period of testing and preparation for it, a conclusion which promoted secularism and materialism. People began to look to improved technology for control of the environment. Scientific progress in agriculture and medicine, for instance, made new methods preferable to prayer as a way of securing a good crop or a cure of disease. There was a powerful demand for freedom and equality, and Churches and priesthoods were attacked as bastions of tyranny, privilege and outmoded superstition. Set free to use his reason, man could make the world a better place without supernatural assistance. Original sin was a slur and a delusion, and man and society were perfectible on earth. It all has a hollow ring now, but during the French Revolution the worship of Reason was installed as the state religion of France.

At the same time there was a counter-current, which sought refuge from

John Wesley, the founder of
Methodism, painted by
Nathaniel Hone in 1766,
when Wesley was in his
sixties. A tireless traveller and
spell-binding preacher, he
attracted huge crowds.
Converts were made in great
numbers and, though Wesley
had no doctrinal quarrel with
the Church of England, he
felt compelled to build up a
separate organization.

rationalism and scepticism in a religion that was emotionally convincing. The Pietist movement in German and Scandinavian Lutheranism turned its back on what it regarded as arid disputes among Christians about doctrine and focused on an ardent devotion to Christ with a sense of warm, personal closeness to the Saviour. The movement influenced John Wesley, the founder of Methodism. Wesley was an Anglican clergyman. As students at Oxford university, he and his friends had been nicknamed Methodists because of the methodical way in which they studied the Bible together and went regularly to church. When he was in his middle thirties, while listening to a reading from Luther, Wesley suddenly felt his heart 'strangely warmed', as he said, with trust in Christ and an assurance of salvation, that Christ had taken away his sins.

In the fifty-three years of life he had left Wesley travelled more than 200,000 miles and preached more than 40,000 sermons, at an average of fifteen a week. He addressed open-air meetings, where he was sometimes pelted with stones and rotten eggs, but he was a spell-binding preacher and huge crowds gathered to hear him. He tried to create in his hearers the same assurance of salvation and liberation from sin that he felt himself. He first impressed on them their sinfulness and worthlessness before God and the doom of hellfire which awaited them, and then that if they would repent and turn to Christ, the Saviour's loving forgiveness would rescue them. Some who heard him burst into tears, cried out or fell to the ground, and then were filled with ecstatic joy.

Converts were made in great numbers, pastors were appointed and Sunday schools established to educate the faithful in Christianity and the Bible. The bishops of the Church of England found the emotional excitement of Methodism repulsive and spiritually dangerous. Wesley and his colleagues were barred from preaching in Anglican churches, and though Wesley accepted the doctrines of the Church of England he felt compelled to build up a separate organization. He ordained his own ministers, his younger brother Charles wrote thousands of hymns for Methodist services and Methodist chapels were built for the local congregations.

Similar 'revival' movements were going on in the United States and Methodism, first carried there in 1760, found fertile soil. In the late eighteenth century and on into the nineteenth, as pioneers moved westwards across the country, the camp meeting became a familiar feature of life in the American West. People gathered to hear a travelling preacher, who would move them to pray, cry, shout, sing and 'get religion'. Methodist and Baptist preachers proved particularly successful at this type of evangelism.

In England in the nineteenth century great efforts were made to bring fervent Christian piety and Christian moral standards to the new working class created by the Industrial Revolution, who had been herded into towns in squalid conditions as fodder for the mills and factories. New churches were built in the industrial towns and Sunday schools were instituted to teach Christian principles to the children of the poor. The Evangelical movement in the Church of England combined zeal to make converts with

The enigmatic figure of Jesus in the gospels can be interpreted in many different ways, and artists have portrayed him in many styles and guises. This *Christus* by a German sculptor, Ernst Barlach, is a typical product of the 1930s.

a determination to improve social conditions. The Evangelicals were at the 'low church' end of the Anglican spectrum, the end nearest to Calvinism. Largely immune to the rationalism fashionable among intellectuals, they had a profound respect for the Bible as the word of God and they regarded good moral behaviour as the test of the good Christian. They had a strong sense of duty and sin. They believed in hell and the Devil. They engaged in Bible reading at home, family prayers and strict Sunday observance. Like the Methodists, they produced a wealth of stirring hymns.

In the 1830s there was a revival at the other, 'high church' end of the spectrum. The Oxford Movement, so called because its prime movers were Oxford academics, challenged rationalism and scepticism by proclaiming the spiritual authority of the Church, descended from the apostles, as against individual judgement. They hoped to bring the Church of England back to its old Catholic heritage and recapture the numinous in Christianity through the revival of medieval rituals, symbolism and devotion. Their own momentum carried some of the leaders into the Roman Church, including the brilliant John Henry Newman, who became a Roman Catholic cardinal. The lasting effect of the movement was to create a strong Anglo-Catholic party in the Church of England which has brought back to many churches ceremonial, vestments, candles, incense, adoration of the host, veneration of the Virgin Mary and the mystique of the clergy as 'priests' rather than 'ministers'. The Evangelicals, who detested all this as popery, were driven into a closer alliance with the Nonconformists – the Methodists, Baptists and others outside the Anglican Church. In the centre were a good many Anglicans who viewed both wings with disquiet.

The Nonconformists grew in strength as the century wore on and in the 1850s approximately as many worshippers went to chapel on Sundays as to church. The Nonconformist chapels inculcated the Calvinist virtues of hard work, self-discipline, thrift and sobriety, and helped to mould the new petty bourgeoisie or 'lower middle class'. It was from the chapels that many of the early leaders of the trade union movement emerged.

The Nonconformists and Evangelicals were the principal driving force behind the energetic missionary effort which in the nineteenth century gave Christianity a greater geographical expansion than it had ever achieved before. Protestant missionary societies sent missionaries to India and the Far East, to Africa, to Australia and the Pacific islands, and to peoples from the Eskimo to the Maori. There was a similar surge of missionary enthusiasm in Germany, Holland and Switzerland, and later a renewed Roman Catholic missionary effort, especially from France. American missionary societies of all denominations joined in the work.

This missionary tide was part of the political and cultural imperialism of the period, when the major western powers carved up huge areas of the world between them. On the whole, the missionaries were more successful in bringing western technology, education and humanitarianism to 'the heathen' than in winning converts. The fact that there were so many varieties of Christianity, some of them mutually competitive, did not help. It was in areas where Christianity was not confronted by any rival major religion that the greatest numbers of converts were gained, especially in

ABOVE The siege of Antioch, during the first crusade. The Jewish concept of holy war was inherited by both Christians and Muslims, and the fighting men on both sides in the crusades were told that heaven would be their reward.

LEFT St Patrick's Cathedral, New York City. This Roman Catholic cathedral was begun in 1858 in the Gothic revival style. Though a large church by any standards, it is now dwarfed by towering skyscrapers. The 19th and 20th centuries have not dealt kindly with Christianity.

RIGHT Pilgrims on their way to Mecca, from a manuscript of the Baghdad School. Hundreds of thousands of pilgrims gather at Mecca from all over the Muslim world. This annual pilgrimage has been an important factor in the strength and cohesion of Islam throughout its history.

وَكَادَ يُزَعْزِعُ الجِمَالَ الشَّمَّ وَأَنْشَدَ

مَا الْحَجُّ سَيْرُكَ تَأْوِيباً وَادِّلاجاً وَلَا اعْتِيَامُكَ أَجْمَالاً وَأَحْمَالاً

الحَجُّ أَنْ تَقْصِدَ البَيْتَ الحَرَامَ عَلَى تَحْرِيدِكَ الحَجَّ لَا تَبْغِي بِهِ حَاجَا

وَتَطَّوِي كَأَهْلِ الإِنْصَافِ مُتَّخِذاً رَدْعَ الهَوَى هَادِياً وَالحَقَّ مِنْهَاجَا

Africa south of the Sahara. The most famous of the missionaries to Africa was David Livingstone, a Scot of typically evangelical outlook – his motto was 'Fear God and work hard' – who hoped to bring Africa the benefits of western civilization as well as the gospel. He was the leading influence on the eventual suppression of the Arab slave trade in Central Africa. He was also a great explorer and his example inspired both further missionary work and further exploration.

In the United States a massive flow of immigrants from Europe – five million between 1830 and 1860, twenty-one million between 1860 and 1914 – brought every variety of Christianity to their new home with them. They included substantial numbers of Irish and Italian Catholics and German and Scandinavian Lutherans. In the United States today Protestants outnumber Catholics, but the Roman Catholic Church is by far the largest single religious organization. The various Baptist bodies constitute the largest Protestant group, followed in terms of numbers by the Methodists, the Lutherans, the Presbyterians and the Episcopalians.

Though Christianity seemed to be vigorous and flourishing in the nineteenth century, it had in fact been struck a succession of hammer blows by science and scholarship. Discoveries in geology and palaeontology (the study of fossil animals and plants) made it difficult to think that the account in the Bible of God creating the world in seven days could be correct. On the contrary, it was becoming clear that the world had formed slowly over millions of years. Work in biology led in the same direction and Charles Darwin's *Origin of Species* did more than any other single book to damage the credibility of the Bible and gain acceptance for the theory of evolution. Protestants and Catholics alike believed in the Bible as the word of God, but if the Bible was not literally accurate, in what way was it accurate? If the world and life had not been created in a few days but had evolved over aeons of time, was God responsible for the world at all, did God even exist?

A new school of biblical scholarship, originating in Germany and known as 'the higher criticism', further undermined the authority of the Bible by showing that it too had evolved, that it had been compiled and edited over centuries and contained the confusions, contradictions and fallibilities characteristic of human authorship. If the Bible was merely the work of men, was there any good reason for relying on it? The higher criticism also suggested that St Paul rather than Jesus was the real founder of Christianity.

Belief in God, belief in the Bible and belief in Christ were all threatened. Many Protestants, especially on the evangelical wing, responded with fierce hostility and denunciation. The Roman Catholic Church also reacted vigorously. Pope Pius IX convened a council at the Vatican, which asserted the existence of God and the divine inspiration of the Bible, and also proclaimed that the pope, speaking *ex cathedra*, or officially in his capacity as 'Pastor of all Christians', is infallible in matters of faith and morals. This pronouncement was no more welcome to Protestants than Darwin, evolution and the higher criticism.

Christianity was badly shaken. Not only did the prevailing intellectual trend turn even more decisively away from it, but a good many ordinary

Eastern Orthodox clergy at a ceremony outside the church of the Holy Sepulchre in Bethlehem. In eastern Christianity 'orthodox' does not mean right thinking so much as the right way of worshipping, and Eastern Orthodox ceremonials are elaborate and colourful as a revelation of the divine presence among men.

people quietly ceased to take it seriously. Their allegiance had often been more nominal than real in any case, and the advances of technology and democracy were making life more comfortable and opening up opportunities for personal advancement which accelerated the growth of materialism. In Russia, and later in eastern Europe, Christianity was allowed to exist only on sufferance after the coming of Communism and the Eastern Orthodox Church was severely damaged.

All the same, there are still today large numbers of believing Christians. The changed climate has produced attempts to modernize the religion, to bring it up to date with thinking in other areas, to rid it of the lumber accumulated over centuries. Among many examples are the abandonment of Latin in the Mass and the rewriting in a modern style of Protestant services. This is not an approach which commends itself to all Christians, some of whom value tradition, and fear that being modern means setting the religion adrift on the swirling tides of currently fashionable political and social attitudes.

Perhaps the principal consequence of the nineteenth-century trauma has been to make Christians more tolerant, of each other and of other religions. There has also been a marked emphasis on practical Christianity, on the duty to help the poor and unfortunate, to an extent which, to critics again, threatens to turn the religion into just one more welfare agency. Questions of doctrine have come to seem less important to many Christians than emotional commitment and the leading of a Christian life. The danger to Christianity has stimulated the attempt to unite all Christians in one Church. The modern ecumenical movement began among the Protestant missionary societies, which were dismayed by the damaging effects of rivalry between different denominations. The International Missionary Council was formed by various Protestant bodies soon after the First World War. Soon after the Second World War the World Council of Churches was formally constituted in Amsterdam with a programme of drawing mankind away from both Communism and laissez-faire capitalism. This was again a Protestant organization, but both the Roman Catholics and the Eastern Orthodox gave it some encouragement. The Roman Catholic Church became more ecumenical in its approach, notably under Pope John XXIII. The difficulties of uniting Christendom are formidable, however, because the differences between the major denominations are not founded on petty-minded disputatiousness, but on deep divisions of attitude, temperament and tradition.

OVERLEAF Muslim services, by contrast, are much simpler, and both music and images are forbidden. Evening prayers at the mosque of Marhagat Khan, built in 1670, at Peshawar, Pakistan.

8. Islam

Islam is estimated to have close to 600 million followers today, or about one in every seven human beings. It is the dominant religion of all the Arab states and of Turkey, Iran, Afghanistan, Pakistan and Indonesia. There are also substantial numbers of Muslims in Africa south of the Sahara, in the Soviet Union and the Balkans, and in China. In the United States, the Black Muslim movement was founded in the 1930s. In Britain numerous mosques have been opened in recent years, while churches have been closing for lack of support.

The name Islam means 'submission' or 'surrender' and its adherents are Muslims, those who submit themselves to the will of God. They dislike being called Muhammadans because they resent any implication that they worship Muhammad, which they do not. The simple creed of their faith, occupying the same place in Islam as the Shema in Judaism, is 'There is no god but God, and Muhammad is God's messenger.' This is whispered in every newborn baby's ear, is repeated frequently by the devout all through life, and should ideally be the last words spoken by the dying.

Muslims worship the same God as Jews and Christians, the god described as the creator of the world in the Old Testament. In Arabic he is called Allah, which means simply 'the god'. The Old Testament prophets and Jesus of Nazareth are respected as forerunners of Muhammad, but Islam claims to correct the errors of Judaism and Christianity. Muslims do not believe that the Jews are God's chosen people and do not accept the Jewish law. Islam is strictly monotheistic and the principal Muslim objection to Christianity is that Christians have breached monotheism in mistakenly supposing Jesus to be divine as the Son of God. Muslims also disapprove of the concept of God the Father, whether it is taken literally or metaphorically, to mean that God stands in a fatherly relation to mankind. Muslim theology has not had to wrestle with the complexities of the Trinity and the relationship between God the Father and God the Son.

The foundation stone of the religion is the holy book, the Qur'an (or Koran), the word of God revealed to Muhammad. It must never be placed

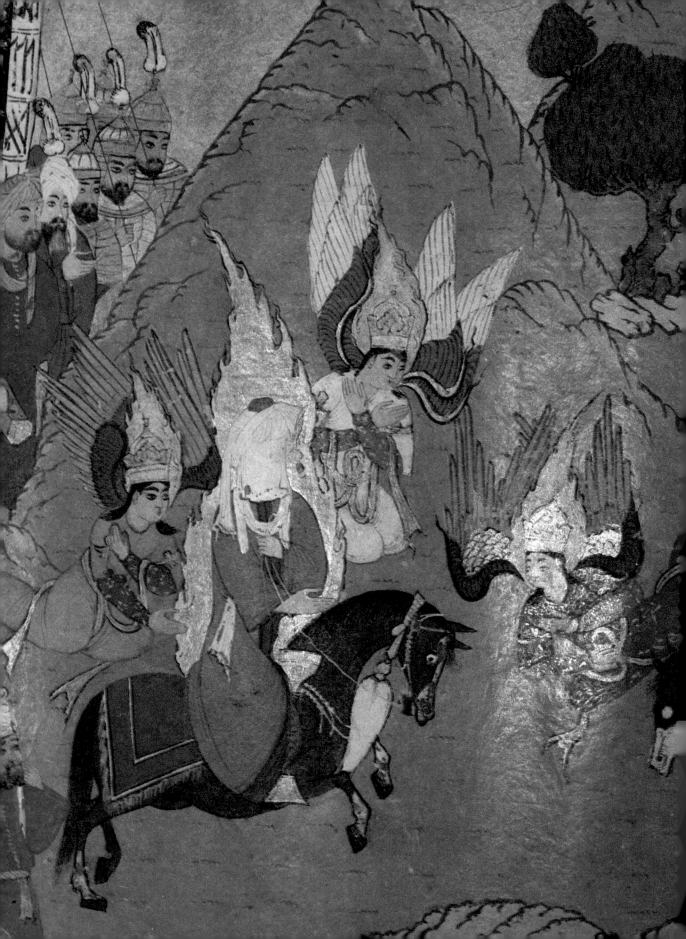

beneath other books, but always on top, and no one should drink or smoke while it is read aloud. Its presence is widely regarded as a protection against misfortune and disease. Many Muslims carry a copy of the Qur'an with them everywhere they go and frequent quotation from it is a Muslim habit. Children are often required to learn the whole book by heart – it is about four-fifths of the length of the New Testament – and it is the basic textbook of all Muslim education. Besides the Qur'an there is a body of tradition going back to Muhammad's time or soon after which is considered authoritative.

Muslim theology is complex and subtle, but at the popular level Islam is an attractively simple and strong religion. There is only one God and the duty of human beings is to worship and obey him. Those who do this, or do their best to, are promised forgiveness of sins and a happy life after death in paradise. Those who do not are promised torment in the fires of hell. Since God is all-powerful, however, everything that happens occurs in accordance with his will, as he has destined it to occur. In effect, you must do your best in life but, ultimately, what happens is not within human control. This commonsense belief can be a powerful source of comfort and strength, reinforced by a maxim from the Qur'an: 'God does not charge a soul with more than it can bear.'

The Five Pillars

The basic requirements of everyday practical religion are known as the five pillars of Islam. The first is to repeat the simple creed and mean it. The second is to pray five times a day. The prayers are essentially expressions of adoration of God, but the worshipper may add his own personal requests. Before praying he must wash and he must face in the direction of the Ka'ba, the house of God in Mecca. During prayers he prostrates himself, with his hands on the ground and his face to the ground. The most commonly repeated prayer is the short first *sura*, or section, of the Qur'an, beginning, 'Praise be to Allah, Lord of the creation, the compassionate, the merciful.'

Prayer is the heart of Muslim religious life and the faithful are called to prayer by the muezzin, crying out in a loud voice, nowadays frequently amplified, from a minaret of the local mosque. The worshipper may pray at home or wherever he happens to be, alone or in a group. If in a group, as in a mosque (a 'place of prostration'), there must be a leader, an imam, so that everything is conducted in an orderly way. An imam is not a priest, Islam allows no priests between man and God. Services are held in the mosque on Fridays, with a sermon by the imam. Islam disapproves of sacred music and there is no singing or chanting in the services. There are no images in the mosques, or at home, because making images of God is forbidden. Instead of an altar, as in a Christian church, there is a semi-circular recess, the *mihrab*, which indicates the direction of Mecca. Worshippers take off their shoes before going into the mosque. If women attend a mosque, they are usually hidden behind screens.

Prayer is the heart of Muslim religious life, and prostration during prayer is a sign of respect and submission to the will of God.

The faithful are summoned to prayer fives times a day by the muezzin, calling from a minaret of the local mosque: 'God is most great. I testify that there is no God but Allah. I testify that Muhammad is God's messenger. Come to prayer, come to security. God is most great.'

LEFT Sulaiman the
Magnificent and his army. It
was under this sultan that the
Ottoman Empire reached the
peak of its power.

RIGHT The great mosque at
Isfahan, Iran, looking south
across the courtyard. It was
built by Shah Abbas I, the
first of the Safavid dynasty of
Persia, late in the 15th
century. All mosques have a
courtyard with one or more
fountains for washing, which
is obligatory before prayer.

The third pillar of the faith is giving to charity. The fourth is fasting, principally during the month of Ramadan, when eating, drinking and smoking are forbidden between sunrise and sunset. Some Muslims observe the fast very strictly, some less strictly and some scarcely at all. The fifth and last pillar is the pilgrimage to Mecca, the *hajj*, which every Muslim should make once in his life if his health and circumstances do not prevent him.

The pilgrimage to Mecca has been a major factor in the strength and cohesion of Islam throughout its history. Every year hundreds of thousands of pilgrims assemble from every corner of the Muslim world. They come as equals and brothers, all in the same white clothing. They fast during the day and they must abstain from violence, sex and all luxurious pleasures. They circle seven times round the small, ancient structure called the Ka'ba, touching or kissing the sacred Black Stone, set in one corner. Other rites include running seven times between two small hills, saying prayers at certain holy places, stoning three pillars, which is said to be stoning the Devil, and the sacrifice of animals, which is followed by a cheerful feast. Many pilgrims bring with them the shrouds in which they intend to be buried and dip them in the sacred well of Zamzam, and many take the opportunity to visit Muhammad's tomb at Medina; though undue lingering there is discouraged by the Saudi authorities, who disapprove of any suggestion of divine honours being paid to the prophet.

The five pillars are all individual requirements, resting on each Muslim personally. Congregations meet to pray in the mosques, but there is no concept in orthodox Islam of a Church, a separate religious institution within society. Society itself is the religious institution. There is no equivalent of the Christian Mass or Lord's Supper and the idea of the worshipper becoming one with God, though it has a history in Islam, has a dangerous tinge of blasphemy in orthodox Muslim eyes. In the mosques, as at Mecca, all the faithful are equal in the sight of God. Although there are certainly distinctions of wealth and class in Muslim countries, there is an egalitarian strain in the religion and Islam has been markedly successful in crossing barriers of race and colour: though far less ready to accept the equality of the sexes.

The Prophet

Islam is the youngest of the major religions. Muhammad (the name means 'highly praised') was born in about AD 570 at Mecca, a prosperous commercial and religious centre of the Hejaz, the north-western part of what is now Saudi Arabia. According to tradition, his father died before he was born and his mother when he was six, and he was brought up by relatives in poverty and obscurity. He was employed in the camel caravan trade and, when he was about twenty-five, he married a well-to-do widow named Khadija, who was fifteen years older than himself. She bore him six children, only one of whom, a daughter named Fatima, survived him. Khadija died when Muhammad was about fifty, and he subsequently took other wives.

As a young man, Muhammad used to go to a cave near Mecca to

LEFT The mosque of Wazir Khan at Lahore, Pakistan, built in the 17th century.

RIGHT A pilgrim encampment outside Mecca.

BELOW View of Mecca, 1882, based on the first photograph ever taken of the city, which was already a pilgrimage centre before Muhammad's time. In the courtyard of the Grand Mosque is the Ka'ba, swathed in black cloth. Set into one corner of it is the mysterious Black Stone. Pilgrims circle seven times round the Ka'ba, touching or kissing the Black Stone.

LEFT The tomb of Muhammad in the Prophet's Mosque at Medina, which pilgrims to Mecca frequently take the opportunity to visit. The present mosque dates principally from the 15th century. Abu Bakr, Umar and Fatima are also believed to be buried here, and Medina, where Muhammad first gained a substantial following, ranks second in sanctity only to Mecca itself. Both cities are prohibited to non-Muslims.

ABOVE Though Mecca is far and away the most important centre of pilgrimage, it is by no means the only one. Thousands of Shi'a pilgrims visit the tomb of the Imam Riza at Meshed in Iran. Riza, who died in 819, is regarded as a martyr by the Shi'a, said to have been poisoned by Caliph Mamun of Baghdad.

meditate and pray. He also learned a good deal about Judaism and Christianity. Arabia at this time was not a backwater, cut off from the rest of the world. Mecca was a station on the trade route from China and India through southern Arabia to the Mediterranean and Muhammad himself went with camel caravans to Syria. Both the Monophysites and the Nestorians had made converts to Christianity in Arabia and established monasteries, and there were Jews and Christian Arabs in Mecca.

The majority of Arabs worshipped nature-deities, to whom sacrifices were offered – human sacrifices in the distant past – but recognized a particularly powerful god, Allah, as the principal deity and the creator of the world. A few were convinced that Allah was the only god and Muhammad seems to have been influenced by them. Mecca, however, owed part of its prosperity to the pilgrims who came there to visit sites which were sacred to numerous deities. Among them were the well of Zamzam and the Ka'ba, which contained images of various gods and goddesses, and also the sacred Black Stone, possibly a meteorite. Very little is known about the pre-Islamic rites at Mecca, but pilgrims circled round the Ka'ba and also ran a sacred race between the two hills.

When he was about forty, Muhammad had a vision. He saw a being who held a text written on silk and commanded him to read it: 'Recite in the name of your Lord who created man.' Muhammad obeyed and the complete text is sura 96 of the Qur'an. Muhammad was doubtful about this experience at first, but subsequent visions convinced him that he was a prophet inspired by Allah, whom he identified as the God of the Old Testament. His mission was to summon people away from the cults of false, imaginary gods and bring them to the worship of the one true God.

Muhammad made a few converts in Mecca, mostly among the uninfluential and the poor. Two more prominent citizens who joined him were Abu Bakr and Umar, who were to play leading parts in the movement. Many Meccans ridiculed him and accused him of trying to turn them into Jews or Christians. Their opposition no doubt sprang partly from religious conviction and partly from the fear of a threat to their income from pilgrims – a fear which in time proved to be entirely misplaced.

The new movement made little headway in Mecca, but Muhammad gained converts among pilgrims from Medina (then called Yathrib), another prosperous trading town, with a large Jewish population, close to 300 miles north of Mecca. The prophet was invited to move to Medina, and he and his Meccan followers did so. The year of this emigration, called the Hegira (*hijra* in Arabic), was later made year one of the Muslim calendar.

In Medina Muhammad swiftly made himself the head of the Arab community. His gifts of leadership were considerable and, confident that he was the messenger of God, he began to use force to fulfill his mission. He and his followers raided Meccan caravans and fought battles against the Meccans, in one of which Muhammad was wounded. The nomadic Arab tribes in the surrounding area were won over by a mixture of force, diplomacy and the attractive prospect of plunder. Muhammad was spiritually in the line of the great Jewish prophets and he hoped that the Jews of Medina would join his following, but they denied his claim to be

God's spokesman. His attitude to Judaism changed and he felt that it had strayed from the right path. He expelled the Jews from Medina and told his followers that in prayer they should no longer face towards Jerusalem, the holy city of God in the Old Testament, but towards Mecca. Abraham, he declared was a Muslim and, through his son Ishmael, the ancestor of the Arabs. The Arab and not the Jew, in other words, was God's standard-bearer on earth.

The embryo of the Muslim state was formed in Medina, a community of believers with a leader who was both their religious and their political chief, and with the principle of expanding the territory of the faith by holy war already established. War was not permitted within the community and the Arab penchant for fighting and raiding was turned outwards, against the infidel. The result was soon to give the Arabs a unity and fervour which would carry them to astounding victories.

Eight years after the Hegira, Muhammad was strong enough to take Mecca almost without fighting. The idols at the sacred sites were smashed and only the Black Stone was left in the Ka'ba, which was now dedicated solely to Allah and became the object of the annual pilgrimage which has continued ever since. Missionaries were sent out to tribes all over Arabia. The prophet himself returned to Medina, and there he died and was buried.

Muhammad always insisted that he was in no way divine and possessed no miraculous powers. He had wives and children, he worked at an ordinary job in his younger days, he knew poverty, mockery and disappointment, and he seems to have had a strong sense of humour, a rarity among prophets. His personality gave him a hold on the affection and loyalty of his followers which must have been powerfully strengthened by

The birth of Muhammad, from a 14th-century manuscript. The fire streaming from the infant Muhammad's head is the mark of his spiritual power. Both mother and child are veiled to hide their faces, which it would be considered idolatrous to show.

LEFT Abraham receiving the
messengers from God
(Genesis, chapter 18), from a
Muslim manuscript. Sarah,
Abraham's wife, is looking at
herself in a mirror. Muslims
worship the God described as
the creator of the world in the
Old Testament, and
Muhammad maintained that
Abraham was a Muslim and,
through his son Ishmael, the
ancestor of the Arabs.

his visions and the ecstatic states in which he spoke words which, he said, rang painfully in his head like the clangour of a bell. It is these words, remembered and written down by his followers, which make up the Qur'an.

Muhammad is regarded by Muslims, as he regarded himself, as the last and greatest of the line of prophets stretching from Moses to Jesus. He is not a divine Saviour, but he will intercede for the faithful at the Last Judgement. There has always been a popular tendency, however, to think of him as something more than a man. To the displeasure of theologians, his birthday is widely celebrated with processions and readings from the Qur'an, and pious legends have clustered round his memory. They include tales of miracles and of spirits flocking to hear him and to be converted to Islam, and the story of how he was transported in an instant by night from Mecca to Jerusalem and ascended to the seventh heaven, where he saw God himself. Jerusalem became the third holiest city of Islam, after Mecca and Medina, which are both barred to non-Muslims.

The Qur'an

The canon of the Qur'an (which means 'recitation' or 'discourse') was settled within twenty years or so after Muhammad's death and it is unique among the scriptures of the major religions in the closeness of the connection between the founder and the holy book. Parts of the Qur'an were recorded in Mecca and parts later in Medina. It is written in Arabic of inspiring beauty and force, and for Muslims it is infallible, because it was dictated to the prophet by God's Spirit, through angels.

Page from an Egyptian copy
of the Qur'an, 14th century.
The Qur'an, the holy book of
Islam, was dictated to
Muhammad by God, through
angels as intermediaries.

Every sura of the Qur'an except one begins, 'In the name of Allah, the compassionate, the merciful', but the main emphasis is on the overwhelming power and majesty of God. Because Allah is both all-powerful and compassionate, man can safely put his trust in him, and in him alone. The omnipotence of God is so stressed as to suggest that he is responsible not only for the good in the world but also for the evil. The consequence, as in Judaism, is that the Devil, whose Arabic name is Iblis, plays nothing like as prominent a role in Islam as in Christianity.

There are vivid passages about the Last Judgement, which may occur at any moment, when all mankind will be physically resurrected. Unbelievers will be condemned to appalling agonies in hell. The righteous will go to live for ever in paradise, a place of beautiful gardens and shady trees and sparkling fountains, of delectable food and drink and sexual delights in the company of beautiful girls, the dark-eyed houris, and handsome boys. There is a marked contrast here with the Christian heaven, from which erotic satisfactions are excluded. Muhammad taught that death, for the faithful, is not something to fear, but the gateway of paradise, and Muslim warriors fought with all the fiercer courage because they believed that the joys of paradise would be their reward. These delights were interpreted spiritually by Muslim theologians, but taken literally at popular levels.

The Qur'an and the main line of Islamic tradition has no great obsession with sin and lacks the revulsion from sex and the body which is one current, though only one, of Christian feeling about life. There is no concept of original sin in the Qur'an, no belief that all human beings are stained with guilt from birth. Such crimes as murder, theft and adultery are forbidden, of course, but the only unforgivable sin is to fall away from monotheism. Pork and wine are prohibited, and so is gambling. On the positive side, God requires justice and fair dealing, kindly treatment of women, slaves and orphans, generosity to the poor, respect for parents and hospitality to travellers. Arab society in Muhammad's time was patriarchal and the Qur'an is in no doubt about the inferior status of women. The primary purpose of sex is the procreation of children and so a man may have up to four wives at a time (fewer than current custom allowed) and any number of concubines. There are numerous other rules and regulations, which became the basis of Muslim law, the Shari'a or 'highway', which is regarded as God's law for all mankind. In theory the Shari'a regulates every human activity, because Islam is not only a religion but a complete social system. Respect for the Qur'an and for tradition has tended to make Muslim law an inflexible and conservative force.

Expansion and Division

The Qur'an left Muslims in no doubt of their duty to propagate the faith by 'striving (*jihad*) in God's path', and that this meant by war as well as by persuasion. 'March in the name of Allah.' The Arabs marched indeed, or rather rode swiftly on camels and horses. Damascus and Jerusalem fell to them, Egypt was conquered and the Sasanian Empire of Persia collapsed in

Interior of the dome of the Rock, Jerusalem. The mosque stands on the site of the Temple and also on the rock from which, according to tradition, Muhammad was carried up to the seventh heaven.

Ceiling of the Dome of the Rock. Muslim architects took over the dome from the church architecture of eastern Christendom, and the dome seems admirably suited to symbolize God's all-encompassing power.

Interior of the mosque at Cordoba. With images banned from the mosques, to prevent idolatry, Muslim builders carried the use of abstract and geometrical ornament to a high peak of elegance.

defeat. A hundred years after the prophet's death his followers ruled an area larger than the Roman Empire at its height: from Spain and Morocco across North Africa to Egypt, Arabia, Palestine, Syria, Mesopotamia and Iran. They saw their success as the evident handiwork of God.

The Arab armies were recruited largely from the nomadic Bedouin. Their warcry was *Allahu akbar*, 'God is most great', and they were inspired by religious fervour and a sense of unity in a divine mission, but love of fighting and lust for plunder also drove them on, and there were other factors in their success. They were frequently welcomed as deliverers by people oppressed under Byzantine or Persian rule, and by Monophysite and Nestorian Christians who were at odds with the orthodox Church. Arab government was often milder than what it replaced. Though prisoners of war were customarily offered the choice of Islam or death, the majority of the conquered were given a third alternative. They could practise their religion, though not make converts, provided they paid a special tax. All faiths except Islam were second-rate religions in Muslim areas and many converts were made, largely for reasons of practical advantage but partly because Islam was attractive in its own right.

The first caliph or 'successor' to Muhammad as political and religious leader, though not as prophet – there could be no more prophets – was Abu Bakr. He was followed by another close friend of Muhammad, the stern and ferocious Umar, of whom the prophet once jokingly said that the Devil himself would dodge down an alley if he met Umar in the street. The third caliph, Uthman, was a member of the Umayyad clan of Mecca.

The speed and extent of the Arab success created its own problems. The power and wealth gained by the leaders made the office of caliph a prize disputed by the able and ambitious. Uthman was murdered while at prayer in his own house. His successor was Ali, the husband of Muhammad's daughter Fatima, but Uthman's nephew Muawiya, the governor of Syria, blamed Ali for Uthman's death. There was a civil war between them, which ended when Ali was assassinated and Muawiya became caliph and founded an Umayyad dynasty which ruled from Damascus. Ali's son Husain rebelled against Muawiya's successor, Yazid. His small force was surrounded and cut to pieces, after refusing to surrender, and Husain himself was beheaded.

There have always been different sects and schools of thought in Islam, many of them short-lived, but these struggles for power caused a schism which has lasted ever since, between the Sunnis and the Shi'a. The Sunnis accepted Muawiya and subsequent caliphs because their overriding concern was to preserve the unity of Islam. They were the majority and consequently it is with them that the orthodox tradition of Islam rests. A minority, the Shi'a, believed that the succession to Muhammad ought to be hereditary and belonged with the descendants of Ali. They gained some support among non-Arab Muslims, especially in Persia, who resented the domination of Islam by Arabs. The Shi'a are the dominant party today in Iran, Iraq and Pakistan. They commemorate the martyrdom of Husain, for so they regard it, every year during the month of Muharram, with mourning and processions, in which flagellants lash themselves with chains until the blood runs. A play depicting the death of Husain is presented, and he is regarded as a Saviour. He died for his people's sins and all who mourn for him will be saved.

The Shi'a are generally more hostile to non-Muslims than the orthodox, but they have been strongly influenced by Zoroastrian, Christian and gnostic ideas. Ali is considered the first of twelve infallible imams or 'leaders', the last of whom, Muhammad al-Mahdi, is known as the Hidden Imam or the Expected One. He is said to have disappeared from the world to the mountains near Mecca in about AD 880, and he will return in the future to bring about the triumph of Islam and the reign of righteousness, prosperity and peace. Over the centuries, quite a number of people have claimed to be the Mahdi, 'the rightly guided one'. One of them founded the Fatimid dynasty of Egypt, and another the Almohad dynasty of Morocco and Spain. A more recent example is Muhammad Ahmad al-Sayyid, who proclaimed himself the Mahdi in the Sudan and in 1885 captured Khartoum, where General Gordon was killed. There are numerous Shi'a sects with their own secret doctrines and secret interpretations of the Qur'an. The armed group which in 1979 tried to seize the Holy Mosque at Mecca, which contains the Ka'ba, were members of a Shi'a sect.

The Ismailis, who claim to combine the best of Islam, Judaism and Christianity, were originally an offshoot of the Shi'a. Hasan ibn as-Sabbah split off from the Ismaili movement in the eleventh century and founded the notorious sect of the Assassins, which from its mountain strongholds in Persia and Syria sent out killers drugged with hashish (hence the word 'assassin') to murder its enemies. The head of the sect was known as the Old Man of the Mountains. The Druzes of Lebanon and Syria are also an offshoot of the Ismailis. They await the return of their divine Saviour, Caliph Hakim of Egypt, who mysteriously disappeared in 1021.

Conflicts with other sects and schools of thought helped to hammer out the orthodox doctrines of Islam in the period from the seventh to the tenth centuries. There were the Kharijites, a puritanical sect which survives in North Africa, Oman and Zanzibar, who maintained that various sins including unlawful killing, desertion in battle, usury and practising magic were unforgivable. The orthodox view, however, is that only polytheism is unforgivable and that Allah in his mercy may well forgive the sins of true believers. There was also the vexed question of predestination and free will. The Qur'an says that all events are predestined by God, including whether a man is a Muslim or not, which raises the problem of God's justice in condemning to hell those he has caused not to be believers. There are other passages, however, which suggest that human beings have free will, to obey or disobey God. Various philosophers attempted to resolve the contradiction. After prolonged argument, the orthodox solution was subtly propounded by the great theologian al-Ashari of Baghdad, that all man's actions are predestined by God, but man acquires responsibility for them by willing them. In effect, it seems, men do not have free will, but they think they do, and in making decisions which they believe are their own they become responsible for their decisions and are justly rewarded or punished by God.

ABOVE Members of the Ahmadiya sect, in Cairo. The sect was founded in 1908 by Ahmad al-Qadiani. His followers regard him as the Mahdi, who came to usher in the world-wide triumph of Islam. Ecstatic singing and dancing of this kind is also practised by the Sufi dervish orders.

LEFT A Muharram procession in Pakistan. During the first month of the Muslim year the Shi'a mourn for the death of Husain, whom they believe to have been the rightful caliph as a direct descendant of Muhammad. He is regarded as a Saviour, who died for his people's sins.

The Sufis

The Umayyads of Damascus were overthrown by another Arab dynasty, the Abbasids, though an Umayyad house remained in power in Spain. Under the Abbasid caliphs Islamic civilization came to its golden flowering under the influence of Persian culture and Greek philosophy. Harun al-Rashid, poet and scholar, the caliph of the *Arabian Nights*, ruling in fabled magnificence from the peerless city of Baghdad, was the richest and most powerful man on earth. But the empire could not be held together and the subsequent political history of Islam is tangled in the extreme. Independent dynasties established themselves in the outlying provinces, including the Fatimids, who ruled Egypt and much of North Africa. The power of the Abbasid caliphs waned. The Seljuq Turks built up a new Muslim empire in western Asia in the eleventh century and it was their threat to the Byzantine Empire which provoked the Crusades. Meanwhile the territory of Islam was still expanding. Muslim African states were established across a band of country to the south of the Sahara and Turkish leaders carried the faith into southern Russia and the north-west of India.

Sufism, which is a general term for Muslim mysticism, sprang up largely in reaction against the worldliness which infected Islam when its leaders became the powerful and wealthy rulers of multitudes of people and were influenced by foreign cultures. Harun al-Rashid, eating off gold and silver, toying with a harem of scented beauties, surrounded by an impenetrable retinue of officials, eunuchs and slaves, was a far cry from the stern simplicity of an Umar, who lived in a modest house, wore patched clothes and could be approached by any of his followers.

Dissatisfied with both materialism and the tangles of theology, individuals and small groups began to lead lives of austerity in semi-retirement from the world. The typical early Sufi lived in a cell in a mosque and taught a small band of disciples. The extent to which Sufism was influenced by Buddhist and Hindu mysticism, and by the example of Christian hermits and monks, is disputed, but self-discipline and concentration on God quickly led to the belief that by quelling the self and through loving ardour for God it was possible to attain a union with the divine in which the human self melted away. Secret methods were worked out for achieving this in trance, by meditation, breathing techniques and physical exercises. Some mystics rashly claimed that in attaining union with God they had actually become God, claims which horrified the orthodox as blasphemy. 'Glory be to Me,' one mystic said, and another, al-Hallaj, was crucified in AD 922 for saying, 'I am the Truth.' The execution made other Sufis more cautious in their public pronouncements, but they continued to believe that the human self is an illusion and that the supreme aim is to shed one's personal identity through absorption into the One Reality. They often expressed their yearning for the divine in love poems, in which God is addressed directly or more often under the female name of Laila, which means 'night'.

A bridge across the gap between orthodoxy and Sufism was constructed by Abu Hamid al-Ghazzali, regarded as the greatest of orthodox Muslim theologians, who taught at the university in Baghdad. Sickening of philosophy as sterile, he went into retirement in his late thirties to investigate mysticism, and became a mystic himself. He decided that the experience of union with God, though spiritually immensely valuable, was not the same thing as becoming identical with God, any more than two lovers who in their ecstasy feel themselves one have in fact become the same person. The mystic should return from the experience, still himself, but strengthened and revitalized.

Once Sufism became respectable, wealthy sympathisers endowed semi-monastic establishments in which the Sufi shaikh, or master, lived with his disciples and their wives and children – for celibacy was not a requirement. The secret teachings and techniques were known only to the shaikh and his initiated disciples, but initiates also gave open teaching to people from the local area and gathered what might be called 'lay' followers, who came to the monastery for instruction and help. Some monasteries sprouted daughter-houses and Sufi orders or 'paths' developed, which from the twelfth century spread throughout the Muslim world. Many of them still survive. The members of an order are called dervishes or faqirs.

Sufi shaikhs claimed absolute authority over their disciples and were regarded with awe as holy men, credited with miraculous powers and venerated virtually as godlings. People prayed for help to famous shaikhs of the past and made pilgrimages to their tombs. They were treated, in fact, as favourite saints were treated by Christians, and their cults introduced polytheism into a monotheistic system. Respect for the supernatural abilities of dervishes was increased by the physical powers which they demonstrated in states of ecstasy. The Rifaiya or 'howling dervishes' chanted in a circle with violent movements of the body and showed their utter reliance on God and their immunity to pain by fire-walking, swallowing red-hot coals, eating glass, falling on sharp knives and handling snakes. The Maulawiya or Mevlevi order of 'dancing dervishes', founded by the great Persian poet and mystic Jalal ud-Din Rumi, are famous for the swirling dances through which they induce ecstasy. Some Muslim faqirs, like Hindu sadhus, inflict extraordinary tortures on themselves and are believed to acquire supernormal powers.

Ironically, what began as an attempt to recapture the simplicity of early Islam turned into a jungle of popular polytheistic and magical cults. It is for this reason that Sufism is banned in Saudi Arabia, and in Turkey the number of dervishes has been drastically reduced. Elsewhere in the Muslim world the Sufi orders are flourishing. There has been a marked growth of interest in Sufi mysticism in the West since the Second World War, a development often viewed with a somewhat sardonic eye by Muslim Sufis themselves.

Westernization and Tradition

The territory of Islam was still expanding in the fourteenth and fifteenth centuries. Muslim traders and missionaries carried the faith to Malaysia, Indonesia and China. Islam became the dominant political power in India under the sultans of Delhi and the Mughal emperors. Further to the west, the Ottoman Turks, who came originally from Mongolia, settled in Asia

The beautiful mosque of Omar Ali Saifuddin in Brunei. Traders and missionaries carried Islam to Malaysia and Indonesia in the 14th and 15th centuries. The ruler of Brunei was converted to Islam in the 15th century.

Minor in the thirteenth century, displaced the Seljuqs and built up their own Muslim state. Sultan Muhammad II stormed Constantinople in 1453 and made it his capital as Istanbul. The Ottoman Empire reached its zenith under Sultan Sulaiman the Magnificent, who ruled the Balkans, Asia Minor, Syria, Egypt, Arabia, Mesopotamia and Persia. But this empire too began to splinter and entered on the long, slow decline which by the nineteenth century had made the Ottoman sultan 'the sick man of Europe'.

An important new reforming impulse emerged when Muhammad ibn Abd al-Wahhab rose like some prophet of old in the deserts of Arabia in the eighteenth century and fiercely condemned the cults of holy men, the tendency to treat the prophet as a divine figure and the moral laxity which had infected the faith. He traced the political eclipse of Islam to its spiritual degeneration and preached a return to the Qur'an and early tradition. Puritanical, militant and intolerant, the Wahhabi movement was the driving force behind the rise to power in Arabia of the house of Saud. Ibn Saud captured Mecca and Medina in 1924 and the new kingdom of Saudi Arabia was proclaimed in 1932. It remains the most conservative and traditionalist of the Muslim states.

The impact of western political and cultural imperialism on Muslim countries in the eighteenth and nineteenth centuries had, broadly speaking, three main consequences in the realm of religion. One was a modernizing and westernizing trend. The second was an upsurge of nationalism and a revival of pride in the glories of the Islamic past. The third was a conservative reaction against contamination by western influence. Muslim intellectuals influenced by western science and humanitarianism found themselves uneasy with Islam's approval or tolerance of holy war, slavery, polygamy and the subordination of women. In Egypt Muhammad Abduh urged Islam to make use of modern scientific knowledge. In India, Sayyid Ahmad Khan, a pro-British Muslim leader, suggested that Islam and Christianity had much in common and that Muslim education needed to take account of western thought. At the same time, his westernizing programme meant that he saw no possibility of a union in India between Muslims and Hindus.

An even more influential Indian Muslim, Muhammad Iqbal, wanted a reformulation of Islam in the light of western knowledge and criticized what he called blind acceptance of tradition. He was far from starry-eyed about the West, which he said was eaten up with greed and power-hunger, but he believed that the genius of Islam could absorb what was best in the West to create a new force for human progress. He too saw no possibility of a union with Hindus and called for the formation of a separate Muslim state in India, which later became a reality with the creation of Pakistan.

This trend of opinion was naturally not to the liking of the orthodox. Another westernizing syncretic movement, which began in Persia in the nineteenth century, has become a <u>separate religion</u> altogether as Bahaism. Its founder was Mirza Ali Muhammad, a member of one of the Shi'a sects, who in 1844 declared that he was the Bab (Gate) and had superseded the prophet Muhammad as the forerunner of a coming Messiah who would reform religion and the world. He was executed by firing squad in 1850 and his disciples hid his body for fifty years until it was entombed on Mount Carmel, which has become a place of Bahai pilgrimage. In 1863 one of the Bab's disciples, Mirza Husain Ali, proclaimed that he was the expected Messiah as Baha Ullah (Splendour of God), the latest of a succession of divine manifestations on earth who included Zoroaster, Krishna, the Buddha, Jesus and Muhammad. He disapproved of holy war, slavery and the subjection of women. Although Baha Ullah spent much of his life in exile and confinement, the movement spread and branches were established in Europe and the United States, where there is an impressive Bahai temple in Chicago. The Bahais believe that the same truths can be discerned behind all the major religions, and they hope to restore to humanity the ability to achieve unity by love. Theirs is the new faith for a new age which will see the world united under one government in love and peace.

The most drastic attempt to westernize Muslim society was made in Turkey under Mustafa Kemal Atatürk, an army officer who became virtual dictator in 1923, when the Ottoman Empire was given its quietus and the last sultan went into exile in Malta. Islam was at first declared the state religion of the new Turkish Republic, but this was swiftly altered. The

Worshippers gathered for prayer at the al-Aqsa mosque in Jerusalem. Though the faithful are required to pray five times daily, it need not be in a mosque. The worshipper can pray at home or wherever he or she happens to be, alone or in a group. If in a group, as in a mosque, there must be a leader, an imam, to ensure that the proceedings are orderly.

legal and educational systems were freed from the grip of traditional Islamic law, and dervish monasteries were closed down and a thorough-going programme of modernization turned Turkey into a secular state.

The orthodox were horrified and no other Muslim government has attempted anything so far-reaching, but the other Muslim countries have gradually become westernized to some degree. The immense wealth which oil has brought to some of them makes resistance to western trends difficult, but resistance there is. A powerful tide of conservative and anti-western feeling has been running, as in Iran under the Ayatollah Khomeini, with a drive to return to the beliefs and standards of the early days of the faith. No other religion has in fact remained so close to its original inspiration, and Islam has preserved its traditional identity and withstood the pressure of materialism and religious scepticism more effectively than any of its rivals.

The Bahai temple at Haifa in Israel. Bahaism began as an Islamic splinter-movement and has developed into a separate religion. Its principal leader, Baha Ullah, proclaimed himself the latest in a succession of divine manifestations who included Zoroaster, Krishna, the Buddha, Jesus and Muhammad.

9. Religion in the Secular Age

In the past, most people did not choose their religion. They found it ready-made for them by being born in a particular place and time, and accepted it as part of the whole inherited conglomerate of ideas in which they grew up. Even when a new religion came on the scene, it made comparatively little headway unless it gained the support of the government. Given the backing of the regime, it was widely accepted, largely for practical reasons, and became part of a new inherited conglomerate in which subsequent generations were brought up.

The position in the Protestant West, and increasingly in the rest of the world, is obviously very different. People now choose or reject religion for themselves, and many reject it. Though the membership figures of the principal religions and denominations exaggerate the extent of genuine commitment to them, there are still plenty of believers. But there are also numerous agnostics and atheists, and probably larger numbers who have a vague belief in a God who never does anything and requires no response on their part. To keep a hold on any substantial following a god must have power – power to act on his worshippers' behalf – and for many people today God is either unreal or powerless to intervene in a world controlled by other forces.

Religion is no longer a matter of state, and the idea that religious unity is vital to the cohesion of a society is considered out of date. Religion is a private matter, and secularism – concentration on this world rather than the next – is the prevailing orthodoxy of modern government. Discrimination against people on religious grounds is condemned as wrong, religious tests for public office have disappeared, the influence, prestige and numbers of the clergy have declined, religious indoctrination in schools is viewed with suspicion and so is censorship to protect religious principles. Where events were once felt to lie in the hand of God, they are so no more, and the state which has gladly ceased to support religion finds itself uncomfortably lumbered with the responsibility for planning and the blame for everything which goes wrong. Many of these changes are welcomed by the religious as

Meditation at a 'Tibetan' monastery in Cumbria, England. In the 20th century, and especially since the Second World War, the West has seen a rising tide of interest in oriental religions, mysticism and meditation, among people in search of a satisfying spiritual system to fill the vacuum created by the dominance of science and the decline of Christianity.

당과 수 령께 무 한 히 충 직 한 혁 명 전 사 가 되 자!

Poster glorifying Mao Tse-tung and the unity and progress of the Chinese people under his leadership. The figure of Chairman Mao dominates the scene like a colossal Buddha-image or the figure of Christ in the Vézelay Last Judgement. So strong is the need for religion that anti-religious movements attract religious emotions and play a religious role.

well as by the irreligious, but both camps display symptoms of serious unease. Now that religion has ceased to be intertwined with every aspect of life, the stiffening seems to have gone out of society and something valuable and necessary in life has been lost.

Allowing for exceptions, the influential thinkers of the past accepted one religion or another as true and socially desirable. The exceptions include materialist philosophers in India and China, some of the Greek philosophers and the Roman writer Lucretius, who was already saying in the first century BC that religion sprang from fear of death and the unknown, exploited by unscrupulous priests to give themselves power. Today Lucretius's view is quite widely popular and the most influential modern thinkers have not regarded any religion as true or socially desirable.

The obvious examples are Marx and Freud, both of whom discarded their own Jewish religious inheritance, or tried to. Marx believed that God was merely man writ large and religion a projection on to the outside world of man's needs and desires. It had survived as 'the opium of the people', employed by the ruling classes to keep the masses obedient. Ironically, the criticism applies just as strongly to Communism as to any religion.

The paradox is that the need for religion is so strong that anti-religious movements play a religious role, attract religious emotions and turn into quasi-religions. In the Soviet Union, eastern Europe and China, Communism is employed as religion used to be, to knit society together and control thought and behaviour, and it is people born under Communism who find a religion ready-made for them today. The proletariat are Communism's chosen people and the class struggle is their holy war. The Marxist future utopia of happiness, prosperity and universal concord appeals to the same emotions as the Messianic age of Judaism and Christianity, and its historical inevitability is the equivalent of God's providence, or plan for the world, the factor which makes sense of the confusing muddle of life. The driving force behind events is the mysterious Trinity of the dialectic – thesis, antithesis and synthesis – three principles in one principle, immeasurably greater than man, to which he must bow and with which he will co-operate, if he knows what is good for him. The doctrines of Communism are dogmas, which the believer must accept regardless of his private judgement, and any of the faithful who cannot follow the party line are heretics, denounced as fiercely as any deviationist Arian or Monophysite of the past. Communism is a kind of Church, depending for adherents on faith, emotional commitment and the need to believe in a force greater than oneself, with the party members as its clergy, the revolutionary martyrs as its heroic saints, and the mummified corpse of Lenin in Moscow as its revered object of pilgrimage.

On a less awe-inspiring scale, much the same is true of Freudianism, with its own dogmas and self-contained system, dependent on faith and emotional commitment. Its substitute for the sacred is the unconscious mind, whose mysteries are infallibly interpreted by psychoanalyst-priests. Freud thought that the religious world is imaginary and that God is a human father projected larger than life-size on the screen of the outside world. To account for the origin of religion, he devised his own strange myth of the primal murder, when the earliest family of human beings supposedly killed their father and ate him in a ritual meal. Freud considered religion a fantasy, but the label can as justly be tied to his own system.

While religious needs have been attracting converts to anti-religious systems, vigorous new religious cults have sprung up, in Japan, in Africa, in the Pacific islands and in the Americas. Modern Spiritualism, for example, which began in the United States in the 1840s, developed as a religious movement on the fringes of Christianity, providing apparent proof of life after death by communicating with those who had passed over to 'the other side'. There are Spiritualist churches in the United States and Europe today, and in South America new cults have emerged which combine Spiritualist, Roman Catholic and African ingredients. Deities from West Africa, originally taken to South America by slaves, are identified with Jesus, the Virgin Mary and Christian saints, and believers attempt to help souls which are confused and frightened after death.

In North America and Europe the proliferation of new movements has been accompanied and often inspired by the rising tide of interest in mysticism and oriental religions among people in search of a satisfying spiritual system to fill the vacuum created by the dominance of science and the decline of Christianity. The Theosophical Society and the Vedanta Societies are examples, there was the flirtation with Zen, and there is the current vogue of Transcendental Meditation. Not all the new groups are eastern-oriented, however. Within Christianity itself the modern Pentecostalist movement has followed the example of the early Christians and found a source of inspiration and evidence of the continuing power of the Holy Spirit in ecstatic speaking in tongues, prophesying and miraculous healing. The modern witchcraft movement, by contrast, has recreated the supposed pagan religion of pre-Christian Europe, and there are adherents of various systems of pagan mysteries.

One common factor in the appeal of these very different groups is the desire for there to be mysteries. They meet a demand for a spiritual reality which is not approached with microscope in one hand and test-tube in the other, or through worship of the restrained conventional kind in church or synagogue, but is experienced in direct personal communion. They satisfy a need for the numinous, the mystical, the sacred dimension, through which, it is hoped, individuals can achieve fulfillment and 'salvation' by becoming their ideal selves.

For the future, the long history of religion and the continuing demand for it suggest that no society will ever be able to do entirely without it. Religion has not withered away, even under the quasi-religion of Communism or the materialism of the West. In the West, if history repeats itself, the time looks ripe for the rise of a new popular religion. The conditions which accompanied the emergence of major religions in the past are present again. The growth of large-scale institutions, the disappearance of familiar landmarks, the confusion of moral standards, urbanization, cosmopolitanism and increased social and physical mobility have again created anxiety and a need for greater psychological security than established institutions supply. Science, technology and materialism have made the world more comfortable physically, but less comfortable spiritually.

Judging from history, however, there is a serious obstacle. In the past, new religions established themselves only with the support of political regimes. This is as true of modern Communism as of Buddhism and Christianity. The governments of the West do not look likely to give vigorous backing to any religion. As long as religion remains a private matter, it is questionable whether a new major faith can come to power.

Members of the Hare Krishna movement at a festival in Trafalgar Square, London, in 1969. This Hindu sect was founded in 1965 and its devotees, chanting and dancing, are now a familiar sight in the streets of Western cities.

Chronological Tables

Table 1: India and Pakistan

	BC	
Aryan invasion of India	c. 1500	
	c. 1500–500	Vedic period
	c. 1200	the *Rig Veda*
	c. 700	the earlier *Upanishads*
	c. 500	Buddha: Mahavira
Alexander the Great in India	327–325	
the Maurya dynasty, founded by Chandragupta 1 Maurya	321–185	
	c. 300?	the *Bhagavad Gita*
reign of Asoka	268–231	
	AD	
the Gupta Empire	320–535	
Arab conquest of the Indus region	712–745	
	c. 800	Sankara, Vedanta philosopher
reign of Mahmud the Great of Ghazni	999–1030	
reign of Muhammad of Ghur	1160–1206	
Sultanate of Delhi	1206–1526	
	1440–1518	Kabir, founder of Hindu sect
	1469–1539	Nanak, first guru of Sikhs
	1479–1531	Vallabhacarya, founder of Vaishnava sect
	1485–1533	Caitanya, founder of Vaishnava sect
Vasco de Gama sails to India round the Cape	1498	
Portuguese established at Goa	1510	
the Mughal Empire	1526–1858	
reign of Akbar	1556–1605	
British settlement at Madras	1639	
reign of Aurangzeb	1658–1707	
death of Sivaji, Maratha war leader	1680	
	1708	death of Gobind Singh, Sikh leader
	1772–1833	Rammohan Roy
	1780–1839	Ranjit Singh, Sikh leader
	1824–1883	Dayananda Sarasvati
	1828	the Brahmo Samaj founded by Rammohan Roy
	1836–1886	Ramakrishna, Vedantist mystic
the Indian Mutiny	1857	
India becomes British crown colony	1858	
	1862–1902	Vivekananda, disciple of Ramakrishna
Gandhi	1869–1948	
	1875	the Arya Samaj founded by Dayananda Sarasvati
Queen Victoria crowned Empress of India	1877	
Partition: India and Pakistan separate states	1947	

Table 2: Buddhism in India

	BC	
	c. 563–483	the Buddha
	c. 540–468	Mahavira, founder of the Jains
the Maurya dynasty, founded by Chandragupta I Maurya	321–185	
reign of Asoka	268–231	
	251	first Buddhist mission to Sri Lanka
death of Brihadratha, last of the Mauryas	185	
	AD	
the Kushana Empire	1st–3rd centuries	
reign of Kanishka	78–103	
	80–150?	Asvaghosha, biographer of the Buddha
	c. 200	Nagarjuna: the Lotus Sutra
	c. 400	Asanga: Vasubandhu: Buddhaghosa
reign of Harsha in northern India	606–648	
the Pala dynasty in Bengal and Bihar	760–1142	
Muslim conquest of northern India	11th–12th centuries	

Table 3: China

	BC	
Shang dynasty	c. 1766–1122	
Chou dynasty	c. 1122–256	
	604	traditional date of Lao Tzu's birth
	551–479	Confucius
	c. 371–289	Mencius, Confucian philosopher
	c. 298–230	Hsun Tzu, Confucian philosopher
Ch'in dynasty	221–206	
Han dynasty	206 BC –AD 220	
reign of Wu Ti	141–87	
	AD	
	1st century	Chang Ling, Taoist leader
Sui dynasty	581–618	
reign of Wen Ti	581–604	
T'ang dynasty	618–907	
Sung dynasty	960–1279	
	1130–1200	Chu Hsi, Neo-Confucian philosopher
Genghis Khan	1167–1227	
Kublai Khan	1216–1294	
Yuan (Mongol) dynasty	1279–1368	
Ming dynasty	1368–1644	
	1552–1610	Matteo Ricci, first Jesuit missionary in China
Ch'ing (Manchu) dynasty	1644–1912	
reign of Ch'ien Lung	1735–1796	
the Opium War	1840–1842	
T'ai P'ing rebellion	1850–1864	
Sun Yat-sen	1866–1925	
Mao Tse-tung	1893–1976	
Boxer Rising	1900	
the Kuomintang founded by Sun Yat-sen	1905	
Chinese Revolution	1911	
the Chinese Republic	1912–1949	
Chinese Communist party founded	1921	
(Communist) People's Republic of China	1949	

Table 4: Japan

	AD	
Prince Shotoku	574–622	
Nara period	710–794	
	767–822	Saicho, founder of Tendai Buddhist sect
	774–835	Kukai, founder of Shingon Buddhist sect
Heian period	794–1192	
	1133–1212	Honen, founder of the Jodo sect
	1141–1215	Eisai, founder of the Rinzai school of Zen
	1173–1262	Shinran, disciple of Honen
Kamakura period	1192–1333	
	1200–1253	Dogen, founder of Soto school
	1222–1282	Nichiren, founder of Nichiren sect
Ashikaga Shogunate	1338–1573	
Oda Nobunaga	1534–1582	
Tokugawa Ieyasu	1542–1616	
	1549	first Christian mission to Japan
Tokugawa Shogunate	1603–1867	
	1730–1801	Moto-ori Norinaga, nationalist writer
	1776–1843	Hirata Atsutane, nationalist writer
	1780–1850	Kurozomi Munetada, founder of Kurozomikyo
	1798–1887	Nakayama Miki, founder of Tenrikyo
Meiji government	1868–1912	
	1871–1944	Makiguchi Tsunesaburo, co-founder of Soka Gakkai
	1900–1958	Toda Josei, co-founder of Soka Gakkai
accession of Emperor Hirohito	1926	
Second World War	1940–1945	
American military government	1945–1950	
Japanese sovereignty restored	1952	

Table 5: Zoroastrianism

	BC	
Aryans move into Iran	c. 1500	
Median Empire	612–549	
	588	traditional date of Zoroaster's revelation
Achaemenian Empire	559–330	
reign of Cyrus the Great	559–529	
reign of Darius the Great	521–486	
reign of Artaxerxes II	404–359	
Alexander the Great conquers Iran	330	
Parthian Empire	c. 140 BC – AD 224	
	AD	
Sasanian Empire	224–636	
Arab conquest of Iran	636–652	
	936	traditional date of arrival of the first Zoroastrians (Parsis) in India

Table 6: Judaism

	BC	
	c. 2000?	Abraham
	15th or 13th century	Moses
reign of David	1012–972	
reign of Solomon: building of the Temple	c. 970–931	

kingdom of Israel	931–721	
kingdom of Judah	931–587	
	9th century	Elijah
	8th century	Amos: Hosea: Isaiah: Micah
	6th century	Ezekiel: Deutero-Isaiah
Palestine part of the Achaemenian Empire	539–333	
Palestine ruled by the Ptolemies of Egypt	323–197	
Palestine ruled by the Seleucids of Syria	197–142	
reign of Antiochus IV Epiphanes	175–164	
Hasmonean revolt against Syrians	168	
Hasmonean monarchy	142–63	
	c. 70 BC –AD 10	Hillel, famous teacher
Palestine comes under Roman rule	63	
reign of Herod the Great	39–4	
	AD	
	c. 50–135	Akiba, famous teacher
fall of Jerusalem: destruction of the Temple	70	
destruction of Jerusalem	135	
Arab conquest of Palestine	637	
	892–942	Saadya ben Joseph, philosopher
	c. 1085–1140	Judah Halevi, philosopher
the First Crusade	1096	
	1135–1204	Moses Maimonides, philosopher
the Jews expelled from England	1209	
the Jews expelled from France	1394	
the Jews expelled from Spain	1492	
	1729–1786	Moses Mendelssohn, philosopher
Jewish pale in Russia established	1791	
	1830–1915	Solomon Schechter, Conservative leader
	1860–1904	Theodor Herzl, founder of Zionist movement
	1897	first Zionist congress
the Balfour Declaration	1917	
the Second World War	1939–1945	
state of Israel proclaimed	1948	

Table 7: Christianity

	6 or 4 BC – c. AD 30	Jesus of Nazareth
	AD	
	c. 50–60	letters of Paul
	c. 64–67?	deaths of Peter and Paul
sack of Jerusalem by Romans	70	
	c. 70–100	gospels of Mark, Matthew and Luke
	c. 100	gospel of John
reign of Constantine the Great	312–337	
council of Nicaea	325	
	c. 330–379	Basil the Great, bishop of Caesarea
	354–430	Augustine, theologian
reign of Theodosius the Great	379–395	
partition of the Roman Empire	395	
end of the Roman Empire in the west	476	
	c. 480–547	Benedict, founder of the Benedictine order
coronation of Charlemagne in Rome	800	
Vladimir of Kiev	978–1015	
schism between western and eastern Christianity	1054	
	1073–1085	Pope Gregory VII
the Crusades	1096–1270	

	1170–1221	Dominic, founder of Dominican order
	1181–1226	Francis of Assisi, founder of Franciscan order
	1198–1216	Pope Innocent III
the Albigensian war	1209–1229	
	1224–1274	Thomas Aquinas, theologian
	c. 1260–1327	Meister Eckhart, mystic
the papacy at Avignon	1309–1377	
	1320–1384	Wycliffe, reformer
	c. 1369–1415	Huss, reformer
the papal schism	1378–1417	
fall of Constantinople	1453	
	1483–1546	Luther
	1484–1531	Zwingli, Swiss Protestant leader
	1491–1556	Ignatius Loyola, founder of Jesuits
	1506–1552	Francis Xavier, Jesuit missionary
	1509–1564	Calvin
council of Trent	1545–1563	
	1620	the Pilgrim Fathers
	1624–1691	George Fox, founder of Quakers
	1703–1791	John Wesley, founder of Methodism
	1801–1890	John Henry Newman, Roman Catholic cardinal
	1813–1873	David Livingstone, missionary and explorer
Darwin's *Origin of Species* published	1859	
Vatican council	1869–1870	
International Missionary Council founded	1921	
World Council of Churches constituted	1948	
	1958–1963	Pope John XXIII

Table 8: Islam

AD

	c. 570–632	Muhammad
	622	the Hegira, emigration to Medina
	630	Muhammad takes Mecca
Abu Bakr caliph	632–634	
Umar caliph	634–644	
Uthman caliph	644–656	
Ali caliph	656–661	
Umayyad dynasty of Damascus	661–750	
death of Husain	680	
Abbasid dynasty of Baghdad	750–1258	
reign of Harun al-Rashid	786–809	
	873–935	al-Ashari, theologian
	1058–1111	al-Ghazzali, theologian and mystic
the Crusades	1096–1270	
Sultanate of Delhi	1206–1526	
	1207–1273	Rumi, mystic
the Ottoman Empire	1301–1923	
reign of Sulaiman the Magnificent	1520–1556	
the Mughal Empire	1526–1858	
	1703–1792	al-Wahhab, founder of Wahhabi movement
	1817–1892	Mirza Husain Ali (Baha Ullah)
	1817–1898	Sayyid Ahmad Khan, Indian Muslim leader
	1849–1905	Muhammad Abduh, Egyptian reformer
	1876–1938	Muhammad Iqbal, Indian Muslim leader
Mustafa Kemal Atatürk, Turkish dictator	1880–1938	
Ibn Saud	1880–1953	
creation of Pakistan	1947	

Bibliography

Suggestions for Further Reading

The number of books on the subject, especially on Christianity, is huge. This is a short selection of books which readers who want to pursue the subject further will, I believe, find interesting and useful. Many of them have extensive bibliographies.

General

S.G.F. Brandon, *Man and His Destiny in the Great Religions*, Manchester University Press, 1962

William James, *The Varieties of Religious Experience*, Dolphin Books, New York; Fontana, London, 1960, reprint

Trevor Ling, *A History of Religion East and West*, Macmillan, London and New York, 1968

Johannes Maringer, *The Gods of Prehistoric Man*, Knopf, New York; Weidenfeld & Nicolson, London, 1960

Rudolf Otto, *The Idea of the Holy*, Oxford University Press, 2nd edn, 1950

Ninian Smart, *The Religious Experience of Mankind*, Scribner's, New York, 1969; Collins, London, 1971

R.C. Zaehner, *Mysticism Sacred and Profane*, Oxford University Press, 1957

R.C. Zaehner (ed), *The Concise Encyclopedia of Living Faiths*, Hawthorn Books, New York, 1959

Indian Religions

A.L. Basham, *The Wonder That Was India*, Sidgwick & Jackson, London, 1954

Nirad C. Chaudhuri, *Hinduism*, Chatto & Windus, London, 1979

N. Owen Cole and Piara Singh Samba, *The Sikhs: Their Religious Beliefs and Practices*, Routledge, London, 1978

Edward Conze, *Buddhism: Its Essence and Development*, Cassirer, Oxford, 3rd edn, 1957

Edward Conze (ed), *Buddhist Scriptures*, Penguin Books, Harmondsworth and New York, 1959

K.N. Jayatilleke, *The Message of the Buddha*, Allen & Unwin, London, 1975

Trevor Ling, *The Buddha*, Temple Smith, London, 1973

Stuart Piggott, *Prehistoric India*, Penguin Books, Harmondsworth and Baltimore, 1952

D.L. Snellgrove and H. E. Richardson, *A Cultural History of Tibet*, Weidenfeld & Nicolson, London, 1968

R.C. Zaehner, *Hinduism*, Oxford University Press, 1962

R.C. Zaehner (ed), *Hindu Scriptures*, Everyman's Library, London and New York, 1966

R. C. Zaehner (ed), *The Bhagavad-Gita*, Clarendon Press, Oxford, 1969

China and Japan

Masaharu Anesaki, *History of Japanese Religion*, Routledge, London, 1963, reprint

Anthony Christie, *Chinese Mythology*, Hamlyn, London and New York, 1968

Raymond Dawson, *Imperial China*, Hutchinson, London, 1972

Werner Eichhorn, *Chinese Civilization*, Faber, London, 1969

Japanese Religion, Agency for Cultural Affairs, Kodansha International, Tokyo and Palo Alto, 1972

D. Howard Smith, *Chinese Religions,* Weidenfeld & Nicolson, London, 1968

D. Howard Smith, *Confucius*, Temple Smith, London, 1973

D.T. Suzuki, *Zen Buddhism*, Doubleday, New York, 1956

Zoroastrianism

Mary Boyce, *Zoroastrians: Their Religious Beliefs and Practices*, Routledge, London, 1979

John R. Hinnells, *Persian Mythology*, Hamlyn, London and New York, 1973

R.C. Zaehner, *The Dawn and Twilight of Zoroastrianism*, Weidenfeld & Nicolson, London, 1961

Judaism

W.F. Albright, *From the Stone Age to Christianity*, Johns Hopkins Press, Baltimore, 1957

S.G.F. Brandon, *Creation Legends of the Ancient Near East*, Hodder & Stoughton, London, 1963

David L. Edwards, *A Key to the Old Testament*, Oxford University Press, 1967

Isidore Epstein, *Judaism*, Penguin Books, Harmondsworth and New York, 1959

J. Lindblom, *Prophecy in Ancient Israel*, Blackwell, Oxford, 1962

Noah Lucas, *The Modern History of Israel*, Weidenfeld & Nicolson, London, 1974

Max L. Margolis and Alexander Marx, *A History of the Jewish People*, Meridian Books, New York, 1958, reprint

Helmer Ringgren, *Israelite Religion*, S.P.C.K., London, 1966

D.S. Russell, *The Jews From Alexander to Herod*, Oxford University Press, 1967

G.G. Scholem, *Major Trends in Jewish Mysticism*, Thames & Hudson, London, 1955

Adin Steinsaltz, *The Essential Talmud*, Weidenfeld & Nicolson, London, 1976

G. Vermes, *The Dead Sea Scrolls in English*, Penguin Books, Harmondsworth and Baltimore, 1968

Christianity

Roland H. Bainton, *The Horizon History of Christianity*, American Heritage, 1964: published in Britain as *The Penguin History of Christianity*, Harmondsworth, 1967, 2 vols

Jack Beeching, *An Open Path: Christian Missionaries 1515–1914*, Hutchinson, London, 1980

Peter Brown, *The World of Late Antiquity*, Thames & Hudson, London, 1971

J. G. Davies, *The Early Christian Church*, Weidenfeld & Nicolson, London, 1965

George Every, *The Mass*, Gill & Macmillan, Dublin, 1978

Geoffrey Faber, *Oxford Apostles*, Penguin Books, Harmondsworth and Baltimore, 1954, reprint

Michael Grant, *Saint Paul*, Weidenfeld & Nicolson, London, 1976

Robert M. Grant, *A Historical Introduction to the New Testament*, Collins, London, 1963

John Hick, *Evil and the God of Love*, Macmillan, London, 1966

Michael E. Marty, *Protestantism*, Weidenfeld & Nicolson, London, 1972

John L. McKenzie, *The Roman Catholic Church*, Weidenfeld & Nicolson, London, 1969

Ninian Smart, *The Phenomenon of Christianity*, Collins, London, 1979

Helen Waddell, *The Desert Fathers*, Constable, London, 1974, reprint

Timothy Ware, *The Orthodox Church*, Penguin Books, Harmondsworth and New York, 1963

Marina Warner, *Alone of All Her Sex: The Myth and Cult of the Virgin Mary*, Weidenfeld & Nicolson, London, 1976

Islam

A. J. Arberry, *Sufism*, Allen & Unwin, London, 1950

A. J. Arberry, *The Koran Interpreted*, Allen & Unwin, London, Macmillan, New York, 1955

N. J. Dawood (ed), *The Koran*, Penguin Books, Harmondsworth and Baltimore, revised edn, 1966

Alfred Guillaume, *Islam*, Penguin Books, Harmondsworth and New York, 1956

Philip K. Hitti, *A Short History of the Arabs*, Princeton University Press, 1943

Martin Lings, *What Is Sufism?*, Allen & Unwin, London, 1975

Fazlur Rahman, *Islam*, Weidenfeld & Nicolson, London, 1966

Wilfred Cantwell Smith, *Islam in Modern History*, Princeton University Press, 1957

W. Montgomery Watt, *Muhammad, Prophet and Statesman*, Oxford University Press, 1961

Religion in the Secular Age

Jacob Needleman, *The New Religions*, Doubleday, New York, 1970; Allen Lane, London, 1972

Bryan Wilson, *Religion in Secular Society*, Penguin Books, Harmondsworth and Baltimore, 1969

Bryan Wilson, *Contemporary Transformation of Religion*, Oxford University Press, 1976

Acknowledgments

Photographs were supplied or reproduced by kind permission of the following (page numbers in italics indicate colour pictures):

Ashmolean Museum 100; Barnaby's Picture Library endpapers, 24 right, 30, 64 above and below, 97 (photo Hubertus Kanus), 115 right (photo Hubertus Kanus), 119, 126–7 (photo Hubertus Kanus), 226–7, 234–5; Bayerisches Staatsbibliothek 175; BBC Hulton Picture Library 88, Bibliothèque Nationale, Paris 190, 210 above, 211; Bildarchiv Foto Marburg 197, 208; Bodleian Library 126 below; W. Braun 132; British Library 136 below, 139, 144 above, 174 right, 186–7; British Museum 26, 42, 95 right, 96, 99 left, 102 above left (photo Michael Holford), 108, 130 left, 142, 186 top right, 188–9, 216, 228 above, 229; Bury Peerless 48; Mike Busselle 230–1; Camera Press 74–5, 82 below right, 92, 105, 240; Chester Beatty Library 172, 222; Dr J.A.L. Cooke, Oxford Scientific Films 136 above; Dept. of Environment 8–9; Douglas Dickins, FRPS 12, 15, 24 left, 31, 32, 34 above and below, 37, 38, 43 above right, above left and below, 56, 66 left, 68, 69, 70, 71, 72 above and below, 73 left and right, 78, 82 left and above right, 102 below, 103, 112–13, 131 right, 158, 159, 161, 210 below, 214–15, 219, 232, 236–7, 239; Edinburgh University Library 129; Mark Edwards 14–15, 54–5; John Freeman 183; Freer Gallery of Art 58–9, 61; Giraudon 155, 173; Ian Graham 29, 35, 40, 46–7, 80, 115 left, 116, 120–1, 223, 224 above; Sonia Halliday 110 below, 150–1, 177, 194–5 above, 218; Robert Harding Associates 99 right; David Harris 160, 164 left; High Commission of India 52, 54 below; Michael Holford 86, 90; Indian Tourist Office 44, 49, 50 left, 221 above; Israel Government Press Office 162 below; Israel Museum 148 below right; Japan Information Centre, London 118; Jewish Museum, London 163; Behram Kapadia 106 below, 107, 143 left and right; Keble College, Oxford (photo Jeremy Marks, Woodmansterne Ltd) 147; A.F. Kersting 189 right, 192; Keystone Press Agency 81, 122–3, 226 left, 244; Archives photographiques Larousse 10 above; Leiden University Library 148 left; Library of Congress 204 left; Louvre 193 (photo Giraudon), 202–3; William Macquitty 89; Mandel Archive 134, 144–5, 148–9, 164 right, 204 right, 225 above, 228 below, 242; Mansell Collection 1, 16, 62–3, 91, 114, 131 left, 138 above, 170, 180, 203 above, 205, 224–5, 234 below; Middle East Photographic Archive 156, 182, 212–13, 221 below, 238; Musée de l'Homme 10–11; Musée Guimet 5 (photo Giraudon), 18 (photo Giraudon), 20 (photo Giraudon); Musée de S. Germain 6; Museum of London 196; National Gallery 154, 184–5, 186 left, 198; National Portrait Gallery 207; The Pierpont Morgan Library 2; Popperfoto 50 right; Rockhill Gallery, Kansas 110 above; Alfred Rubens Collection 167; Scala 152 left; Seattle Art Museum 117 left; Ronald Sheridan 23, 106 above, 138 below, 140–1, 146–7, 162 above, 168–9, 231 below; Staatsbibliothek Bamberg 178–9; Swiss National Tourist Office 200; Victoria and Albert Museum 22, 25, 27, 28, 34 above right, 39 (photo Michael Holford), 41, 45, 66 right, 67, 76, 77, 83, 93, 94, 98, 117 right, 146 below (photo Michael Holford); Warburg Institute, University of London 124; Weidenfeld and Nicolson archive 3, 8 below, 84, 104, 111, 130 right, 135, 152 right, 174 left, 191, 194–5 below; Wellcome Museum 102 above right (photo Michael Holford); Werner Forman 95 left, 101; Professor Y. Yadin 157

Picture research by Patricia Mandel

Index